EXPLAINING CAMERON'S COMEBACK

EXPLAINING
CAMERON'S
COMEBACK

EXPLAINING CAMERON'S COMEBACK

ROBERT WORCESTER
ROGER MORTIMORE
PAUL BAINES
MARK GILL

David.   31-12-15

Happy New Year

Bob Worcester

Indie**Books**

Also in this series

Explaining Labour's Landslide
Explaining Labour's Second Landslide
Explaining Labour's Landslip
Explaining Cameron's Coalition

Explaining Cameron's Comeback

By Robert Worcester, Roger Mortimore, Paul Baines and Mark Gill

ISBN: 978-1-908041-27-2

Published by IndieBooks
4 Staple Inn, London, WC1V 7QH

www.indiebooks.co.uk

This edition © IndieBooks 2015

Printed by TJ International, Padstow, Cornwall

Table of contents

Lists of tables, figures and cartoons

List of tables

List of figures

List of cartoons

Foreword

Once again the team of Worcester, Mortimore, Baines and Gill have looked back on the British General Election of 2015 in this, the fifth book of the "Explaining" general elections series in which we have listened to the voters rather than the players. Instead of grinding axes and puffing, done by interviewing mainly politicians and media, we are trying to bring objective and systematic findings from our opinion polling to understand what happened, and where we can ascertain it, why what happened happened.

We allow no politics of our own to colour our analyses, and have neither incentive nor inclination to edge or spin what we find in the data.

The beginning of the honeymoon of new party leaders, and the 'long election', are increasingly recognised as being important in deciding which party, and which leader, win the election. This time, from mid-term to the call of the election itself on 30 March 2015, the two major parties seemed to be deadlocked, so it appeared that all was to play for and another hung parliament was likely to be the outcome. This apparent stalemate continued right up to election day, with little change in the standing of the parties right up to 7 May.

For many years I have sounded off on radio and television, in this election on social media as well, to pundits and public, at all three party conferences each year speaking at the GovNet fringe meetings to literally hundreds of the party faithful on each occasion, and to many audiences at universities, and other places who have sought my views on the political scene, to "Watch the share, not the lead". Seldom did that advice stick. Headlines shouted "Labour two points ahead" followed by broadcast reports of "XYZ newspaper poll shows Labour on course to win election" (six months before the vote) or worse.

I tend to watch the share of the party in power, whichever party that may be: in the 2010-15 parliament it was the Conservatives, as the major partner of the coalition government.

In mid-term, with Ed Miliband Leader of the Labour Party and David Cameron Prime Minister, our monthly polls showed Labour consistently ahead, but not by much, and occasionally behind. At that time, the economic mood of the country was pretty bleak. In the Party Conference in 2014 with the election to be the following year, I gave delegates some very bad news. Their share of the vote in 2010 was 37%, and even with that level of support the outcome was a hung parliament.

From March 2013 to August 2014 the Tory share of the polls from the major polling organisations was 32%. I said at the Conservative Party conference that if the Tories didn't get their share of support up to 35% they would not be in the game, never mind still in No. 10 Downing Street. And if they got up to 36% they'd end up behind, with no telling whether Labour could form a government to keep them out. At 37%, they'd lead, as they did 2010–15, a coalition. At 38%, a small Tory majority. And so they nearly did, with a vote share of 37.7%, enough for a tiny majority.

I showed them this slide. Two questions were asked, their voting intention, asked by all the polling organisations, and their expectations of the state of the economy as measured in the Ipsos MORI monthly surveys since 1979.

Figure 1: Watch the share, not the lead

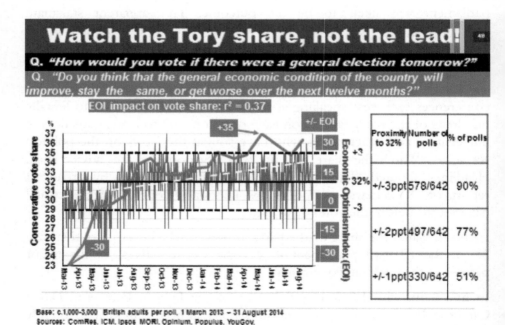

Why March 2013, why August 2014?

Because between those two dates our 'EOI', Economic Optimism Index, went from a −30 net score to +35, a 32.5% swing over the year and a half, just over 32 people in 100 had changed their minds from being deeply pessimistic about the future of the economy to being quite optimistic. Yet the Tories were getting little credit in their standing in the country, and were pretty well becalmed at 32%.

As the table on the right of the graph shows, over half of all the 600+ polls taken over that 18 months had the Conservatives at 32% plus or minus just 1%, three quarters of the polls had them at plus or minus 2%. Nine in ten had the Tories at 32%, within the normal three percent 'margin of error'.

True, there had been a slow rise over the period, and if it continued to the election on 7 May 2015 on the same projection, they might get to 36%, but would the economy prove the optimism? Would another issue work against them? It was too close to think they'd walk it, for sure. This pattern continued into 2015, and to the vote, so we thought.

We thought wrong.

So what did happen? Elections are won and lost on the margin. Much is made of Nate Silver's record in the last American election of calling the right winner in all 50 states. Actually it's dead easy to call say 45 of the states correctly, as it is most of the constituencies in the UK. In the US, in most elections if you can get Ohio, Pennsylvania, Florida and one or two others right, and you've got a lot of help from a lot of polls to help you, with a bit of nous and a bit of luck, it falls into your lap. The same for the UK, most are either Conservative or Labour and most of the others are predictable.

At least they used to be. Not this time, nor likely to be in 2020 either, and in fact, less likely if there are new constituency boundaries next time.

So, what happened in 2015? In the pages that follow, particularly in the Introduction and in the chapter on the polls, these are the points we make:

It wasn't so much that Cameron won it, but for a number of reasons we spell out, Labour lost :

- One in ten intending Labour voters didn't cast their votes.

- Nearly all intending Conservative voters did. (It wasn't "shy Tories", it was "reluctant Labour" who gave Cameron his comeback.)

- Eleven different polling organisations came up with the same finding, and as they did, you must draw the conclusion that the result was solid at the time the interviews were done (Table 39) or there was a systematic and pervasive methodological error. We do not think there was.

Two things happened, both 'Kinnock moments', which I believe led to some Labour 'intenders' deciding at the last minute that while they would never vote for the Tories, they couldn't vote Labour either and wouldn't vote for any of the others.

Figure 2: Negative Conservative campaigning on the SNP issue

They just couldn't stand the idea that Nicola Sturgeon would be pulling the Miliband strings, telling him, as she said she intended to do, what he could and couldn't do, as in this memorable Conservative campaign poster, widely seen and widely reported in the press and on 'What the papers say' television and radio programmes. and…

…the 'Ed Stone' (or 'Labour's Tombstone' as I call it) was widely ridiculed and emphasised the general concern about Ed Miliband's suitability as prime minister.

The outcome of the election, a Conservative 10-seat win, leaves this government with a majority which is just under half the 21-seat majority of John Major's government in 1992, which afterwards caused strain on every contentious vote in the House of Commons, as it only needed a dozen 'rebels' to vote against it, or two dozen to abstain or be absent and unpaired while the Labour and Liberal Democrats had full turnouts, to lose the vote. It's not quite that simple, but it was clear for the Leader and Shadow Leaders and surely the whips on all sides, and the strain showed. Now it's just that much worse, but with a clearly divided Labour Party, with many of its more moderate members acting on their conscience and/or constituencies rather than party loyalty, it's possible that there will be less strain than back in Major's day.

In the chapters that follow we offer an Introduction which begins with election night. On the night I was interviewed by Martyn Lewis, who just after midnight said *"I just can't believe that exit poll"*. I replied *"Martyn, five years ago almost to the minute you said those very same words and by 3 am, you had to eat them as the exit poll was proved right by then"*. He admitted he had. The 2015 exit poll was not so accurate as in the past, and its extrapolation by the Curtice team ended at 316, not a majority, but had the Lib Dems, UKIP and the SNP within a seat or two. The outcome shows how important a single percentage point difference in the share of the two main parties can be.

When the results of the exit poll were announced I recalled my inaugural address at LSE a few weeks following the 1992 election, which was titled "The polls have a lot to answer for". I started my lecture with these words: *"The polls have a lot to answer for; for one thing the most exciting election night in many years."*

We've used many tables of numbers and graphic illustrations which are the tools of our trade. Polling is a simple business, all we have to do is ask the right sample, the right questions, and add up the figures correctly. In addition though, we have to communicate the results effectively. This country's education system graduates numerate people who can use long division but not write, and literate folks who can't add up. So we try to explain what, joking aside, is a pretty complicated story in the language that suits the latter, and leave the former to pore over the numbers in the tables, and we also add in graphics, especially pie charts and bar graphs, which visually convey the messages that we are trying to get across.

Cartoon 1: Banx, *Financial Times*, 31 March 2015

The polling results during the election did convey early on three clear (and indeed accurate) messages, which were greeted by some as improbable: the collapse of the Liberal Democrats, the double digit performance of UKIP, and the near-annihilation by the Scot Nats of all other parties' candidates standing for election, with a triumphant 56 seat win *out of the 59 parliamentary seats in Scotland.*

With this record, then, why am I met every day with someone who asks "How did the polls get it so wrong?" or even by the Royal Statistical Society running a conference on "What does failure of the polls tell us about the future of survey research?" Come on guys, if anyone should understand stats it ought to be the statisticians. The answer to the silly question is not a silly answer, it is, in short, that it wasn't a failure of the polls, it was a failure of the pundits and forecasters, the media and the psephologists (and too many of the pollsters) who were quick to cast the blame on the polls, ignoring as they did that translating leads (with a wide margin of error, double the margin of the party shares) into seats (tricky business that) and using what can never be a precise measure of what people do on the day as many don't know what they'll do themselves.

There are headlines in newspapers over articles that are wildly misleading, sometimes over well-written articles by journalists who have experience of writing polls, but too many people don't understand, it is the sub-editors and editors who write the headlines, often to fit few words to summarise complicated stories. One of the worst was a headline on a story anticipating a by-election that was not called for another month, for an election a month after that saying on the basis of a voting intention poll in that constituency, "Labour to win by-election', when the candidates had not yet been selected. And television poll coverage can be worse.

This is a book that will in one way have a short shelf life of five years, until the next election. If you're quick, you might pick up a copy of our previous book, *Explaining Cameron's Coalition,* used, for £1.76 plus postage, or £25 new (we'll beat that, @£10!). But for students of politics, studying or nerdy, the books in this series are truly 'contemporary British history'.

Later chapters include a masterful summary of 'How British general elections work' written by Professor Roger Mortimore, our colleague in the production of all five of the series and a contributor to others in the parallel 'Political Communications' series I started in 1979 to augment the worthy *British General Election of…* books beginning in 1945 and carried on through every election since, mainly by David Butler and now by Dennis Kavanagh.

We then look at the Coalition Government of 2010–15 that we've titled "Trench warfare: anatomy of the stalemate", looking closely at people's values, attitudes and opinions, focussing on the images of the leaders, tied in importance with issues in the 2010 election but, surprisingly, dropping to below both issues and party images, and the images of the parties, now not just three and 'others', but five. We call this the 'Political Triangle' although for several decades it's been a tetrahedron in shape, resting on a base of people's values. I take pride in having invented this concept in

1972 for Harold Wilson's two 1974 campaigns, working as the private pollster to the Labour Leader for 19 years, and have not only exploited it since for e.g. the *Sunday Times* in this country but have exported it to several other countries where I've been advisor to their leaders.

The leader image 'perceptual map' has in addition to the three party leaders this time the added interest of comparing Nigel Farage with the 'main stream' leaders of the Tories, Labour and Lib Dems, to convey at a glance how 'out on a limb' Farage is from the others, only differentiated in the minds of the electorate as having a lot of personality, but also is thought to be 'more style than substance'. (Figure 15: Leader Image)

The party image is also clearly reflecting voters' minds, showing UKIP as a party isolated, and described as 'extreme' as far away from the other parties as can be, with the only other attribute more closely related to UKIP being that it is perceived as 'different to the other parties'. This contrasts with the Conservatives being seen as having a "Good team of leaders" and being "Fit to govern" which the Tories have all to themselves. (See Figure 16: Party Image)

The dedicated team that has put together this book cut their collective teeth on its predecessor, *Explaining Cameron's Coalition*, and were joined then, as now, by my son Kenton, whose doctorate came from Columbia, who is now a professor of political science at Marymount Manhattan College in New York City, and who has a serious side line to his teaching of Plato's Republic and other courses balanced by an interest in the influence and power of editorial cartoons, and whose contribution in the 2010 book caught the eye of David Mellor who together with Ken Livingstone have a most entertaining Saturday morning show on LBC. Relatively little has been written on this subject by British academics, although Professor Colin Seymour-Ure is an exception, founder chairman of the University of Kent's massive cartoon archive.

Kenton's contribution this time adds another layer of understanding of how editorial cartoons can forecast, irritate, lampoon and portray both the election itself and the players in it. It is, in both countries, an untapped and ill-understood source of political marketing and political expression which needs examination and understanding. I'm hopeful that one day we will have sponsorship to carry out such a contribution to enable Kent and his Dad to collaborate on the research to put some statistical flesh on the anecdotal bones to understand just what the impact of editorial cartoons has on people's perceptions of the leaders, the parties and issues important in determining how people vote.

Cartoon 2: Christian Adams, *Daily Telegraph*, 2 April 2015

As always, we thank the many colleagues, both at Ipsos MORI and the ROW (the Rest of the World) for the time and encouragement to continue on with developing the rich asset we hope this fifth book in the series offers to serious scholars in the field of political science, contemporary British history, communications and other academic disciplines affected by elections:

Ipsos MORI's country manager Ben Page; Bobby Duffy, who heads up Ipsos MORI's Social Research Institute; the head of politics Gideon Skinner and the head of politics from our Edinburgh office, Mark Diffley, who joined us in London for most of the campaign; the core political research team, Glenn Gottfried, Harry Evans, Mike Wheeler, Jerry Latter and Dom Oliver, and our data processing wizards Joe Broughton, Darren

Thickpenny, Lynn Sullivan and Darshana Ghelani; Hannah Millard, Aalia Khan, Hannah Williams, Jim Kelleher, Ross Edghill and Duncan Struthers in the communications team; Graham Keilloh and Mike Clemence, the exit poll team, and Simon Atkinson, who directed it; Claire Emes, who oversees all our digital research; Josh Keith, Steven Ginnis, Natasha Morgan, Tim Silman, Suzanne Hall, Fay Sadro and Connor Leckey, who ran our online community Election Uncut for the BBC; Paul Carroll, who directed the Ipsos MORI 'worm' for the broadcasters' coverage of the debates, with Chris Rigby, Greg Davies and Mark Denley, and Fiona Nolan and Kate Foley who handled the recruitment; Lucy Setterfield in Edinburgh; Carl Phillips, Guto Hunkin and and Rebecca Writer-Davies in the Reputation Centre; Stewart McGeoghegan, Ian Douglas and Una Dumigan at our telephone interviewing centre; the Exit Poll Field team, Jessica Bultitude, Vanessa Fiorentini, Desmond Glass and Alastair Townend; all our interviewers, both on the telephone and on the ground in the Exit Poll; our secretary/PAs, Kerry Colville and Rosalind Hazell; and not least our front-line, the hardworking receptionists at our Borough Road offices (now no more), Salli Barnard and Lyn West.

And tributes to our clients, without whose support we would not have have had the data on which the book is based: in particular Joe Murphy at the *Evening Standard*; Paul Royall, Sally Watson, Judy Machin and Magnus McGrandle at the BBC; Gordon Macmillan and Stephen Townsend at STV; and Claudia Chwalisz and Michael McTernan at Policy Network. And to the exit poll clients: Sue Inglish, Sam Woodhouse and David Cowling (BBC), Emma Hoskyns (ITV News) and Nick Phipps (Sky), plus John Curtice, Stephen Fisher, Colin Rallings, Michael Thrasher, Nick Moon and their teams, all integral parts of the exit poll.

Thanks also to Professor Vernon Bogdanor, whose ready willingness to plow through an early draft of the manuscript and give us his thoughts and endorsement that what we're trying to do is worthwhile is greatly appreciated. Particularly important is his reminder not to forget to say that no one can predict the future of elections (or indeed referendums) with accuracy, as people are human, and change their minds, on the margin, but elections are won and lost on the margin, and as I often say, changing minds of the electorate is what elections are all about. Certainly the pundits and the forecasters and the punters and bookies can't (unless the race is fixed, whether on horses or on party leaders, but this is not an issue in this country as it is in many). And to ITN's Alastair Stewart, knowledgeable and with great political nous, who both could make the numbers dance and was such a pleasure to work with on election nights (and when we got our ITN exit polls spot on, much to the relief of both Alastair and myself).

Also to our new publisher James Humphreys of Indie*Books,* who has taken such a keen and personal interest in helping us speed up the publishing process and make new technology accessible. And to Carole Baines for proof-reading the work.

Sincere thanks to them all, collectively and individually. And as well I want to thank personally my co-authors, Roger Mortimore who as in all these volumes worked diligently and effectively to 'get it right', and carried the lion's share of the load, and our friends Cranfield Professor Paul Baines, who is a leading scholar in the study of electoral behaviour and elections, and specifically in political marketing, and Mark Gill, former head of the polling unit at Ipsos MORI, who has been working with and for me for over a decade both in this country and abroad advising political leaders and media clients.

Sir Robert Worcester KBE DL, Founder, MORI, December 2015

Cartoon 3: Peter Schrank, *Independent on Sunday*, 19 April 2015

Introduction

Election night

On 7 May 2015, Prime Minister David Cameron led the Conservative Party to a surprise victory in the UK general election, securing a narrow overall majority of ten seats, after his near failure at the previous election in 2010 had forced him to go into coalition with the Liberal Democrats. This book seeks to explain how he succeeded. It shows how the national swing of votes, although small, was from the Conservatives to Labour and yet the Conservatives gained seats and Labour lost them.

Figure 3: The general election result: votes and seats

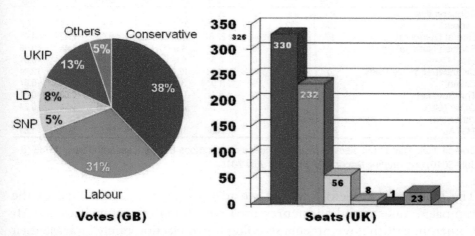

Votes (GB)   Seats (UK)

Source: Calculated from election results as reported by the BBC (www.bbc.co.uk)

In the pages that follow, we show how the contest which is traditionally at the centre of an election, vying for floating voters in marginal constituencies, had congealed into a stalemate, with neither major party able to make significant gains from the other. We show how this came about because the Conservatives convinced the key voters that they had succeeded in resuscitating the economy or that Labour could not be trusted to run it, coupled with Labour's failure to shift the agenda of political debate onto different issues through which they might challenge more effectively. In addition there was a dramatic realignment of the third-party votes – away from the Liberal Democrats, towards the UK Independence Party and the Scottish National Party – meaning that the eventually-decisive battles of the election were fought in a different part of the electoral landscape, where Labour and the Conservatives barely engaged face-to-face with each other at all. This influenced both the form and content of the election campaign, producing a contest that many proclaimed 'boring' (although we didn't think so) and 'negative' (which it was, but for reasons that may be more understandable having read our analysis).

Table 1: British general election result 2015, compared with 2010

	SEATS (n)			SHARE OF VOTE (% – GB only)			VOTES (millions – GB only)		
	2010	2015	Chg	2010	2015	Chg	2010	2015	Chg
Conservative	306	330	+24	36.9	37.7	+0.8	10.68	11.29	+0.61
Labour	258	232	−26	29.7	31.2	+1.5	8.60	9.35	+0.75
Liberal Democrat	57	8	−49	23.6	8.1	−15.5	6.83	2.42	−4.41
Scottish National Party	6	56	+50	1.7	4.9	+3.2	0.49	1.45	+0.96
Plaid Cymru	3	3	0	0.6	0.6	0.0	0.17	0.18	+0.01
UK Independence Party	0	1	+1	3.2	12.9	+9.7	0.92	3.86	+2.94
Green	1	1	0	1.0	3.8	+2.8	0.28	1.15	+0.87
The Speaker	1	1	0	0.1	0.1	0.0	0.02	0.03	+0.01
Other (GB)	0	0	0	3.3	0.8	−2.5	0.98	0.24	−0.74
Other (NI)	18	18	0						
TOTAL	650	650		100	100		28.98	29.98	+1.00

Source: Calculated from election results in House of Commons Library Research Paper 10/36 (8 July 2010) and Briefing Paper CBP7186 (28 July 2015)

The Conservative victory was, if we rely on the media coverage of the campaign, unexpected and represented something of a comeback for Mr Cameron. British governments standing for re-election rarely increase their vote shares or numbers of seats, and Mr Cameron did both for his party – the first Prime Minister to do so after a full term in Downing Street since the Great Reform Act.[1] True, the historical precedents for Labour were

---

[1] Labour under Harold Wilson increased both seats and vote share in 1966 and October 1974, but this was after only just over a year in office in the first case, and eight months in the second. The Conservatives did so in 1955, but Anthony Eden had replaced Winston Churchill as premier only weeks before the election. Clement Attlee improved Labour's vote share but lost seats in 1951, as did the Marquess of Salisbury for the Unionists in 1900. Margaret Thatcher achieved the opposite for the Conservatives in 1983. Lord Palmerston increased Whig votes and seats in 1857, but had been Premier for less than half of the previous parliament.

not much better – no ousted government had bounced straight back from defeat to win an overall majority at the first attempt since the 1920s. But Labour seemed to have enough momentum to make another hung parliament at least likely, and almost all of the media speculation revolved around the possibility of the SNP holding the balance of power, and on whether they would or could put Ed Miliband, Labour's leader, into Number Ten. The Conservative campaign consisted very largely of warning of the dangers of this possibility, spreading photo-montage images of Miliband in former SNP leader Alex Salmond's top pocket or as a puppet whose strings were being pulled by the current SNP leader, Nicola Sturgeon.

Such apparently-desperate negative campaigning, according to the conventional wisdom, could only alienate the uncommitted voters. Cameron's refusal to take part in as many TV debates as the other leaders and the public wanted was also seen as defensive, and likely to hurt him further. On election night, when the Exit Poll predicted correctly that the Conservatives would be easily the largest party, jaws dropped.

What opinion polls can tell us

David Cameron's victory was also unexpected because the pre-election opinion polls were interpreted as indicating the near-certainty of a hung parliament and the clear possibility that Labour would be able to oust the Conservatives from office. Since this book is largely concerned with what polls can tell us about the election and the voters, we need to address the impression that "the polls got it so wrong".

In the first place, the Exit Poll on election day was once again accurate (as they have been previously), and the pre-election polls correctly foreshadowed a lot of dramatic developments which would otherwise have been entirely unexpected, including:

- the collapse of the Liberal Democrat vote share;

- the size of the UKIP vote share; and

- the SNP's near-annihilation of the other parties in Scotland.

A good deal of the perceived error in the pre-election polls came from the interpretation, not from the polling itself. In particular, the perceived error came from misguided translation of national voting shares into seat projections: properly read, there was nothing in the polls to suggest that Ed Miliband's Labour Party was heading for victory; despite this, many forecasters and pundits concluded that he was.

Nevertheless, it is perfectly true that the polls throughout the campaign consistently showed a higher Labour vote share and a lower Conservative share than transpired on election day. But polls are snapshots, not predictions: if people change their minds on how to vote after they have answered a poll that does not prove that the poll was wrong at the time it was conducted. However, when the polls have been saying roughly the same thing for weeks, and no less than 11 different polling organisations say it again in the final polls before the election (which, as far as we can make them, *are* predictions), and the election result comes out differently, then the suspicion naturally arises that they were never right. In 2015 almost all the polls showed the two main parties roughly neck-and-neck, but when the actual votes were counted the Conservatives had a clear lead.

Were the polls wrong all along? In one sense, yes: we don't believe that there was some dramatic last-minute swing of voters to the Tories after the pollsters had finished asking their questions. But nor do we believe that the polls were undercounting the number of Tory voters. **The over-projection of Labour's performance came entirely from the expectation that Labour supporters would be more likely to turn out and vote than they had been in 2010, and this proved not to be the case.**

We believe that throughout the campaign we measured the level of party support correctly, but were let down by not properly allowing for turnout. There were not hordes of voters who told the pollsters that they would vote Labour and instead voted for some other party, or of those who voted Conservative having told us they would do something else. But there were people who told us, quite correctly, that they supported Labour, and also told us that they were absolutely certain to vote yet failed to do so when it came to the point.

These eventual-non-voters we treated as voters throughout the campaign. But at what point does a voter become a non-voter anyway? These were real people, who at any point up to 10 p.m. on election day might have stirred themselves to cast the Labour vote that they always more or less vaguely intended to cast. Is it too deterministic to say that they were fated from the start not to reach the polling station, branded as inevitable abstainers, and that the polls should have treated them as such?

This point is crucial because, if this is true, the polls were adequate, their samples were representative, and the problem was only in translating answers to the voting intention questions into a projection of behaviour. We need also to maintain a sense of proportion: embarrassing though the difference between the final 'predictions' and the result may be for the pollsters, the average difference between vote share and prediction for the two main parties was barely three percentage points for each (and much lower for all the other parties) – very few of the conclusions that we wish to draw from the polls' other findings would be affected in the least by an error of that size. There is no reason to doubt the reliability of the polls for this purpose, and they can perfectly well be used to explore the pattern of public opinion that underlies the election outcome, even if they proved faulty in predicting some voters' behaviour.

Because tracking voting intentions is by no means the only function of opinion polls (and is in fact one for which polls are least well suited, since a useful measure of voting requires a greater precision than polls can ever be confident of providing). More usefully, they give a much broader range of information which helps understand elections and the public's engagement in politics: perceptions of the parties and their leaders, people's reactions to events and to proposed policies, and the interaction between all these factors in influencing voting behaviour. They serve, too, between elections, to measure public attitudes to the government and its policies. They can help us understand who votes, and which way, and why, and what the parties and candidates might do to change that, why some governments succeed and others fail. Above all, they help us to understand voters, to get into their minds and see what makes them tick.

After every election there is a shelf-full of election post-mortem books, popular and academic. Some concentrate on the politicians, some on the policies, some on the campaigning. But elections are first and foremost about voters, what they want, what they know, what they believe, what they think. These drive votes and decide elections – without them, the politicians, the policies, the campaigning, could count for nothing. Concentrating on what the opinion polls can tell us about the voters gives a unique perspective, which in some ways is more revealing than all the others. It is this that is, ultimately, the purpose of this book and of the series to which it belongs.[2]

This book tells the story of the 2015 election from the point of view of the voters as revealed by the polls. The opinion polls we cite in this book are mainly those conducted by Ipsos MORI[3], the company for which most of us work or have worked (although we turn to evidence from the other polling companies whenever it seems to us to shine light on some question that our own polls have not fully covered). By focusing on what the opinion polls can tell us about the election, and the government of the UK in the five years preceding it, we shine the spotlight upon public opinion and on what the voters and non-voters themselves thought about it. Polls (or surveys, we do not distinguish between the two terms) provide evidence that is not available from any other source – the neutral and objective measurement of how many of the public hold a particular view, and how that relates to the other views they hold, who thinks what and what they know or think they know, and why.

We argue that polls provide a far more reliable reflection of public opinion than either journalistic commentary or politicians' claims, because with all their faults, polls are rarely very far from the truth. In 2015, there seems to have been a widespread supposition before the election that the polls were saying that Labour was likely to be the easily biggest party in terms of parliamentary seats. By comparison with the final outcome, of a Conservative majority with Labour almost a hundred seats behind, this was indeed utterly wide of the mark. But the polls were saying nothing of the sort. The average of the final polls put the Conservatives and Labour absolutely neck-and-neck in votes (in fact four polls put the Tories slightly ahead, two put Labour ahead and four had the two dead level). In the voting, the Conservatives led by 6.5 percentage points, 37.7% to 31.2%,

---

[2] The previous books in the series are Robert Worcester and Roger Mortimore, *Explaining Labour's Landslide* (London: Politico's Publishing, 1999); Robert Worcester and Roger Mortimore, *Explaining Labour's Second Landslide* (London: Politico's Publishing, 2001); Robert Worcester, Roger Mortimore and Paul Baines, *Explaining Labour's Landslip* (London: Politico's Publishing, 2005); Robert Worcester, Roger Mortimore, Paul Baines and Mark Gill, *Explaining Cameron's Coalition* (London: Biteback, 2011).

[3] Fuller details of the Ipsos MORI polls that we cite, and of all Ipsos MORI's published polls, can be found online at www.ipsos-mori.com. In every case, data are weighted to match the profile of the population unless otherwise stated.

meaning that the average error for each of the two parties was just over 3 points – not good, certainly, but not as ludicrously wide of the mark as many commentators supposed.

It was the psephologists and the pundits who were translating parity in vote shares into a comfortable Labour lead in seats. (In fact we, and almost all the other pollsters, were resisting all efforts to predict numbers of seats from our polls, as we always do. This is simply something that cannot be done with any accuracy from national vote shares, and the 2015 election offers a classic illustration of why this is the case.)

Perhaps there was some justification for the misinterpretation. For several general elections before 2015, the electoral system was biased towards Labour and against the Conservatives, so that if the two parties were neck and neck in votes, Labour would be well ahead in seats. But that did not hold in 2015, and in retrospect we can see that nobody should have supposed that it would. The bias in the electoral system swung away from Labour in 2015, and the Conservatives were favoured instead. Why? Because the Conservatives picked up a lot of extra seats from the collapsing Liberal Democrats without needing much of an increase in votes to do so, and at the same time Labour's collapse in Scotland made only a small dent in their national share of the vote but a far more catastrophic loss of seats: overall, a big net swing in seats for a small net swing in votes.

The polls showed that both of those things were going to happen, but few pundits really believed either. They thought the SNP earthquake was exaggerated, and the Liberal Democrats would hang onto a lot of their seats even if they lost votes elsewhere. Properly read, the polls should have indicated that the Tories would be easily the biggest party even at an equal split of the votes. But few interpreted their results in this way.

In fact, the polls got a lot right. They correctly measured the collapse of the Liberal Democrats, rightly showing that they would lose two-thirds of their support in the course of a single parliament, a quite unprecedented occurrence. And, similarly, the polls correctly showed the equally dramatic rise of UKIP and the SNP. UKIP's increase in votes, of course, was already foreshadowed by their victory at the European Parliament election in 2014 and by their impressive showing in holding two parliamentary seats at by-elections in the autumn, but nobody was sure how that strength would translate into general election votes. The polls got it right, however: on average they predicted 13%, and 13% was what UKIP got (despite Britain's First-Past-the-Post system only delivering them one parliamentary seat in return).

In the SNP's case, there was not even the evidence of previous years' elections to rely on – nothing in what the voters had previously done at the ballot box prepared for more than a modest increase in the SNP's vote share, which would have implied no more than a handful of gains in seats. But the opinion polls showed a sudden and staggering swing from Labour to the SNP in the immediate aftermath of the Independence Referendum in 2014, so big that it suggested that Labour might be virtually wiped out in Scotland at the general election, losing almost every seat. There were plenty of people to tell us we were wrong; but that turned out to be exactly what happened on the day, with the SNP missing just three seats and Labour reduced to a solitary Scottish MP, Ian Murray for Edinburgh South.

However, we don't want to give the impression that we are happy with the performance of the polls. The error was not as large as some people seem to think it was, but it was still too wide. An enquiry set up by the British Polling Council is currently investigating all the polls at the 2015 election, and we hope that when it reports in 2016 that its conclusions will be helpful in ensuring that the polls at future elections are nearer the mark than they were at this one. Nevertheless, we are fairly sure we know already why Ipsos MORI's polls came out the way they did.[4] As we mentioned above, we measured the Conservative vote correctly, but we overestimated the Labour vote and underestimated the number of non-voters, and that was caused by the answers Labour supporters gave us about how sure they were that they would actually vote. (We set out our evidence for this viewpoint in more detail in a later chapter.)

Taking account of what we now know about the election result, we believe that we can trust what our polls, and the other polls, tell us about public

---

[4] There is no guarantee, of course, that different polls were not affected by different problems, so the BPC Enquiry may well still tell us things we didn't know based on the evidence of the other polls that we have not yet seen in detail. And, unfortunately, knowing what went wrong may not necessarily indicate an immediate solution to prevent that happening again – that may still take much further work.

opinion before and during the election within any reasonable margin of error. They can show us why people preferred one party to another, what the public thought about the issues, the leaders and the election campaign, and to some extent what might have happened if the parties had played their hands differently or the course of events had unfolded differently.

Before we begin to consider the polls, we begin by examining the election result that we hope to explain further.

Anatomy of a Conservative victory

The Conservative victory in 2015 was not the result of a single phenomenon but a conflation of events with different types of voters. In a sense this is always true in any election. It is a familiar if trite statement that there is no such thing as a general election, rather there are 650 constituency elections going on at once. But usually there is a fairly simple pattern. Modern elections are mostly national, and the vast majority of the constituency battles reflect the national mood and the national campaign. Even so, it is seldom one-dimensional. The marginal seats may be different from the safe seats, certain regions may buck the national trend, local issues and local candidates may be significant in a few places. But, still, these are usually mere details. A single narrative can still explain most of what is going on and give a broad understanding of the result. In 2015, however, the picture was more complex than usual.

The strategic considerations

The starting point for understanding the 2015 British general election is the result of the election in 2010. British politics is relatively stable and so it is always easier to understand the results in terms of change from one election to another rather than assuming that the parties start from scratch in recruiting voters each time.

Election victories are counted in constituency seats, not aggregated totals of votes. So we begin from the fact that the Conservatives won 306 seats in 2010: they would therefore need 20 gains for an overall majority of the 650 seats in the House of Commons. Labour would need 68 gains, from any of the other parties, to get a majority of their own; but, failing that, if nothing else changed then 25 net gains directly from the Conservatives would make Labour the largest party, and as few as 15 or so might leave them the better placed to reach agreement with the smaller parties and form the next government.

In the simplest scenario, if uniform swing ruled (and it doesn't), we could easily calculate what this meant in votes. The Conservatives could make the 20 gains they needed with a 2% swing from Labour in all their target seats – in other words, if two voters in every hundred there switched from Labour to Conservative (or if that was the net effect after a more complex pattern of switching between parties). Another way of expressing the same change is to say that Labour's lead would be reduced or the Conservative lead increased by 4 percentage points. (The change in the gap is always double the swing, because the voter who swings gets counted twice, being knocked off one side's total and also added to the tally on the other side). So the other way of looking at it is that the Conservatives needed to capture every Labour seat where they were less than 4 points behind in 2010. Labour's task was harder, having been further from victory at the last election. Labour would need slightly more than a 5% swing from the Conservatives to make the 68 gains they needed for a majority.

However, it was plain that a great deal had changed since 2010, and uniform swing might be a very poor guide; the constituencies which had had the closest results in 2010 might not still be the ones most vulnerable in 2015. Liberal Democrat support had collapsed to barely a third of its previous level, while UKIP, the Scottish National Party and to a lesser extent the Greens had all dramatically increased their support. This would probably not break down evenly in vote share across the country, so swings might well be far from uniform. Consequently, to make sense of the strategic situation in 2015 it is necessary to break the election down into at least four separate battlegrounds as follows:

1. the constituencies in England and Wales that were marginal between the Conservatives and Labour (roughly 120 seats, depending on how one defines "marginal");

2. the constituencies in England and Wales won by the Liberal Democrats in 2010 (46 seats);

3. the supposedly-safe seats held by one or other of the two major parties in England and Wales[5] (roughly 400 seats); and

4. Scotland (59 seats).

A few seats came into none of these categories (notably the 18 in Northern Ireland), too exceptional to fit into any national pattern[6]. None

---

[5] Which, realistically, included all the theoretically-marginal seats where the Liberal Democrats had been the challengers.

[6] They include Plaid Cymru's seats and any targets they might hope to win, the solitary Green seat in Brighton and the three by-election gains by smaller parties (two for UKIP, one for George Galloway). Northern Ireland's 18 constituencies, which are not contested by the major parties, were

would stand or fall on trends that would show up in the national opinion polls, so we shall not dwell on them further.

The battle for constituencies

As always, the biggest potential pickings for the two major parties were in the constituencies that were marginal between them, where many seats can be picked up for a relatively small swing in votes. Almost all of these constituencies are in England and Wales. These are the constituencies where a general election is usually decided, and either party might have won or lost the 2015 election here had things turned out differently.

But this was not the only potentially important battleground. It was clear from the opinion polls and from the results of local and European elections that Liberal Democrat support had collapsed to a fraction of its former level. The Liberal Democrats had won 57 seats in 2010 – as such there was a possibility that many of these would be vulnerable to challenge by Labour or the Conservatives. (The only exception to this was in Scotland, where it was clear that a very different dynamic was in place, and Labour was hardly better placed to gain from the Liberal Democrat collapse than were the Tories.) In fact, if the Liberal Democrats were to lose those votes evenly across the country, they would also lose the vast majority of their seats. In most of these constituencies the Conservatives were in second place in 2010 and would expect to be the beneficiaries. On the other hand, if (as the polls suggested) more of the former Liberal Democrats were intending to switch to Labour than to the Conservatives, there was also the possibility that Labour might achieve enough of a swing to come through from third place and win some of these constituencies; but this was a fairly remote hope as the Conservative vote was already substantial in many of these targets, and Labour would need to pick up much more than the evaporating Lib Dem vote to come close to winning the seat.

However, the position in the Liberal Democrat constituencies was complicated by the reputation that Liberal Democrats had built up over many years for successfully nursing their constituencies through diligent

---

not included in the polls; as ever, they marched to an entirely different beat and are outside the scope of this work. What could be counted upon was that none of the MPs from the Province would be either Conservative or Labour.

local work, their 'pavement politics', and so building up a formidable and resilient personal vote for their sitting MPs. Uniform swing has never been a good predictor of the number of seats won by the Liberal Democrats. (In fact, in 2010, they made a net loss of seats even though their vote share increased slightly, while in 1997 they more than doubled their number of seats even though their share of the vote went down.) At past elections, Lib Dem incumbents had often succeeded in holding onto their seats against the national tide. Many observers believed that they would be able to do so again, so that even if the party lost two-thirds of its vote nationally, as the polls suggested was likely, a good many of its MPs would survive; constituency polling seemed to point to the same conclusion.

The third potential battleground was the supposedly-safe seats held by both the major parties in England and Wales. Since the last general election, UKIP had risen from being a bit-part player to a genuine challenger, heading for anywhere between 10% and 20% of the vote depending on which poll you looked at and how you interpreted it. They had come first in the 2014 European Parliament election, and had two seats in the House of Commons – both retained triumphantly in by-elections after their defecting Conservative MPs voluntarily submitted themselves to the verdict of their constituents and appealed for a new mandate. UKIP's chances of gaining further seats would not depend on their national share of the vote, but on how effectively they could concentrate their appeal in the few constituencies they targeted. The polls suggested that most of UKIP's increased support was coming from former Conservative voters, and naturally enough their targets were therefore mostly Conservative-held seats, especially on the East Coast of England, around the Thames estuary and along the proposed route of the controversial rail expansion, HS2; but they also, reportedly, fancied their chances in some Labour strongholds in the North of England, and some Labour sympathisers were certainly taking the threat seriously.

Nor were UKIP the only party who could benefit from the political vacuum created by the Lib Dems' loss of credibility as a destination for the protest vote. The Greens made their mark more slowly and less dramatically than UKIP, but by the time the general election approached they were also a safe bet to increase their share of the vote significantly, and possibly to pick up one or two extra seats in addition to the one they already held in Brighton.

The final piece of the jigsaw puzzle was Scotland. With less than a year to go to the election, Scotland looked set to have little if any importance to the wider result. Labour winning the bulk of the seats there seemed a foregone conclusion – they had not failed to win at least 40 seats north of the border since 1959, and at the last few elections (since the Scottish Conservatives had ceased to be a credible force) very few seats had changed hands. The Liberal Democrats had a handful of MPs, and apparently stood to lose most of them – their collapse of support since 2010 had been even more calamitous in Scotland than in England and Wales – in which case Labour would inevitably be the beneficiary. The Scottish National Party were performing impressively in local elections and at Holyrood, having won majority control of the Scottish government in 2011, but they seemed unlikely to make much impression on Westminster seats, given the impressive margins by which Labour had held most of its constituencies in 2010.

After the Independence Referendum in September 2014, however, there was a sudden and dramatic change. Labour support plummeted and that for the SNP rose. The Westminster voting intention polls abruptly fell into line with those for the Scottish Parliament, suggesting a swing of up to 25%, with the SNP heading towards winning half the Scottish vote. This completely changed the situation. With vote shifts on anything like this scale, all Labour's seats in Scotland were potential SNP gains, and the SNP rather than Labour would also pick up the seats left by the eclipse of the Liberal Democrats. Scotland therefore had to be regarded as having as many seats where the result was uncertain as any of the other categories.

Floating voters in the centre-ground marginals

This situation, of an election which needed to be fought on several different fronts, posed challenges for both Labour and the Conservatives. There was no guarantee that the key voters holding the balance of power in different types of constituencies would have the same policy preferences, the same priorities or even the same values. What might appeal to one group could alienate another – and, of course, trying to say different things to different voters can backfire badly, even if a party is cynical enough to try it. Both parties found themselves needing to decide how far to appeal to their 'core vote' and how far to shift to the political centre-ground to attract floating voters. That dilemma is always present to a certain extent, but normally parties target marginal constituencies because this is where most seats would be won or lost for a given movement in votes.

Generally it is assumed that the results in these constituencies are determined by the decisions of the 'floating voters', who might vote Conservative, Labour or not vote at all, and that moderate, centrist policies have most appeal to this group. Usually the focus of the two major parties' efforts is on competing with each other for the same group of voters, and the natural strategy is to converge on the ideological centre-ground (wherever that is for the time being), with differences between the parties becoming less and less marked.

In 2015, however, there were signs that this strategy was not proving productive. Labour needed positive gains for any hope of victory. They were making few inroads into Conservative support. The polls suggested that only tiny numbers of voters had switched from the Conservatives to Labour and as many if not more had switched in the opposite direction. On further investigation, the reason for this became clear – supporters of the two parties were more polarised than is typically supposed. Both sides had kept the support of the bulk of those who had voted for them in 2010, and few of these had misgivings about their support. Even on issues where the Conservatives were weak among the rest of the public, they were still strong among their own voters; similarly, Labour voters backed their party even on the issues that other voters saw as the strongest reasons for not voting Labour. To use a military analogy, this was trench warfare: both sides were well dug in, and there was no obvious prospect of either making much ground. Had this been the only hope for either party of achieving the swing they needed to win the election, there would have been nothing much they could do beyond sitting tight and waiting for somebody to invent the electoral equivalent of the tank.

But swing is not only made up of direct switching from one party to another, it also takes account of gains and losses from other parties. Even if Conservative candidates held onto all their votes, that would not save their seats if their Labour opponents could find enough extra votes from some other source to reach a higher total, and it was clear that support for the Liberal Democrats had collapsed since 2010. In the vast majority of Conservative-Labour marginals the Liberal Democrats had run third at the last election, often with a substantial share of the vote. Most of these votes were now presumably up for grabs, and if Labour could do better than the Tories at securing them they might be able to win a good many extra seats as a result. Moreover, Labour had every realistic hope of doing exactly this: since it was discontent with Nick Clegg's joining the coalition that was at the root of the disillusionment of many Lib Dem voters, the bulk of those who had abandoned the party were likely to be more sympathetic to Labour than to the Conservatives.

Competition between Labour and Conservatives for the support of former Liberal Democrats was likely to take place in the ideological centre-ground, just as was any direct competition for each other's voters. But in 2015 another new element complicated the picture – the emergence of UKIP and, later in the parliament, the Greens as credible competitors for votes. Traditionally, the Conservatives have faced no significant threat on their right wing, Labour none on their left wing: there has been a third party challenge of varying strength to be dealt with in the centre (particularly since the 1980s and the rise of the Liberal-SDP alliance), but their flanks have been largely secure. This has meant that all their campaigning guns could safely be pointed in broadly the same direction, and explains why falling back on the heartlands for their target audience has frequently been seen as a defeatist retreat. But for several years before this election it had become clear that in 2015, the Conservatives faced the threat of losing substantial numbers of their votes to UKIP. True, Labour was also losing some support to UKIP, and it was even argued that many of the votes that the Conservatives were losing in that way were 'naturally' Labour votes in any case; but the Conservatives were losing most.

On the other hand, the Conservatives had nothing much to fear from the Greens but Labour did: the danger was not only from direct switching from Labour to Green, but also that the Greens might pick up the support of left-wing former Liberal Democrats who would otherwise have voted Labour. This left each of the major parties with a threat on their flank – the Conservatives, it was generally felt, could best counter the UKIP threat by moving to the right, while Labour could defend itself against the Greens by shifting to the left.

Neither UKIP nor the Greens were ever likely to take many parliamentary seats, despite the paranoia of some MPs in 'safe' constituencies who felt threatened by them; but both could and probably would take votes in constituencies they couldn't win, including the Conservative-Labour marginals, and these votes, like those of the former Liberal Democrats, might be enough to swing the result between the two bigger parties.

The final part of the equation in the Conservative-Labour marginals was turnout. At the 2010 election, only two-thirds of the registered electorate bothered to vote. Many of those who did not, of course, were entirely neutral between the parties, seeing no good in any of them; and a few may have been so genuinely torn between more than one party or candidate that they could not make up their minds. But there was still, almost certainly, a large pool of potential voters who if they voted would only vote one way, but who hadn't voted at all; naturally, therefore, any party that could mobilise their own non-voters could gain an advantage.[7] It is an article of faith in both parties, especially among activists, that their own non-voters tend towards the extremes of the party ideologically, frustrated because their party has moved too far towards the centre, not seeing the point of voting because they no longer feel there is enough difference between Conservative and Labour for it to matter. Therefore the 'get out the vote' element of their campaign objectives, as well as the defence of their flanks against the emerging new parties, might be served best by emphasising the differences between the parties and their more extreme or radical stances. With no significant movement directly between the Conservatives and Labour, it was the net outcome of these turnout questions and vote movements involving other parties that would determine the swing and therefore the destiny of these marginal seats.

This strategic situation determined which voters it would be most productive for each party to target and try to persuade. In most elections, the Conservatives would have been best advised to concentrate on wavering Labour supporters, and vice versa. But in 2015 this was not the case. The Conservatives could achieve most by appealing to those voters who knew that they preferred a Conservative-led government to a Labour

---

[7] This is a big part of the explanation for the apparent paradox that consistently before the election the polls seemed to show no movement between the Conservatives and Labour and yet showed Labour having pulled level with the Conservatives in support. From the very start of the parliament we found that Labour supporters were almost as likely as Conservatives to tell us that they were "absolutely certain" to vote at an immediate election, whereas previously there had been a big differential in the Conservatives' favour. Had this materialised at the ballot boxes, it would have delivered a substantial swing to Labour without the need to win over any Conservative supporters at all.

one, but might nevertheless not vote Conservative – right-leaning Liberal Democrats and former Liberal Democrats, most of those who were considering voting for UKIP, and those who might not vote at all. Labour's optimum strategy was the mirror image of this, with the SNP, Greens and Plaid Cymru in the corresponding role to UKIP. Essentially, there was no overlap between the Conservative and Labour target groups, and so no reason for the parties to compete directly with each other for the hearts and minds of the same voters.

This in turn, as we shall see in a later chapter, meant that the most natural direction for each party's campaign was a negative one, attacking their opponents. Both Conservatives and Labour needed to remind voters who already knew which government they preferred how important it was to them that the other side didn't win, and that they risked allowing that to happen if they voted for the smaller parties or didn't vote at all. A vote not cast for the Conservatives or Labour would be a wasted vote. Hence, campaigns based around emphasising the dangers of five years of the other party's rule were likely long before the parties began to put out their messages. We don't know whether the parties' campaign chiefs reached their decisions by the same process of reasoning as we did, but the prominence of negative elements in the messages of both main parties certainly did not surprise us.

The results

In 2015, the Conservatives' support went up by about 600,000 votes on 2010, and Labour's by roughly 750,000 votes, in a slightly higher overall turnout. This left the Conservatives on just under 38% of the vote in Great Britain, Labour on 31%, a swing to Labour but of less than half a percent, the lowest ever net election-to-election movement between the two. UKIP took more than one vote in eight, well ahead of the Liberal Democrats whose support had fallen by nearly two-thirds, to 8%. The next biggest party were the SNP, with almost 5% nationally, accumulated entirely in Scotland of course, where they took half of all the votes. The Greens, disappointing by comparison with their standing at the start of 2015, had 4%.

This much we know from the official results. The polling data throws more light on the underlying dynamics by indicating how the switching between different parties added up to the final result[8]. It seems clear that there was very little switching directly between the two main parties, adding up to perhaps 1.5% of the public in total, but that what there was favoured the Tories, probably by around two-to-one (in other words, roughly half a million who voted Labour in 2010 switched to the Conservatives in 2015, and quarter of a million moved in the other direction).

However, the movements to UKIP and from the Liberal Democrats were much bigger. Decisions of former Liberal Democrats probably decided the election. Labour was the biggest beneficiary, taking 19% of the 2010 vote, according to our polls, while the Conservatives took 14%; but 6% went to the Greens and 6% to UKIP, and 4% to other parties (mostly Plaid Cymru and the SNP). Labour's failure to carve out a bigger advantage here, even though most of those defecting from the Liberal Democrats seem clearly to have preferred a non-Conservative government, proved costly in the Conservative marginals that Labour hoped to capture. This contributed significantly to the Conservatives' achieving an overall majority, if a tiny one.

Labour suffered a smaller net loss than the Tories to UKIP (there may have been up to four times as many switchers to UKIP from the Tories as from Labour). But Labour also lost significant numbers to the SNP and the Greens (and also lost out because of the many left-of-centre Liberal Democrats that switched to Green rather than Labour); combined with the Tory net gain direct from Labour, this kept the overall swing down to such a minimal level.

The voting trends were not uniform, however, and the variations in the pattern had a strong influence on the outcome of the election in seats, which did not flow in the same directions or the same proportions as the votes. For one thing, there was a strong regional dimension. Labour did much better than average in London, and a little better in the North of England, but was humiliated in Scotland where its share fell by 18 points in the face of the SNP landslide. The Conservative performance was less

---

[8] These projections are based on Ipsos MORI's aggregated election polls, which are weighted to match the final result and turnout at regional level. However, they should only be regarded estimates – not least because they depend upon people telling us how they voted in 2010, which we know has never been entirely reliable.

19

uneven, worst in Scotland but even there their number of absolute votes increased and their share was down only slightly.

Table 2: Voting by region

	2015 vote						Change since 2010					
	Con %	Lab %	LD %	UKIP %	Grn %	Nat %	Con %	Lab %	LD %	UKIP %	Grn %	Nat %
All GB	38	31	8	13	4	5	+1	+2	−16	+12	+2	+4
East Midlands	43	32	6	16	3	0	+2	+2	-15	+13	+2	0
Eastern	49	22	8	16	4	0	+2	+2	-16	+12	+2	0
Greater London	35	44	8	8	5	0	+0	+7	-14	+6	+3	0
North East	25	47	6	17	4	0	+2	+3	-17	+14	+3	0
North West	31	45	7	14	3	0	-1	+5	-15	+10	+3	0
Scotland	15	24	8	2	1	50	-2	-18	-11	+1	+1	+30
South East	51	18	9	15	5	0	+2	+2	-17	+11	+4	0
South West	47	18	15	14	6	0	+4	+2	-20	+9	+5	0
Wales	27	37	7	14	3	12	+1	+1	-14	+11	+2	+1
West Midlands	42	33	6	16	3	0	+2	+2	-15	+12	+3	0
Yorks & Humber	33	39	7	16	4	0	-0	+5	-16	+13	+3	0

Source: Calculated from election results in House of Commons Library Research Paper 10/36 (8 July 2010) and Briefing Paper CBP7186 (28 July 2015). Rows do not sum to 100% as votes for other parties (0.9% of total) are included in percentages but not shown.

Despite much mention during the campaign of George Osborne's plan for a 'northern powerhouse', and the promised investment to achieve that, Conservative share of the vote was up slightly in the North East (the least obvious beneficiary of such policies), but level in Yorkshire and actually down in the North-West – apart from Scotland, the Tories' worst regional performance of the election; even in London they did marginally better, and raised their vote share by a whisker over what was achieved in 2010. This led to the unprecedented outcome that each of the four nations of the UK gave most votes to a different party:

- the Conservatives won in England;
- Labour won in Wales;
- the SNP won in Scotland; and
- the Democratic Unionists won in Northern Ireland.

In the marginal seats in England, Labour did well in the seats it already held and which might have been Conservative targets, but more poorly in the ones held by the Conservatives which Labour hoped to win and where, on average, the Conservative vote increased by more than Labour's. The Liberal Democrat vote collapsed fairly uniformly across almost all its seats and in every region, while UKIP made equal gains almost everywhere except Scotland and, to a lesser extent, London, but not sufficiently concentrated anywhere to capture any seats.

To understand the impact of these overall patterns, we must return to considering the four distinct battlegrounds outlined earlier.[9]

The Conservative-Labour marginals in England and Wales

In the Conservative-Labour marginals there was little overall swing, and each party did better in the constituencies it already held. Coincidentally, there were exactly the same number of seats in England and Wales, 59, where the Conservatives led Labour by a margin of less than 10% of the vote (the traditional definition of a 'marginal seat') as the number where Labour led the Conservatives by a similarly-slim margin.

- In the Conservative marginals, Conservative support rose on average by 4.2 points and Labour's by only 1.6, a 1.3% swing to the Conservatives; but

- In the Labour marginals, the Conservative vote share on average stayed exactly level while Labour's rose by 3.0 points, a 1.5% swing in the other direction

If every seat in these categories had swung in exactly the same way all would have been retained by the party that already held them. A few seats were captured, nevertheless, against the general tide: Labour won ten previously Conservative constituencies, all but one in London or the north of England; but countering this, the Conservatives picked up eight Labour seats, scattered across the country, including the prized scalp of Ed Balls at Morley & Outwood, on the outskirts of Leeds.

---

[9] In all these analyses, we exclude the five exceptional constituencies whose inclusion would distort the averages because of their special circumstances – the Speaker's seat at Buckingham, and four others where the comparison with the 2010 results is misleading. (These were the two seats captured by UKIP and one by Respect in by-elections, and Thirsk & Malton where the election in 2010 was delayed by the death of a candidate and so fought on a different day with an uncharacteristically low turnout.)

Most of the more marginal Conservative seats were ones that the party had captured from Labour in 2010, so the increase in the Conservative share of the vote probably arose largely from the incumbency advantage that almost any new MP can expect. (This reflects not only the personal vote that the new MP has built up, but the loss of the personal vote of the previous Labour MP, which was working to Labour's advantage when he or she was defending the seat in 2010.)

Table 3: Conservative/Labour marginals in England and Wales

Average constituency vote share change, 2010-15

Constituency type (2010 result)	Seats	Change in vote % share					Turnout change	Seats won				
		Con	Lab	LD	UKIP	Grn		Con	Lab	LD	PC	Grn
All seats*	568	+1.3	+3.4	−15.8	+10.8	+3.0	+0.4	327	230	7	3	1
Lab 1st Con 2nd	139	−1.0	+3.6	−13.3	+12.9	+2.3	−0.0	8	131	0	0	0
Con 1st Lab 2nd	134	+2.7	+0.8	−13.6	+10.8	+2.1	+0.9	124	10	0	0	0
Lab 1st, Con 2nd, margin 0-10%	59	0.0	+3.0	−13.7	+11.5	+2.3	+0.1	8	51	0	0	0
Con gains from Lab	8	+4.1	−0.5	−14.5	+11.7	+2.1	+0.6	8	0	0	0	0
Con 1st, Lab 2nd, margin 0-10%	59	+4.2	+1.6	−14.1	+9.2	+2.0	+1.4	50	9	0	0	0
Con 1st, Lab 2nd, margin 10-15%	28	+3.1	−0.7	−13.2	+11.3	+1.9	+0.1	27	1	0	0	0
Lab gains from Con	10	+2.1	+8.5	−15.0	+6.0	+1.3	+1.9	0	10	0	0	0

Source: Calculated from election results as reported by the BBC (www.bbc.co.uk) for 2015 and by the House of Commons Library in Research Paper 10/36 (8 July 2010) for 2010
*Omits Buckingham, Bradford West, Clacton, Rochester & Strood and Thirsk & Malton.

This was true in almost all of the minority of seats the Conservatives lost as well as the majority that they held: only in two of the seats they lost was the Conservative vote actually down (and in one case the seat was already Conservative in 2010 while in the other the Labour candidate in 2015 was the former MP, in both cases reducing the potential incumbency effect). In fact in three of the ten (Brentford & Isleworth, Ealing Central & Acton and Dewsbury), the Conservative increase was as good or better than in the average Conservative-held marginal, but Labour won with a double-digit improvement in its own share.

Labour's ten gains stand out from the other Labour targets mainly because Labour's performance here was dramatically better (with an average 8.5 percentage point increase in vote share), while that of UKIP was rather worse; the Conservatives under-performed across these ten constituencies, averaging only a 2.1% point increase, but not dramatically so. The lower

UKIP increase in these constituencies implies at least the possibility that Labour succeeded here in persuading some of those who would otherwise have voted for UKIP to vote tactically for Labour instead, although some of these seats were in London where the UKIP increase was low. Certainly the lower-than-average Green Party vote increase suggests some tactical squeezing of that vote, although probably not enough to be decisive on its own.

In the small number of Labour-held seats that fell to the Conservatives, the story is one of both Conservative over-performance and Labour under-performance. Labour's best performances were in its safest seats; in the marginals it was defending its average increase in vote share was +3.0 points, lower than the +3.4 it averaged in all of its seats. But in the eight that got away, Labour's share fell in five and rose by less than half a point in another two; only in one case, Derby North, was the increase (+3.5) in line with that in the seats that were held and the defeat attributable solely to a better-than-average Conservative performance. Nevertheless, the Conservative vote was up in all eight cases (ranging from +2.3 in Bolton West to +5.4 in Southampton Itchen), compared to the lack of any increase achieved across the Labour-held marginals on average, and the − 1.1 fall averaged across Labour-held seats as a whole. But the Green, UKIP and Liberal Democrat performances here were not much different from that in the other Labour marginals, suggesting that unusual levels of tactical voting were not the decisive factor.

However, these few results were the exceptions, out of line with the general trend, probably because of local factors but in any case making up the inevitable, essentially random, element of variation that occurs in any election. The real story of the marginal seats was that of the vast majority where swings were mostly towards the incumbent and the victorious party was the same as in 2010. Of the 87 seats where Labour was second to the Conservatives in 2010 but trailed by less than 15% of the vote, the Conservatives retained 77 in 2015.

This story of 'no change' may superficially seem dull by comparison with that of the seats that changed hands, of the upheaval in Scotland and the windfalls delivered by the withering of the Liberal Democrats, but its importance cannot be over-stated. In reality, it is here that elections are decided. 2015 was no different just because the decision was one of 'no change'. **The success of the Conservatives in holding their lines,**

conceding no significant net gains to Labour after five years in government pursuing policies that might generally be expected to be unpopular, was the foundation on which Cameron's Comeback was built. It certainly did not seem obvious in 2010, perhaps not even likely, that it would happen.

Every British government since the 1950s serving a full term had lost vote share at the next election; elsewhere in Europe, government after government that tackled the economic effects of the global financial crisis by pursuing austerity policies was being turfed out in favour of socialist and populist opponents promising a less stringent spending regime (as, for example, in France and Greece). Electoral success depended entirely on the government being able to claim sufficient economic success that those voters who had preferred a Conservative government in 2010 felt austerity measures had been justified, and were therefore prepared to vote for the same economic diet in 2015.

From Labour's point of view, this was the only 'theatre of war' where they had any realistic prospect of making the gains they needed to return to government. In 2010, the disaster in Scotland was unforeseen and the fate of the Liberal Democrats uncertain, but unlikely to offer Labour many easy pickings. The 87 marginal Conservative seats would have to provide most of the 68 gains Labour needed for a majority or, at the least the 30 or 40 seats that would ensure Labour was the dominant party in a hung Parliament. But Labour did not even make a perceptible dent in these Conservative defences. **In essence, the 2015 election was won and lost here.**

Of course, the Conservative success was not simply one of solid defence and minimal movement. The net changes in the major parties' shares of the votes were generally small and the swings between them mostly insufficient for seats to be captured, but the underlying churn of votes was certainly much bigger. Here, as elsewhere in the country, the Liberal Democrats fell, UKIP and the Greens rose, and where parties maintained their vote share it was by bringing in through one door enough extra votes to compensate for the ones they lost out of another.

With so much media attention before the election on the possibility of defections to UKIP costing the Conservatives seats, and so much of the Conservative focus during the campaign emphasising the dangers of a hung Parliament, clearly intended to counter this risk, it is worth noting UKIP's performance in the key marginals. On average, UKIP did worse, but only a little worse, in the more marginal Conservative-held seats than in safer Conservative seats where a UKIP vote could make a protest – and at least conceivably elect a UKIP MP – without the danger of handing the seat to Labour. This may be an indication that the Conservative campaign succeeded in provoking second thoughts or at least tactical voting among some of those who were attracted by UKIP, but if so the benefits were modest, about 1.5% of the vote. There were only four seats that the Conservatives won narrowly enough from Labour for this to have made a difference, and one of these was Thurrock where in fact a double-the-average shift to UKIP almost handed the seat to Labour in a three-way fight. Moreover, there is no sign of any tactical voting for the Tories by UKIP supporters in the Labour-held marginals that the Tories were trying to win.

This does not entirely preclude the possibility that the campaign was a success – far more voters than might be supposed are unaware of the tactical situation in their constituencies, so any swing that was achieved might have operated across the board rather than being particularly concentrated in the marginal constituencies. It is certainly true that UKIP's final share of the vote was a little lower than their standing a few weeks before the election as suggested by most of the polls. On the other hand, the concentration of lower UKIP gains in marginal Conservative constituencies may mean no more than that those who would otherwise have voted UKIP were particularly susceptible to the incumbency effect and liable to give the benefit of the doubt to a new MP. But the evidence is at best unclear.

The safer Conservative and Labour seats

In the seats where the margin between Labour and Conservative was a double-digit percentage of the vote, the main interest was the possibility that UKIP or the Greens might pull off a prodigious swing and either take the seat or hand it on a plate to the party that trailed in 2010 by siphoning off too many of the incumbent's votes.

UKIP was defending two seats, both won by the Conservatives in 2010, where in each case the MP had defected to UKIP and then called a by-election, both in Autumn 2014. They held one, Clacton, taking 44% of the vote, and lost the other, Rochester & Strood, with 30%. But constituencies which have had recent sensational by-elections are notoriously unusual in their behaviour at the subsequent general election, and this throws little light on what was happening elsewhere.

Excluding the exceptional cases, as we have already noted, UKIP increased its share of the vote on average by a little under 11 points. Impressive as this was, it was not of course sufficient to deliver any seats on uniform swing – gains could come only where the party managed a much better-than-average performance.

Table 4: Conservative/Labour safer seats in England and Wales

Average constituency vote share change, 2010-15

Constituency type (2010 result)	Seats	Change in vote % share					Turnout change	Seats won				
		Con	Lab	LD	UKIP	Grn		Con	Lab	LD	PC	Grn
All seats*	568	+1.3	+3.4	−15.8	+10.8	+3.0	+0.4	327	230	7	3	1
Con 1st, Lab 2nd, margin 10%+	75	+1.4	+0.2	−13.2	+12.0	+2.2	+0.4	74	1	0	0	0
Con 1st, LD 2nd, margin 10%+	145	+2.4	+2.7	−17.9	+10.5	+3.5	−0.3	145	0	0	0	0
Lab 1st, Con 2nd, margin 10%+	80	−1.8	+4.0	−13.0	+13.9	+2.3	−0.1	0	80	0	0	0
Lab 1st, LD 2nd, margin 10%+	55	+0.1	+7.5	−18.3	+10.0	+4.4	+1.5	0	55	0	0	0

Source: Calculated from election results as reported by the BBC (www.bbc.co.uk) for 2015 and by the House of Commons Library in Research Paper 10/36 (8 July 2010) for 2010
*Omits Buckingham, Bradford West, Clacton, Rochester & Strood and Thirsk & Malton.

But in only ten constituencies did UKIP manage to double this average, and increase their vote share by at least 21.6 points. (Table 5.) Five of these were safe Labour seats in the North of England, three were safe Conservative seats and two were marginals; these last five were all on the East coast or the Thames estuary, as indeed were the two by-election gains. In every case the defending party held the seat and only in Thurrock, as already mentioned, was the result particularly close, although Nigel Farage in Thanet South also got within six points. Hartlepool, with a slightly lower vote increase (+21.0) allied with a better base performance in 2010, also saw the UKIP candidate finishing second and less than 10% of the vote behind, but only the defeat in Rochester & Strood had any effect in changing the post-election complexion of the House of Commons.

Table 5: Best UKIP performances

	Change in UKIP vote share 2010-15 %	Con %	Lab %	UKIP %	Others %
Clacton*	+44.4	36.7	14.4	**44.4**	4.5
Castle Point	+31.2	**50.9**	13.8	31.2	4.1
Rochester & Strood*	+30.5	**44.1**	19.8	30.5	5.7
Heywood & Middleton	+29.6	19.1	**43.1**	32.2	5.6
Thanet South	+26.9	**38.1**	23.8	32.4	5.7
Dagenham & Rainham	+26.3	24.4	**41.4**	29.8	4.4
Boston & Skegness	+24.3	**43.8**	16.5	33.8	5.9
Thurrock	+24.3	**33.7**	32.6	31.7	2.0
Rotherham	+24.3	12.3	**52.5**	30.2	5.0
Rother Valley	+22.5	23.3	**43.6**	28.1	5.0
Makerfield	+22.4	19.5	**51.8**	22.4	6.2
South Shields	+22.0	16.6	**51.3**	22.0	10.1

Source: Calculated from election results as reported by the BBC (www.bbc.co.uk) for 2015 and by the House of Commons Library in Research Paper 10/36 (8 July 2010) for 2010
*Seats already held by UKIP after by-elections in 2014

Nor did the Greens do any better, unsurprisingly in view of the modest share of the national vote they eventually received. They had already in demonstrated their ability to channel their support into winning an individual constituency, Brighton Pavilion in 2010, and they tightened their grip there in 2015 with an 11-point increase in vote share. Elsewhere their best result was in Bristol West, a Liberal Democrat seat, and presumably most of the plummeting Liberal Democrat vote there switched straight to them, but their 27% share of the vote fell well short of preventing the previously second-placed Labour from winning, with 36%.

In Norwich South, a faint Green hope in 2010 but which had ended as a three-way marginal with the Greens in fourth place on 15%, they failed to make any net gains from the Lib Dem collapse at all, and in fact finished with a slightly lower 14% in 2015: presumably tactical voting was operating here to prevent the risk of the Tories slipping through the middle to victory. (As this was the only constituency in the country with a substantial existing Green vote and the remotest possibility of a Conservative victory, there are no comparable seats where a similar pattern might have been detected.) Yet apart from the Speaker's seat at Buckingham, not contested by the major parties, this was still the Greens' next nearest miss, 25% behind the winners. In none of the safe seats, Conservative or Labour, did any meaningful challenge materialise, even to the extent of providing a platform for future elections. The Greens achieved a ten-point increase in a handful of the safest seats (Hackney North & Stoke Newington, Holborn & St Pancras, Sheffield Central and, slightly incongruously, the Isle of Wight), but like UKIP failed to make even a ripple in the water of the bigger picture.

The Liberal Democrat seats

If the foundation of the Conservative victory was in the traditional marginals, the difference between another coalition and a single-party majority was settled in the seats won at the previous election by the Liberal Democrats. Nick Clegg's party entered the election defending 57 seats. Of these 11 were in Scotland, and all but one fell under the SNP juggernaut; consideration of these we can defer for the moment. Of the other 46, they held only 7, with 27 being won by the Conservatives and 12 by Labour. **Without those 27 seats the Conservatives would have had only 303, well short of a majority** and in fact fewer than they won in 2010.

Table 6: Liberal Democrat held seats in England and Wales

Average constituency vote share change, 2010-15

Constituency type (2010 result)	Seats	Change in vote % share					Turnout change	Seats won				
		Con	Lab	LD	UKIP	Grn		Con	Lab	LD	PC	Grn
All seats*	568	+1.3	+3.4	−15.8	+10.8	+3.0	+0.4	327	230	7	3	1
LD 1st Con 2nd	34	+2.0	+4.3	−16.6	+7.7	+3.5	+1.1	27	1	6	0	0
LD 1st Lab 2nd	11	−3.3	+12.3	−17.8	+7.3	+4.5	+2.3	0	11	0	0	0
LD 1st PC 2nd	1	−0.5	+3.9	−14.2	+7.7	+3.8	+3.6	0	0	1	0	0
LD 1st, Con 2nd, margin 0-10%	17	+3.5	+2.5	−16.6	+8.1	+3.4	+1.3	17	0	0	0	0
LD 1st, Con 2nd, margin 10%+	17	+0.5	+6.1	−16.5	+7.3	+3.6	+0.8	10	1	6	0	17

Source: Calculated from election results as reported by the BBC (www.bbc.co.uk) for 2015 and by the House of Commons Library in Research Paper 10/36 (8 July 2010) for 2010
*Omits Buckingham, Bradford West, Clacton, Rochester & Strood and Thirsk & Malton.

But these Conservative gains were not achieved by sweeping increases in Conservative support in these constituencies: they were, for the most part, pure windfalls. Liberal Democrat support plummeted almost everywhere, with little difference between seats where the nearest challengers were Labour and those where they were Conservatives, and little difference between the plainly marginal constituencies and the apparently safer ones. The UKIP vote rose in all these classes of constituencies, as did to a lesser extent the Green vote; and Labour's vote was well up almost everywhere, and by the most where they were already in second place. But the Conservative vote rose on average by only 2 points in the constituencies where they were challengers and fell in the other categories.

Nevertheless, the Conservatives had no need to achieve a significant increase in their own vote with the Liberal Democrat vote disintegrating to such a large extent; they needed only to stay ahead of Labour and watch as the Liberal Democrat vote fell past them and left them in the lead. (Indeed, in three of their gains, the Conservatives' own vote share also fell.)

In only a very few of the Liberal Democrats' seats was the pattern much different from this. In four of the six seats where the Liberal Democrats survived, the Conservative vote was also sharply down, and except in Southport the Liberal Democrat loss was also lower than average: in Southport and Carshalton & Wallington, the result was close and the Conservatives might have won had their vote held up better, but they ended a poor third in Sheffield Hallam (Nick Clegg's seat) and Leeds North West. In Norfolk North and Westmorland & Lonsdale, the majorities in 2010 were big enough to withstand the loss of votes being suffered elsewhere, although Tim Farron in the latter seat suffered a lower-than-average loss in any case.

The scale of the Liberal Democrat losses were one of the surprises of the election, not because the national opinion polls didn't predict them – they did – but because most people expected that the party's famed local campaigning and the personal vote commanded by its MPs would allow them to save many more seats than the overall swing would suggest. We have to admit we were among them: we thought it perfectly possible that the party's vote share might drop into single figures and yet by over-performing in the constituencies that they had won at the last election they might still emerge with twenty or even thirty seats. But this was not to be. Across England and Wales as a whole, the Liberal Democrat vote share was down 16 points; in the seats they were defending it was down 17 points on average, and in only five seats did they manage to keep the fall to under 10 points (four of which they lost anyway).[10]

So the near-extinction of the Liberal Democrats capped the Conservative victory, giving them the extra seats they needed for an overall majority. But it did not contribute to the defeat of Labour. Even had the personal vote of the Liberal Democrat MPs held up better, the outcome would only have been that the Conservatives were still much the largest party, albeit in a hung Parliament, and the probable consequence would have been a renewal of the coalition or a Conservative minority government dependent to some extent on Liberal Democrat acquiescence. Labour lost its chance because of what happened in Scotland.

Scotland

The Scottish National Party's stunning performance, winning 56 out of 59 seats in Scotland, was perhaps a slightly hollow victory as the Conservative success nationally meant the SNP were not left holding the balance of power in Parliament as they had hoped, and as much of the media had predicted. But this, of course, made their achievement no less remarkable and the impact no less painful for Labour. The SNP, which in 2010 had secured only 20% of the Scottish vote, took 50% this time. Labour, the Conservatives and the Liberal Democrats were left with a single seat each.

This, also, was predicted by the pre-election opinion polls but widely disbelieved or discounted. Before the Independence Referendum held in September 2014, there had been no apparent signs of such a political revolution, even though the SNP had secured a majority at the previous Scottish Parliament elections; conventional wisdom was that a good many Scots would 'lend' their vote to the SNP for less important elections but would never vote nationalist for Westminster. But attitudes apparently changed dramatically in a couple of weeks following the referendum, despite the fact that the nationalist cause had lost and Scotland had voted to stay within the Union.

The general election showed a veritable tide of votes flowing to the SNP with little local variation. They gained votes least successfully in the

---

[10] Ironically they did better in Scotland, limiting the loss to single figures in more than half their seats, but that proved useless in the face of the huge swing from Labour to the SNP in every case.

constituencies they already held, presumably because in those seats they had already squeezed out some of the juice that they were to find elsewhere; in fact six of their seven lowest gains were in their six existing seats. But even here their performance was hardly disappointing. In Na h-Eileanan an Iar (the Western Isles), their least successful result, they put on 9 points; in Dundee East, best of their six defences, they put on 22. In every other constituency in Scotland bar Ochil & South Perthshire, their increase in vote share was at least 25 points. More than a quarter of the voters in every one of those constituencies had voted for some other party in 2010, and voted for the SNP in 2015. Britain has never seen anything like it.

It was Labour, of course, who were the main sufferers, both in votes lost and in seats. Of the 41 constituencies Labour was defending in Scotland, their share of the vote rose in just one, Edinburgh South, and that was the only seat they kept. In all but three of the rest, their share fell by at least 10 points. The loss of these forty seats changed Labour from being a possible contender for power if things went their way in England to being inevitable also-rans.

The changing bias in the electoral system

The combination of the outcomes in these four groups of constituencies created one of the anomalous results for which Britain's First-Past-the-Post electoral system is renowned. Nationally, there was a net swing of votes, admittedly a small one, from Conservative to Labour; yet the Conservatives' number of seats went up, Labour's went down, and power passed from a coalition in a hung Parliament to a Conservative majority government.

The reason, nevertheless, is straightforward enough, and owes as much to the peculiarities of the outcome in 2010 as in 2015. At the 2010 election, the operation of the electoral system was considerably biased in favour of Labour and against the Conservatives, as it had been for a good many years; in 2015, the bias shifted so that the Conservatives now have the advantage. In 2010, assuming uniform swing from the actual result, if Labour and the Conservatives had won equal numbers of vote across the country then Labour would have won 307 seats and the Conservatives only 254, an advantage to Labour of 53 seats; in 2015 had the votes been equal, the Conservatives would have had the advantage by 302 seats to 255, a gap of 47. The bias had swung by exactly 100 seats.

Our breakdown of the result into its various 'theatres of war' shows how this happened. In the bulk of the seats that are marginal between the Conservatives and Labour, not much changed: there was a modest swing to Labour, and Labour made a very small net gain in seats. But in Scotland, Labour lost a great many seats while their loss of votes, viewed as a percentage of their national total, was small. Meanwhile, in England and Wales the Conservatives picked up a row of seats from the Liberal Democrats, without requiring much increase in their vote to do so, and this increase was in any case offset by a net loss of votes to UKIP which in the end cost them no seats at all.

Who voted which way?

To dig a little deeper into what happened, we need to go beyond the official results and consult the polling data to discover who voted for which party and how that has changed. For this purpose we use our Election Aggregate, which draws together data from all our polls during the campaign and is then adjusted in the light of the final result and turnout to provide estimates of the breakdown of the votes[11]. Its findings (Table 7) are mostly what one would expect after an election when the big parties concentrated on appealing to their existing supporters rather than reaching out to supporters of their opponents. Essentially, 2015 saw a further polarisation of the vote: each made most of its gains among the groups where it was already strongest, and tended to lose support where it was already weakest. For example, the Conservatives increased their share of the vote among the middle class (ABs and C1s) but slipped among the working class (C2s and DEs); Labour's vote share went up nine points amount 18-24 year olds, but down by the same amount among the 65-and-

---

[11] Ipsos MORI interviewed 10,227 GB adults aged 18+ on 10 April-6 May 2015. Interviews were conducted face-to-face or by telephone. Data were weighted to reflect the profile of the population and the election result at regional level. (Note that because our method of estimating voting behaviour has been updated since 2010 to allow for differential levels of electoral registration, figures for 2010 have been re-estimated using the new method so as to comparable. In the tables, "change since 2010" refers to these estimates and not to those given in *Explaining Cameron's Coalition*, which in some cases were slightly different.)

overs. The 'gender gap' also widened slightly, with the Conservative lead over Labour a point up among men and a point down among women, but this was not so simple a phenomenon as much of the press coverage during the 2010-15 period implied. And both Labour and the Conservatives improved their standing significantly among ethnic minority voters, who remained almost immune to the appeal of UKIP. Each of these factors, in their own way, contributes to understanding how David Cameron was able to come back with a Conservative victory.

Table 7: How Britain voted, 2015

| | 2015 vote | | | | | | Change since 2010 | | | | | |
	Con %	Lab %	LD %	UKIP %	Grn %	SNP %	Con	Lab %	LD %	UKIP %	Grn %	SNP %
All GB	37.7	31.2	8.1	12.9	3.8	4.9	+1	+2	-16	+12	+2	+3
Gender												
Men	38	29	8	14	4	5	+1	0	-14	+10	+3	+3
Women	37	33	8	12	4	5	+1	+2	-17	+9	+3	+3
Age												
18-24	28	42	4	9	8	7	+2	+9	-28	+8	+8	+4
25-34	33	36	7	10	7	6	+1	+6	-23	+9	+6	+3
35-44	35	35	10	9	4	6	0	+4	-16	+7	+3	+4
45-54	36	32	8	14	4	5	+2	+3	-19	+11	+3	+3
55-64	37	31	9	14	3	5	-3	+4	-12	+9	+2	+3
65+	47	22	8	16	2	3	+3	-9	-7	+12	+1	0
Social Class												
AB	45	26	12	7	4	4	+6	0	-15	+5	+3	+2
C1	42	28	8	11	4	5	+3	0	-16	+8	+3	+3
C2	32	32	6	19	4	5	-3	+3	-17	+14	+3	+2
DE	26	41	5	17	3	6	-5	+2	-13	+13	+2	+4
Housing Tenure												
Owned outright	46	23	9	15	2	4	+1	-1	-11	+11	+1	+1
Mortgage	39	32	9	10	4	5	+3	+3	-18	+8	+3	+3
Social renter	18	49	3	19	3	8	-4	+2	-16	+15	+2	+6
Private renter	28	39	6	11	9	5	-4	+11	-24	+10	+7	+2
Ethnic group												
White	39	28	8	14	4	5	+1	0	-16	+11	+3	+3
Other	23	65	4	2	3	1	+6	+8	-19	+2	+2	0

Source: Ipsos MORI General Election Aggregate
Base: 10,227 GB adults aged 18+ (of which 5,992 were "absolutely certain to vote" or said they had already voted), interviewed 10 April-6 May 2015, weighted to final outcome and turnout. Rows do not sum to 100% as votes for other parties (0.9% of total) are included in percentages but not shown.

Class

One of the biggest changes in British voting behaviour over the past thirty or forty years has been the steady erosion of class-based voting. At one point, Labour's support came almost entirely from households where the chief income earner was a manual worker (what opinion pollsters call the C2DEs or "working class") as opposed to the "middle class" (ABC1s)[12]. But in recent decades those distinctions became less clear. Starting when Tony Blair was leader, Labour began to appeal for middle class votes more successfully than ever before: in 1992, three-quarters of Labour's votes came from the working class, but in 2010 for the first time Labour got more middle class votes than working class votes. This reflected a change in the political landscape and in Labour's approach which was anathema to many of the party's more left wing members and supporters, but it was also a necessary change if Labour was to remain electorally competitive: over recent decades changes in Britain's economic and industrial structure have also caused dramatic changes in the class structure, so that while two-thirds of adults came from working class households back in Harold Wilson's day, now well under half do so – and, moreover, the working class are less likely to vote than the middle class. (In 2015, 67% of ABC1s and 53% of C2DEs voted). That means that a party based entirely on working class votes is doomed to permanent defeat.

And therein lies one of the most alarming problems for Labour in the 2015 result. The recent trend towards class differences becoming blurred was reversed. The Conservatives performed most strongly among their own strongest group, the middle class, while Labour was most successful with working class voters. In fact the Conservative vote was sharply up among ABs, slightly up among C1s, slightly down among C2s and sharply down among DEs; Labour's vote by contrast was flat among ABs and C1s – deriving no benefit from the collapse of the ABC1 Lib Dem vote – but rose somewhat among C2s and DEs. Of the other parties, UKIP were much stronger among C2DEs than ABC1s: much of the Conservative

---

[12] Like most British opinion polls, Ipsos MORI's polls use the classification called 'social grade', originally developed by the advertising industry's trade body, the Institute of Practitioners in Advertising (IPA). Social grade classifies people objectively on the basis of the occupation of the chief income earner in their household, into one of six categories, A, B, C1, C2, D or E. There is a detailed manual classifying every possible occupation into one of these categories, but broadly speaking, As and Bs are higher and lower grades of professionals and managers, C1s are others in clerical or non-manual jobs, C2s in skilled manual jobs, Ds are semi-skilled and unskilled manual workers and Es those on the lowest level of subsistence including those relying on benefits or state pensions. We usually group the first three of these, the ABC1s, under the heading 'middle class' and the remainder, C2DEs, as 'working class'.

strength among the working class has traditionally depended on appeals to patriotism and national identity, and no doubt it was into this constituency that UKIP most successfully tapped. The SNP also seem to have been strongest among DEs, although since Scotland makes up less than a tenth of the total national vote this had only a small impact on the overall figures.

These figures bring out the awkward dilemma with which Labour was faced in 2015, and which remains even more awkward in its aftermath. Labour's traditional supporters, and the group that the party traditionally works to support in government, are the working class and the poor – yet even with Tory support from these groups leaking away, Labour secured only 32% of the votes of C2s and 41% of the votes of DEs. If Labour is to remain true to its history, and to the natural instincts both of Ed Miliband and of Jeremy Corbyn, it is the C2DEs it must aim to recapture first. But even there, the abstainers and those who have defected to the SNP may demand very different policies from those of the working class who have found UKIP to their liking. And attracting either of these groups probably implies continued difficulty in appealing to middle class voters, abandoning the direction which won three elections under Tony Blair without an obviously viable alternative to put in its place. While the Tories lead Labour by 42% to 28% in the C1 vote, and are even level among the C2s, there will be no Labour government.

Age

The changing patterns of class voting have potentially important implications for the future of the parties' positioning, but some of the changes in support by age groups were even more dramatic, and reveal the considerable challenge facing Labour in attracting more support among those age groups we know are most likely to vote in elections. In 2015, Labour strengthened its support among the age group it was already strongest in (up 9 points to lead the Tories by 42% to 28% among 18-24 year olds) and made more modest gains in the 25-64 age bands. Most of these accretions of support came, presumably, from those who had previously supported the Liberal Democrats rather than straight from the Tories, who also benefitted to some degree from Lib Dem desertions, but the net outcome in each case was a swing to Labour, useful ground made up on their opponents.

Labour's problem, however, is that 65-and-overs swung decisively to the Tories – in fact as much as a six per cent swing, and consisting even more of falling support for Labour than of rising support for the Conservatives. Labour has never been strong among the oldest group, of course, but the scale of their challenge is now daunting, with more than twice as many among this age group having voted Conservative (47%) as Labour (22%). The importance of this group is further compounded when we remember just how much more likely older people are to vote than the youngest adults: we estimate that just 38% of 18-24 year olds voted (counting the many who are not even on the register as non-voters, naturally), while 74% of the 65+ group turned out. As has been the case for several elections now, the 'grey vote' is twice as likely to get to the polls, and more than twice as likely to vote Conservative as Labour when it gets there.

Gender

Since before 2010, the media have been reporting at intervals that the Conservatives have developed a "problem with women", but there is absolutely nothing in the polls to back up this claim[13]. At the 2010 election, we found that the Conservatives got the votes of 38% of men and 36% of women. In 2011, we found 36% of men and 34% of women intended to vote Conservative; in 2012 it was 34% and 33%, in 2013, 32% and 30%, and in 2014, 32% and 31%. In the 2015 election, 38% of men and 37% of women voted Conservative. So, true, women were slightly less likely than men to support the Tories, but the gap is no wider than it was – in fact marginally narrower than in 2010. (It's also true that up until the 1980s, the Conservatives had consistently done better among women than among men, certainly since the first opinion polls were conducted and probably since women first got the vote, but that is ancient history now. It was already beginning to be reversed while Margaret Thatcher was still in office, and as far as our figures show, the Conservative share among men has not differed from their share among women by more than two percentage points at any election since 1997.)

---

[13] See our paper Roger Mortimore, Gideon Skinner, and Tomasz Mludzinski, "'Cameron's Problem with Women": The Reporting and the Reality of Gender-Based Trends in Attitudes to the Conservatives, 2010-2011', *Parliamentary Affairs* 68 (2015): 97–115. Also Anthony Wells, 'The Gender Gap', *YouGov*, 11 February 2014, https://yougov.co.uk/news/2014/02/11/gender-gap/, accessed 1 November 2015.

Labour, however, did perform worse among men than women – their vote share was four points higher among women (33% to 29%). This resulted in the gender gap opening slightly, but not – contrary to all those press reports – because of any difference in how men and women reacted to the Conservatives or David Cameron, only because of how they reacted to the other parties.

However, it is a misleading simplification to think in terms of the "women's vote" or the "men's vote". Table 8 shows that when social class and age are taken into account there is a clear – and in some cases widening – gender gap, which is more complex than all women moving in one direction and all men in another.

In the middle class (ABC1s), the Conservatives had performed roughly equally among men and women in 2010, and the change between 2010 and 2015 was also similar (with bigger gains among ABs than among C1s). Labour, however, did appreciably better among AB women than among AB men in 2010, but had 28% of the C1 vote from both men and women; in 2015, the AB gap narrowed while the C1s moved apart, but the differences were small. All in all, there is not much of a middle class gender gap in voting. In the working class, however, the patterns are more interesting: here the Conservatives lost support between 2010 and 2015, but among the men this was entirely in the DEs where the swing by women was mainly concentrated among the C1s; and in each case Labour made correspondingly strong gains in support.

The differences in the gender gap by age are longer established, and have been remarked in the past[14]. Even when women were, taken as a whole, more Conservative than men, the opposite was true in the youngest age group: since the 1980s, the Conservative lead over Labour has been consistently much lower among 18-24 year old women than among men of the same age. This gap almost closed in 2010 but reasserted itself in 2015, so that the difference in voting changes between young women and young men (the former moving away from the Tories, the latter towards

---

[14] We discussed this at some length in our analysis of the 2005 election, Robert M. Worcester, Roger Mortimore, and Paul Baines, *Explaining Labour's Landslip* (London: Politico's, 2005), 224–236. See also Pippa Norris, 'Gender: A Gender-Generation Gap?', in Geoffrey Evans and Pippa Norris (eds.), *Critical Elections* (London: Sage Publications, 1999), 148–163; Rosie Campbell, *Gender and the Vote in Britain: Beyond the Gender Gap?*, ECPR Monographs (Colchester: ECPR Press, 2006).

them) is merely a reversion to the recent norm. Overall, the Conservatives are much weaker among women under 35 than among men of the age, a little weaker among women than men in the 35-54 age band, but stronger in the female half of the 55+ generation. These are broad patterns that have not changed much for a long time, and reflect little on David Cameron or his government's policies. Labour does better among women than among men in every age group, but the difference is much more marked among those aged 25-54 than the older or younger groups. Also of interest, and contributing to this pattern, is support for UKIP, which is roughly the same among men and women aged under 55, but significantly tilted towards men in the oldest group.

Table 8: The gender gap by age and class, 2015

| | 2015 vote | | | | | | Change since 2010 | | | | | |
	Con %	Lab %	LD %	UKIP %	Grn %	SNP %	Con %	Lab %	LD %	UKIP %	Grn %	SNP %
Men	**38**	**29**	**8**	**14**	**4**	**5**	**+1**	**0**	**-14**	**+10**	**+3**	**+3**
AB	46	24	11	9	3	3	+5	0	-16	+7	+2	+1
C1	42	26	8	12	4	5	+2	-2	-15	+9	+3	+3
C2	31	32	5	22	4	5	0	-1	-16	+17	+4	+2
DE	25	40	4	18	3	7	-7	+5	-10	+13	+2	+5
Women	**37**	**33**	**8**	**12**	**4**	**5**	**+1**	**+2**	**-17**	**+9**	**+3**	**+3**
AB	44	28	12	5	5	4	+7	-1	-16	+3	+4	+2
C1	41	30	8	10	5	4	+2	+2	-16	+7	+4	+2
C2	34	33	7	17	3	5	-5	+8	-19	+13	+2	+3
DE	27	42	5	17	3	5	-2	0	-16	+15	+2	+2
Men	**38**	**29**	**8**	**14**	**4**	**5**	**+1**	**0**	**-14**	**+10**	**+3**	**+3**
18-24	32	41	4	8	8	7	+6	+9	-28	+7	+7	+4
25-34	35	32	9	10	6	7	0	+7	-23	+9	+5	+4
35-54	37	31	8	12	4	5	+1	+2	-16	+9	+3	+3
55+	41	25	8	18	2	4	0	-4	-7	+12	+1	+2
Women	**37**	**33**	**8**	**12**	**4**	**5**	**+1**	**+2**	**-17**	**+9**	**+3**	**+3**
18-24	24	43	5	11	9	8	-3	+9	-27	+10	+9	+6
25-34	30	41	5	9	8	5	+1	+5	-24	+7	+7	+3
35-54	33	36	9	11	4	6	+1	+5	-20	+9	+2	+4
55+	45	27	9	13	2	3	+2	-2	-10	+9	+2	0

Source: Ipsos MORI General Election Aggregate
Base: 10,227 GB adults aged 18+ (of which 5,992 were "absolutely certain to vote" or said they had already voted), interviewed 10 April-6 May 2015, weighted to final outcome and turnout. Rows do not sum to 100% as votes for other parties (0.9% of total) are included in percentages but not shown.

Newspaper readership

The relationship between newspaper readership and voting has always been a close one, although even the most strident and loyal of partisan papers are always read by at least of handful of the other side's supporters. In Britain's competitive national newspaper market, a wide range of ideological and policy views are represented, so the alignment between voting and the newspaper's editorial line may come as much from the public choosing to read papers they agree with as from any influence the paper can exert over the beliefs of its readers.

Since we began regularly tracking voting by readership in 1992, more *Sun* readers have voted for the winning party than for any of the losing parties at each general election. The *Sun* is the only national newspaper whose readers have always tracked the national mood in this way – every other title's readers have backed the losers at least once in that time. However, those who say they don't read any newspaper regularly have also always matched the direction of the national result. Both these remained true in 2015, although the Conservative advantage among non-readers this time was wafer-thin (Table 9).

Table 9: Voting by newspaper readership, 2015

	2015 vote						Change since 2010					
	Con %	Lab %	LD %	UKIP %	Grn %	SNP %	Con %	Lab %	LD %	UKIP %	Grn %	SNP %
All GB	37.7	31.2	8.1	12.9	3.8	4.9	+1	+2	−16	+12	+2	+3
Regular readers of:												
Daily Express	44	16	4	33	1	1	−12	0	−14	+28	+1	−1
Daily Mail	57	16	6	18	1	2	0	0	−12	+13	+1	0
Daily Mirror	14	62	2	19	1	1	−4	+4	−14	+18	+1	−1
Daily Record	9	48	2	2	0	38	−4	-20	-3	0	0	+26
Daily Telegraph	72	8	5	11	1	1	+5	0	−15	+7	+1	+1
The Guardian	16	50	13	2	10	7	+7	+4	−25	+1	+8	+5
The Independent	27	41	16	5	7	4	+14	+13	-30	+5	+3	-1
Daily Star	30	50	3	15	0	2	+3	+21	−14	+10	-1	-1
The Sun	39	27	3	23	1	6	-2	-3	−16	+21	+1	+4
The Times	60	17	11	6	2	3	+9	-4	−12	+4	+1	+2
None of these	34	33	9	13	4	6	+1	+2	−16	+10	+3	+3

Source: Ipsos MORI General Election Aggregate
Base: 10,227 GB adults aged 18+ (of which 5,992 were "absolutely certain to vote" or said they had already voted), interviewed 10 April-6 May 2015, weighted to final outcome and turnout. Rows do not sum to 100% as votes for other parties (0.9% of total) are included in percentages but not shown.

The biggest swings in voting behaviour in 2015, however, were elsewhere. Alone among the Fleet Street dailies, the *Express* backed UKIP, and its readers responded positively to that lead with a third of those who reached the polls voting for Nigel Farage's party. This was the only newspaper where the Conservatives lost support apart from a smaller slump among readers of the *Daily Mirror* and its Scottish counterpart, the *Daily Record*; for both of those titles, however, the real story was elsewhere, with a 16% swing of *Mirror* readers from Liberal Democrats to UKIP and a 23% swing of *Record* readers from Labour to the SNP.

The Lib Dems fared very badly across the board, recording a decreased voting intention from 2010 with all newspapers but particularly the *Independent* and the *Guardian* readers, who had been the party's biggest concentration of strength in 2010; despite a 25-point fall in vote share among the latter and a 30-point fall among the former, these remain easily the two papers with the highest proportion of Lib Dem readers, however. UKIP's gains were biggest among *Express* readers but substantial among all of the tabloids. Green gains, by contrast, were particularly noticeable for only a couple of titles, the *Guardian* and (to a lesser extent) the *Independent*, although they made some gains everywhere except with readers of the *Record*.

Conclusion

The mechanics of the election result, therefore, are more complex than usual and partly explain why the Conservative victory took many observers by surprise. Nevertheless, especially with the benefit of hindsight, nothing very mysterious was involved. Given the distribution of the votes, we can see how the Conservatives won, how the Liberal Democrats were all but obliterated, how Labour was swept from its perch in Scotland while failing to compensate with sweeping gains elsewhere, and how UKIP failed to gain any seats.

The above discussion sets out *what* happened. We have yet to turn to investigating *why* the votes were cast as they were. But it is a necessary preliminary. Without it, we cannot gauge the implications of the voting patterns, how each vote matters to the result; once this is understood, we can proceed to considering the voters themselves and the way the parties sought to attract them.

In the remainder of this book, we look in further detail at public opinion, using the evidence of the opinion polls to understand the priorities that drive voters. We see how the public's opinions on various relevant issues are translated into votes, and we see how the parties campaigned to change or reinforce these opinions so as to gain most benefit when polling day arrived. We consider what the public thought of the state of the economy, and why that apparently swung so few votes. We look at what the public thought of Ed Miliband, and whether his leadership had any real impact on Labour's chances of victory. We consider the polarisation of public opinion, which ended with most voters either unable to see much good in Ed Miliband's vision for Britain or unable to see much good in David Cameron's. But first we must start by understanding the complex operation of Britain's electoral system, not forgetting the role which the behaviour of the voters within that system plays in translating theory into practice, and how its apparently capricious behaviour is nevertheless mostly predictable and moulds the priorities of the politicians who must compete for power within it.

The positioning of the parties

How British general elections work

To understand the campaign in any British general election we must begin by understanding how the 'First-Past-the-Post' electoral system works. A party's success in an election is judged not by the number of votes it receives but by the number of seats it wins: a simple majority of those available in the House of Commons (326 at the moment[15]) is a party's passport to power[16]. This may be – usually will be – achieved with considerably less than 50% of the national vote; it may even, as was the case in 1951, be achieved despite the party having won fewer votes than one of the opposing parties. A party may lose seats even though it increases its number of votes, and *vice versa*. But the relationship between seats and votes, although complex, is not entirely arbitrary. In its quest for seats, a party needs to be aware of which votes will help it gain seats and which will not. In other words, some votes are worth more than others.

One of the most stable features of the British electoral system is that some constituencies are 'marginal' while others are 'safe'. There are some constituencies where the long-term trend is for the Conservatives to be much stronger than Labour, suburban seats in the south of England, for example, others where the opposite is the case, such as many industrial or once-industrial seats in the North, in Wales and in Scotland. Marginal seats have closer results, and the reason is usually obvious – they are closer to the average or more mixed in character, and their voting patterns reflect this.

Historically, the vast majority of these marginal seats have been contested between the Conservatives and Labour and, as these are still the only two parties that realistically compete to form or lead a government, the constituencies where these two parties may directly capture seats from each other continue to play the central role in deciding the election outcome.

---

[15] The figure of 323 seats is sometimes quoted, which was the number needed in practice in 2015, allowing for Sinn Fein's MPs not taking their seats and the Speaker not normally being counted on either side.

[16] At least, for as long as it can hold its MPs together in the Commons – but that's another story.

Of course, the identity of these marginal constituencies is not entirely fixed. Over time, the general pattern gradually evolves. The nature of individual constituencies may change, whether by boundary changes or by changes in the character of the local area (e.g. through urban to rural migration). Some would say that the parties change, too, so that the issues that divide them and therefore the identity of their natural support evolves. Certainly the geographical distinction between the strongest areas of Conservative and Labour support is much starker these days than it used to be: a losing Labour Party today will be unlikely to have half a dozen MPs in the South of England outside London, while a losing Conservative Party will be almost wiped out in the North and Wales, to say nothing of Scotland.

And even 'safe' seats are only safe under certain conditions. In a landslide victory, such as Margaret Thatcher's in 1983 or Tony Blair's in 1997, the winning party may reach far into their opponents' natural territory; and in more extreme cases of party collapse, such as the 1931 election after Ramsay MacDonald formed a National government and the rump of his own Labour Party stood out against it, almost any seat may fall.

Moreover, a seat is not necessarily safe because only one of the two main parties can win it. It may come under credible challenge from the Liberal Democrats, from the SNP or from Plaid Cymru, and, indeed, these parties have established safe seats of their own. These days UKIP and the Greens are also contenders, and failing that there is the occasional independent. Chancellor George Osborne's Tatton constituency is one of the 'safest' Conservative seats and has been so regarded for decades, yet when the constituents of Tatton lost faith in their Conservative MP in 1997, the seat fell to former war-reporter turned independent politician Martin Bell; and when Michael Foot sat for Blaenau Gwent it felt inconceivable that Labour could ever lose it, yet in 2005 Peter Law left the Labour Party after being denied the nomination by the imposition of an all-women shortlist, and easily won the seat as an independent. These cases remind us that however justified the criticism that the First-Past-the-Post system devalues the votes of those who live in safe seats, it is ultimately not the system that makes seats 'safe': safe seats are safe because the voters choose to vote that way, and it is always within their power to change that. It is a lesson that Labour in Scotland and Liberal Democrats across the country learned the hard way in 2015.

Nevertheless, given these caveats, it is still broadly true that a party planning for an election can distinguish those constituencies where the result is in doubt from those which they are either certain to win or certain to lose; and, given the inevitable scarcity of campaigning resources, they will be best advised to concentrate as far as they can on the former group. And, much as it worries many observers and perhaps angers many voters, these tend in the short-term at least to be the same constituencies, election after election.

Having established the types of seats to target, the same decision arises again at the more local level. In any given constituency, on which voters do they target most of their efforts? Once again, there are many who will simply not be susceptible to persuasion, and in their case any effort by the parties is entirely wasted. Some will not vote for a particular party under any circumstances; others will vote for a party whether the campaign touches them or not. It is only the third group, who might vote for the party or who might not (and might not even vote at all), whose decisions during the campaign will decide the election, and the party will plainly get the most 'bang for its buck' if it concentrates on getting its message across to them.

This group is classically termed the 'floating voters', torn between voting for Labour and the Conservatives, not strongly committed to either and probably neither very interested in politics nor having much knowledge of the issues. This may make them particularly susceptible to persuasion by beguiling policy promises or by establishing greater trust in a party's leadership and direction than in that of its opponents.

When MORI worked for the Labour Party while Harold Wilson was its leader in the early 1970s, we usually simplified the complexities of the political situation at the time into a rule of thumb, that roughly one constituency in five was marginal, and that one in five of the voters there was a floating voter, so that Labour's key target audience amounted to just one in twenty-five, or four per cent, of the total voters. That same four per cent was of course also the Tories' target audience.

The response to this insight from one of the senior ministers present at one briefing was characteristic — "Four per cent? Hell, we can bribe that many." And that, of course, was exactly what they proceeded to try to do — as almost all governments of both parties have always attempted to do, in one form or another: within whatever they consider the acceptable limits of their own party's character or ideology, they have looked for policies they can adopt, and emphasise in their campaigning, to appeal to the key floating voters. The self-styled idealists who identify political marketing as a threat to traditional politics, and suppose that no party before Tony Blair's New Labour ever moulded its policies to attract the support of floating voters, are talking nonsense. And always, too, there was an eye given to what would play particularly well in the marginal constituencies. (Sometimes in a single particular marginal constituency – which is, arguably, why we now have the Humber Bridge.[17])

The classical democratic theorists seem to have supposed that those deciding between parties or candidates would do so on a wholly rational basis of careful deliberation, based on a full understanding and knowledge of all the issues and entirely independently of personal considerations or benefit. (Stop giggling at the back of the class.)

John Stuart Mill was converted from being a supporter of introducing the secret ballot into an implacable opponent because it would make it easier for a voter to act in his[18] own personal interests rather than for the good of the community, as he explained:

> "Thirty years ago it was still true that in the election of members of Parliament, the main evil to be guarded against was that which the ballot would exclude – coercion by landlords, employers and customers. At present, I conceive, a much greater source of evil is the selfishness, or the selfish partialities, of the voter himself... and to these influences the ballot would enable him to yield himself up, free from all sense of shame and responsibility".[19]

---

[17] The Hull North by-election was held on 27 January 1966, when Labour's majority in the House of Commons was so wafer-thin that the loss of a single seat might have led to the fall of the government. To judge whether the decision to build the Humber Bridge was entirely a bribe to win this by-election, see Richard Crossman, *The Diaries of a Cabinet Minister, Volume One: Minister of Housing 1964-66* (London: Hamish Hamilton & Jonathan Cape, 1975), 394, 437. Barbara Castle was the responsible minister but says very little in *The Castle Diaries, 1964-70* (London: Weidenfeld & Nicolson, 1984), 94–95.

[18] In those days, of course, it was always still "his".

[19] John Stuart Mill, 'Thoughts on Parliamentary Reform', cited by Bruce L. Kinzer, 'J.S. Mill and the Secret Ballot', *Historical Reflections / Réflexions Historiques* 5 (1978): 19–39.

Today the secret ballot has been established for almost a century-and-a-half, and we accept that the secret vote is every citizen's right, to be used as he or she chooses; and, as matter of empirical fact, we know that most will indeed choose the selfish rather than the altruistic option when those are at odds, and moreover that their decision may be neither entirely rational (however that is defined) nor at all well informed. The politician who wants to win an election must take this into account rather than ignore it. The idealist has the luxury of pretending that the world works as John Stuart Mill would have liked it to, but only at the expense of losing the election and seeing people and policies he opposes gaining a monopoly of power.

The differing value of various votes would pose no difficulties for the parties or the democratic system if all voters were alike, but of course they are not. Different voters have different interests, want different things, think in different ways, and are most easily approached by campaigners through different media. If persuading some voters is more valuable to a party than persuading others, it should naturally tailor its campaign (and perhaps, although this is more controversial, its policies) to suit particular groups. But a single national approach calculated to attract one group of target voters may simultaneously alienate some other important group.

This, then, defined the strategic position of the main parties as they approached the 2015 election and left both the Conservatives and Labour with a dilemma in determining their tactical objectives. Each needed to appeal to at least two very different groups of voters in the same constituencies. Each party was concerned to win or at least hold support in the political centre-ground, among the floating voters who were torn between the two; but each also felt threatened at the other end of its spectrum of support – the Conservatives on the right by UKIP, Labour on the left by the Greens. Both also wanted to attract support from former Liberal Democrats whose support for that party might have had a number of different causes: some did so because they were ideologically centrist, some as a tactical vote expressing opposition to one of the two major parties, but some also as a protest vote rejecting the political establishment as represented by both Conservative and Labour. Could they find an approach that worked equally well in attracting votes from all of these groups, or would they be unable to concentrate on one without weakening their chances of success on the other? And if they had to sacrifice success with one group to win over another, which approach would be most successful in net numerical terms?

As noted in the introduction, there was also a further complication. The main battleground of a British election is usually the constituencies that are marginal between Conservative and Labour, and the rest of the election is something of a sideshow, with only a handful of seats likely to change hands. The fortunes of the smaller parties might be important in the event of a hung Parliament (which was a distinct possibility in 2015), but are otherwise only of significance in so far as their performance has an impact on the number of seats in the Conservative and Labour columns.

But in 2015 there was a clear possibility of substantial movement in two other blocs of seats, the 57 won by the Liberal Democrats in 2010, which might now be up for grabs as support for the junior partners in the coalition had melted away, and the 41 seats that Labour won in Scotland, now under threat from the rampant SNP.

In neither of these new battlegrounds was the outcome a foregone conclusion. Many believed that the famed 'pavement politics' of the Liberal Democrats and the personal votes of their sitting MPs might allow them to retain many of their seats even in the face of a dramatic collapse in the party's national vote. And many believed that the opinion polls were much exaggerating the advance of the SNP in Scotland, where only a handful of Labour's constituencies were marginal according to the normal calculations. But both of these battles had to be fought. In each case dozens of seats were at stake. In each case the campaign might make a difference. And in each case there was a risk for the two big parties that the optimum strategy to maximise their chances here was at odds with their best strategy to fight the classic marginal seats. Decisions, decisions!

The Coalition Government of 2010-15

Roots of the political alignment

For all the extra considerations with which the parties had to deal in the 2015 election, the single most important formative factor on the political situation was, as it always is, the relative fortunes of the Conservative and Labour parties. If either were to achieve a dominant lead in public esteem, other factors would be helpless to affect the overall outcome. In fact, neither had done so – as the election approached the result seemed still very much in doubt. To understand why, and to map some of the contours of public opinion as it applied to them, we begin by reviewing the history of the 2010-15 parliament.

Until 2010, Labour were in government. At that election a Conservative-led coalition took their place, elected on a manifesto that denounced Labour's record and promised austerity policies to tackle the deficit in public finances, which Cameron's government proceeded to implement once in power. Labour in opposition for the most part declined to accept blame for the onset of the economic slump and continued to attack the government's policies, arguing for higher public spending and investment to protect public services and to stimulate the economy.

The defining divide between the two main parties, therefore, and the issue on which the voters were in effect asked to choose between them, remained fundamentally the same as in 2010: how much the government should, or could afford to, spend. While numerous sub-issues could be identified, and the political debate was sometimes conducted in those terms – unemployment, inflation, the National Health Service, funding for education – almost all ultimately resolved themselves into details of this same wider question. The few prominent issues which did not fit into this framework, notably immigration, never emerged sufficiently strongly as points of contention between Conservatives and Labour to prompt many voters to choose between them on that basis. The story of how the 2010-15 parliament came and went without changing the essential terms of the political debate is the first key formative influence on the 2015 general election result. If Labour was to win, they had either to change the agenda onto issues that matched their strengths or win the argument for public investment on the economic question. They achieved neither.

Forming the coalition

The first defining moment of the parliament was the concluding of the coalition agreement and the decision of the Liberal Democrats to enter government with the Conservatives. It had a number of consequences for both parties, changed the way that each was to approach the next five years, and naturally involved both in making compromises on policy pledges and ideology. But, importantly, what it did not do was to disrupt the existing political dichotomy between the Conservatives who aimed primarily to restrain public spending and Labour who aimed to maintain it as far as possible. The Liberal Democrats fitted themselves firmly into the austerity camp, although they had some moderating influence on the details of how the policy was implemented, and the dissenters within their ranks were firmly sidelined.

Entering the Coalition proved ultimately disastrous for the Liberal Democrats. There is a temptation to see this outcome as resulting from a trading-off between unpopularity from association with the mainly Conservative policies of the Coalition (particularly the increase in university tuition fees) and popularity from being a moderating influence on those policies, but in fact the reason for the Lib Dem collapse in support was a far simpler one. For many years the Liberal Democrats have been an uneasy coalition between those whose main reason for supporting them was opposition to the Conservatives, those for whom the main reason was opposition to Labour, and those for whom it was opposition to mainstream politics (i.e. both parties). Any decision to join a coalition with either of the major parties would immediately alienate two of these three groups. Only the, probably small, number who could be regarded as genuinely ideological Liberal Democrats would be likely to see anything positive in entering government, giving some possibility of pursuing a distinct Liberal Democrat agenda rather than merely acting as a restraining force on an entirely different party.

One direct consequence of the formation of the Coalition was the passing of the Fixed-term Parliaments Act 2011, which by preventing the Prime Minister from taking a unilateral decision to go to the country early was designed to ensure a greater stability to the government than it might otherwise have achieved. The measure was promoted as a natural modernising reform desirable in itself, and acceptable to both Conservative and Liberal Democrat thinking, but its main practical consequence in the short term was that David Cameron had no freedom to call an early election at some moment which was good for the Conservatives and bad for the Liberal Democrats. In theory, it weakened the Prime Minister by removing one of his discretionary powers; yet, in fact, the impact on David Cameron in the 2010-15 parliament may have beneficial rather than detrimental. Past Prime Ministers – Gordon Brown was a case in point – have sometimes been damaged by the speculation of the possibility of their calling an early election, and one can imagine that had David Cameron still had that power then there would have been a consistent media frenzy (not to mention possible pressure from some of his own backbenchers) from the moment when signs of economic upturn began to proliferate in 2013.

Labour in opposition

Labour's unexpected election of Ed Miliband as leader in September 2010 was the second defining moment of the parliament, but the choice fitted naturally with the direction that Labour was already taking, and may have been a symptom rather than a cause of the party's weakness. During the four-and-a-half years that Ed Miliband was Labour's leader, the party rarely gave the impression of being dominated by him, or that he was leaving his stamp on the party. He was an unspectacular figure, disconcertingly uncharismatic as a figurehead (although reportedly inspiring in speaking to small groups), and ill-suited to elbowing such an established and polished player as David Cameron out of the spotlight.

Worse, perhaps, he came with ideological and personal baggage – these were damaging not through any reflection in the way he performed his job, but because they provided ready-made loopholes through which his opponents could attack. Narrowly elected ahead of his older brother, David, on the back of the trade union vote (he was behind in the votes of both the membership-at-large and the parliamentary party), he could be portrayed as the living symbol of sectional interest, an association which became more damaging as the question of union power became more prominent later in the parliament. His brother not only being older but more experienced in senior posts (David had been Foreign Secretary in the previous government, Ed the Secretary of State for Energy and Climate Change), Ed could be seen as the unnatural choice, fuelling rumours of betrayed pacts that brought back memories of the rivalry between Tony

Blair and Gordon Brown. He could also be seen, more fairly, as the left-wing candidate, although the real ideological distinctions were probably far less than this might have been taken to imply. No matter, it fitted comfortably into a Tory view of the world that wanted to emphasise, at least to its own supporters, the distinctions between government and opposition and to portray the alternative to the Coalition as involving dangerous radicalism.

Nevertheless, all of these impacts may have been marginal. The overwhelming impressions left on the public by Ed Miliband were of weakness and 'weirdness'. As we shall see, he never scored well with the public on likeability, never achieved respectable satisfaction scores for his performance as leader, and never convinced most of the public that he was prime ministerial material. Among those who had voted Labour and intended to vote Labour again he often found a more sympathetic audience, but even they failed to give much endorsement to the way he was doing the job as leader, probably because many had misgivings that he was unlikely to win the election. The rest of the public, from whom he had to recruit extra support if he were to win, remained resolutely unimpressed.

There was also plenty in Labour's approach apart from Ed Miliband's shortcomings to deter Conservative waverers. Labour's strategic failing throughout the parliament was one of positioning: they allowed themselves to appear too left-wing, a point acknowledged by Labour Party grandee Lord Mandelson[20]. In a society far less deferential than it used to be, increasingly led by its experiences in a marketised consumer world to behave as a demanding customer with high expectations, and especially in circumstances where almost all of the public feel economically worse off than a few years previously, a persistent flow of protest issues is almost inevitable. Labour being the more left-wing of the two major parties, they are the natural spokesmen for most of these protests, and when the Conservatives are in government, they have the prospect of exploiting such protests to significant political gain. To do so, however, they need to

---

[20]Adam Withnall, 'Labour Peer Lord Mandelson Says Ed Miliband Has Set the Party Back 30 Years', *The Independent*, 8 May 2015, http://www.independent.co.uk/news/uk/politics/generalelection/election-2015-lord-mandelson-says-labours-campaign-under-ed-miliband-was-a-giant-political-10239305.html, accessed 27 October 2015.

ensure that on those issues where they are identified by the public with one side and the government with the other, they are on the popular side of the argument. Further, when the political situation demands that they target particular voters, it is opinion among those voters rather than sheer weight of numbers in the population as a whole that will determine what political capital, if any, they can gain.

On some issues, the protest or its advocates will be too extreme to be safely backed: association with such causes, when the government is left defending a popular status quo, can only damage Labour – they would be better advised to avoid them becoming an issue of contention between the parties. In the same way, some issues will be too popular and a competent government will join the attack rather than rallying to the defence. Then, unless Labour can succeed in portraying the government as hypocritical on the issue, or can identify the Conservatives with the unpopular side despite their proclaimed stance, there will be no dividend. The art is to ensure that the issues falling into neither of these categories, where Conservatives and Labour are seen to stand in opposite camps, are those which will reflect best on Labour. This boils down very much to how left wing or how moderate Labour is seen to be – and, of course, to how right wing or moderate the Conservatives appear, since they will be aware that precisely the same considerations apply to them. This leaves politicians of either party with a dilemma when their own political convictions and the stance best calculated to win votes are at odds; but such is the nature of democratic politics.

Almost from the first, Labour allowed itself to be associated with movements and causes which could only be seen as threatening by moderate Conservatives and centrists, and increase the resistance of government supporters to Labour's appeal, at least while the government was still able to make the case convincingly for its own policies. In November 2010, a mass student protest against Coalition education policies ended in a riot and an attack on Conservative Party headquarters, and a second, a few weeks later, ended with the desecration of the Cenotaph in Whitehall. A TUC-organised march to protest against cuts on 26 March 2011, said to be the largest demonstration in Britain since the 2003 Iraq War march, ended with protesters clashing with police in

Trafalgar Square, shops and banks in the West End vandalised, and more than 200 arrests[21]. The main body of the protesters had already marched to Hyde Park where they were addressed by Ed Miliband and TUC general secretary Brendan Barber. Small matter that Miliband and Barber were speaking to the peaceful majority and condemned the behaviour of the tiny unlawful minority; the association in the public mind of Labour's links with extremists was clearly made.

The union movement again jeopardised Labour's standing with Conservative-minded voters with a series of public sector strikes, culminating in a mass day of action on 30 November 2011 when schools were closed and hospital operations cancelled. That same autumn came the Occupy London movement, a branch of the international anti-capitalist Occupy movement, attempting to take over the Stock Exchange and then setting up a protest camp for months in the grounds of St Paul's Cathedral, until eventually evicted. Among some more extreme positions, it declared its support for the public sector strikers and the student protest. Their statement ended "This is what democracy looks like"[22], which cannot have endeared the protesters to many of a Conservative frame of mind.

We can gain some impression of the potential contamination of Labour's image by considering the early public reaction to the public sector strikes, at the stage when action was still being mooted. With the strikers expressing genuine grievances from the impact of cuts that many of the rest of the public generally shared, and threatening only legal and constitutional forms of protest to articulate them, this was probably the least radical of the examples we have considered. If Labour was on the wrong side by becoming identified with the protesters in this case, it certainly was in the others.

In June 2011, we found an even divide in opinion over whether public sector workers were right to strike "in protest about job cuts, pay levels and pension reductions", 48% supporting the decision and 48% opposing

---

[21] 'TUC Condemns Post-Rally Violence in Central London', *BBC News*, 27 March 2011, http://www.bbc.co.uk/news/uk-12873191, accessed 2 June 2015.
[22] 'Occupy London Stock Exchange – the Initial Statement', *The Guardian*, 17 October 2011, http://www.theguardian.com/commentisfree/2011/oct/17/occupy-london-stock-exchange-occupylsx, accessed 2 June 2015.

it. (Table 10). However, those who had voted Conservative in 2010 were of a very different mind: just 19% supported the strike, while 78% opposed it.[23] (This was not simply blanket hostility among Conservatives to all union activities – in the same survey, 63% of them agreed that "trade unions are essential to protect workers' interests".)

Table 10: Sympathy for public sector strikes, 2011

Q. This week it was announced that people in a number of public sector jobs will go on strike this summer in protest against job cuts, pay levels and pension reductions. Do you support or oppose their decision to go on strike?

| | | Reported vote in 2010 | | |
	All	Conser-vative	Labour	Liberal Democrat
	%	%	%	%
Support	48	19	74	54
Oppose	48	78	21	44
Don't know	5	2	5	2

Base: 1,003 British adults 18+, 17-19 June 2011
Source: Ipsos MORI Political Monitor

Labour's link with the unions became even more poisonous to their target voters with allegations of vote-rigging by the Unite union in the selection of Labour's parliamentary candidate in Falkirk in 2013. The accusations reported in the media included people being signed up as voting members of the Labour Party without their knowledge and their subscriptions being paid from union funds. The original selection process had to be abandoned, and in the re-run contest voting was restricted to those who had already been members when the sitting MP, Eric Joyce, had announced he would not seek re-election. The chairman of the Falkirk party and the candidate who was eventually selected to fight the seat were both suspended from the party but later re-instated[24]; Ed Miliband was accused of soft-pedalling on the party's internal inquiry after union leaders threatened to boycott the Labour conference; the Grangemouth petrochemical plant where most of the union members worked was almost closed after the management reacted to strike threats which the

---

[23] Ipsos MORI interviewed 1,003 British adults aged 18+ by telephone on 17-19 June 2011.
[24] 'Falkirk Labour: Karen Whitefield Chosen after Selection Row', *BBC News*, 8 December 2013, http://www.bbc.co.uk/news/uk-scotland-25279685, accessed 1 October 2015.

Conservatives linked directly to the Labour selection controversy.[25] Even on the assumption that any irregularities in Falkirk were entirely exceptional and not repeated in other selections, the incident highlighted the influence of the unions within the Labour Party and their willingness to use it to advance sectional union interests. An Ipsos MORI survey of 18-75 year olds shortly before the election found that 68% saw Labour as being "close" and 40% "very close" to the trade unions; by way of comparison, 25% saw them as very close to the working class and only 14% to people with families.[26]

Labour had failed to position themselves in the centre-ground of public opinion on these issues. It seems very clear that the average voter, certainly the average Labour-target voter, would wish for the survival of the political and economic system as a whole, while entirely supporting attacks on those who abused or exploited it.

Table 11: Making the banks suffer

Q. Please tell me which of the following statements comes closest to your opinion?

	All	Reported vote in 2010		
		Conser-vative	Labour	Liberal Democrat
	%	%	%	%
The government should increase taxes on banks, even if it makes the British banking sector much less competitive	50	45	55	61
The government should not increase taxes on banks because they are important to Britain's economic recovery	42	47	39	34
Don't know	8	8	7	5

Base: 1,162 British adults 18+, 21-24 January 2011
Source: Ipsos MORI Political Monitor

The bankers, widely blamed for the 2008 financial crisis, were an obvious example; so unpopular were they that there was widespread support for

---

[25] Priti Patel, 'The Falkirk Scandal: 15 Facts You Need to Know', *The Telegraph*, 28 November 2013, http://www.telegraph.co.uk/news/politics/labour/10480602/The-Falkirk-scandal-15-facts-you-need-to-know.html, accessed 1 October 2015.
[26] Ipsos MORI interviewed 2,024 British adults aged 18-75 online on 24-28 April 2015. The survey was conducted for Policy Network and formed part of the basis for their post-election analysis *Can Labour Win?* (available at http://www.policy-network.net/publications/4963/Can-Labour-Win).

placing punitive financial measures on the banks even at the expense of weakening the economy. In January 2011, we found that 50% of the public thought that the government "should increase taxes on banks, even if it makes the British banking sector much less competitive", while 42% disagreed; among those who had voted Conservative, agreement was not much lower, 45% (with 47% disagreeing).[27]

Here was an issue where it would undoubtedly have profited Labour if they could have positioned themselves on the popular side of the argument and made the Conservatives look diametrically opposed on the other side. But David Cameron deftly joined the attack on the banks and prevented any widespread feeling among the voters who mattered that the Conservatives were the bankers' party.

Very similar, and more prominent as the parliament wore on, was the issue of the 'tax dodgers'. It may have been fortuitous, but the coming to the fore of an issue where the government could wholeheartedly take the popular side against unacceptable business practices can have done them no harm. Throughout the parliament, stories emerged of aggressive tax avoidance by celebrities such as pop star Gary Barlow[28] and major companies such as Google, Amazon and Starbucks[29] and were given due prominence by the media. The Conservatives' unequivocal condemnation of them helped avoid any risk that Labour could easily identify the Tories with big business and themselves as the representatives of the ordinary man-in-the-street consumer. Instead, the Tories could argue – at least to the satisfaction of their own man-in-the-street – that they stood for responsible business and the prosperity that went with it, providing jobs and taking much of the tax burden from the workers, which Labour would jeopardise through irresponsible public spending levels and counter-productive anti-business policies.

The Conservatives may have been lucky, though, to avoid falling foul of public opinion over Syria. The continuing fall-out over the 2003 invasion

---

[27] Ipsos MORI interviewed 1,162 British adults aged 18+ by telephone on 21-24 January 2011.

[28] For the full story, see Lucy Buckland, 'Named and Shamed: After Gary Barlow, Other Celebrity Tax Dodgers', *The Mirror*, 12 May 2014, http://www.mirror.co.uk/3am/celebrity-news/gary-barlow-tax-evasion-celebrity-3531247, accessed 26 October 2015.

[29] Vanessa Barford and Gerry Holt, 'Google, Amazon, Starbucks: The Rise of "Tax Shaming"', *BBC News*, 21 May 2013, http://www.bbc.co.uk/news/magazine-20560359, accessed 26 October 2015.

of Iraq and the damage done by it to Tony Blair's reputation illustrate the potential potency of decisions about military action on the public's domestic political attitudes. In the late summer of 2013, the government argued that British forces should join international military action over the alleged use of chemical weapons in Syria, but the proposal was defeated in the House of Commons. An ICM poll for the BBC immediately afterwards found 71% backed the MPs' veto[30]. Without going into the military and diplomatic rights and wrongs of the decision, it seems quite possible that its effect was to prevent support for and opposition to an ongoing war in the Middle East becoming an election issue between Labour and the Conservatives in 2015, with Labour on the more popular side. The subsequent deterioration of the situation in Syria, and the emergence of Islamic State, may have made events there of much more direct pertinence to British voters by the time of the election, but it was no longer an issue that divided the party leaderships.

It cannot be emphasised strongly enough, of course, that this question of positioning is ultimately one of what the voters perceive to be true, not what is actually true. Furthermore, voters bring their own perspectives and prejudices to the task of making political judgments, and those of one persuasion may come to very different decisions from those of another, even on questions which it might seem to the neutral observer are susceptible to an objective answer. How far to the right or left a leader or party stands is very much a judgment of this type, and we should not therefore be surprised to find considerable differences of opinion between supporters of the various parties. As a case in point, Table 12 shows the public's perceptions of Ed Miliband, three years into his leadership.

In October 2013, we asked the public how they perceived their own political positioning, on a five-point scale running from left wing to right wing, and where they placed the views of the party leaders. As we expected, the public's self-images were spread across the spectrum (27% considered themselves left of centre or left wing, 29% right of centre or right wing and 29% in the centre), and the majority felt David Cameron to be on the right and Ed Miliband on the left. But those who had voted Conservative at the previous election saw Miliband as being distinctly

---

[30] ICM interviewed 1,000 GB adults aged 18+ by telephone on 30 August-1 September 2013: http://www.icmunlimited.com/media-centre/polls/bbc-syria-poll, accessed 5 November 2015.

more left wing than did those who had voted for Miliband's own party – not surprising, perhaps, but a distinct disadvantage if Conservative voters saw a left wing leader as being a deterrent to voting Labour and if Labour needed to capture these ex-Conservative votes.

Table 12: Left-wing positioning of Ed Miliband

Q. Some people describe their political views as being left wing or right wing. How would you describe your own views? And how would you describe the views of...?

	Own views	David Cameron	Ed Miliband		
			All	Con vote in 2010	Lab vote in 2010
	%	%	%	%	%
Left wing	9	5	26	41	21
Left of centre	18	4	28	29	32
Centre	29	13	13	7	16
Right of centre	20	33	6	4	5
Right wing	9	24	5	6	10
Don't know	15	21	21	14	16

Base: 1,004 British adults 18+, 12-15 October 2013
Source: Ipsos MORI Political Monitor

It would probably be misleading to attempt to single out any particular speeches, policy announcements or other incidents involving Miliband and his senior colleagues as the turning points or even influential moments in building up an image of Labour which made it harder to win the election – almost certainly the effect was cumulative, with different moments critical for different voters.

Nevertheless, some mention should be made of one or two of the more notorious, to be representative of and give a flavour of the whole, each offering David Cameron the opportunity to characterise his opponent as extreme, incompetent or weak, any of which are damaging impressions for a potential Prime Minister to give. The controversy over the selection of a candidate in Falkirk in 2013 has already been mentioned, over which Cameron was able to attack Miliband as "too weak to stand up to the Unite union and too weak to run Labour and certainly too weak to run the country"[31] even before many of the more damaging allegations had

---

[31] Eddie Barnes, 'Ed Miliband and the Falkirk Scandal', *The Scotsman/Scotland on Sunday*, 16 November 2013, http://www.scotsman.com/news/insight-ed-miliband-and-the-falkirk-scandal-1-3191702, accessed 11 August 2015.

emerged. During campaigning for the European and local election elections in 2014, Miliband was photographed clumsily making a mess of eating a bacon sandwich, providing a highly-graphic shorthand symbol of criticisms that he was 'weird' or incompetent, which resurfaced during the election campaign itself on the front page of the *Sun*. In Miliband's Party Conference speech in September 2014, which he chose to deliver from memory, he accidentally omitted the passages he had intended to deliver on the deficit and on immigration[32], a gaffe which could hardly have been bettered if Conservative Central Office had written the script.

All of these were errors which on the 'mud sticks' principle could do far more lasting damage to Miliband's, and Labour's, image than any positive achievements could easily do to repair it. Policy blunders may be in theory more easily reversible, but here too we find damaging examples. The promise of a mandatory freeze on consumer energy prices, announced by Ed Miliband at the 2013 Labour Conference, was met with an accusation of 'economic vandalism', and with threats that the policy would drive energy companies out of business or out of the British domestic market.[33]

Labour clearly believed that the policy was a big vote-winner among the 'squeezed middle' (and the sympathetic press hailed it as such, but this was largely based on misreporting of the polling evidence[34]). They may have been unlucky in the way that the appeal of the proposal was subsequently unravelled by a dramatic and unforeseen collapse in energy prices in 2014 and 2015; but it was a gamble in very much the same vein as the wider reliance on Conservative economic failure, with no room for a Plan B if things turned in the government's favour. By the time of the election, it enabled the Conservatives and others to claim that the mere pledge to include the price freeze in Labour's manifesto had cost consumers

---

[32] Patrick Wintour, 'Ed Miliband Admits He Forgot Key Section of Labour Conference Speech', *The Guardian*, 24 September 2014, http://www.theguardian.com/politics/2014/sep/24/ed-miliband-forgets-labour-conference-speech, accessed 12 August 2015.

[33] Kamal Ahmed, 'Top Centrica Shareholder Neil Woodford Accuses Labour Leader Ed Miliband of "Economic Vandalism"', *The Telegraph*, 25 September 2013, http://www.telegraph.co.uk/finance/newsbysector/energy/10332858/Top-Centrica-shareholder-Neil-Woodford-accuses-Labour-leader-Ed-Miliband-of-economic-vandalism.html, accessed 11 August 2015.

[34] Nicholas Watt, 'Labour Support up 14 Points after Miliband's Energy Pledge', *The Guardian*, 31 October 2013, http://www.theguardian.com/politics/2013/oct/31/labour-surge-poll-energy-prices, accessed 20 August 2015; Anthony Wells, 'Bad Poll Reporting Corner', *UK Polling Report*, 31 October 2013, http://ukpollingreport.co.uk/blog/archives/8330, accessed 20 August 2015.

substantial amounts, as power companies failed to pass on reductions in wholesale prices because they feared they might be unable to increase them again if Labour was elected, even if costs rose. "We believe that Labour's price freeze proposal has been instrumental in the failure of the big six energy suppliers to reduce their standard prices, despite the significant fall in wholesale costs", said the spokesperson of one price comparison website. *The Telegraph* mentioned possible losses of £130 a year.[35]

As the election neared, Labour became more equivocal in its economic policies. Miliband pledged at the end of 2014, for example, that a Labour government would cut the deficit year on year (and symbolically chose this as the first of five pledges, indicating the priority which was being placed on it)[36]. But this can only have had the effect of alarming those on the left of the party without placating those in the political centre with whom credibility had already been irretrievably lost. On purely economic issues an impression of irresponsibility may have been even more damaging than a perception that Labour stood too far to the left. By wobbling at the last minute Labour may have had the worst of both worlds, fuelling the disastrous exodus of their supporters to the SNP and weakening them against the Greens and Liberal Democrats, without succeeding in reassuring voters of a more moderate or Conservative bent that Labour could be trusted on economic management.

Liberal Democrats

After the initial decision to join the Coalition, one other event arguably stands out as having a significant effect on the fate of the Liberal Democrats, the U-turn on student tuition fees. Whether it was really a deal-breaker in itself or, as seems more likely, a conveniently clear symbol of a more general feeling of betrayal among Liberal Democrat voters, it was persistently cited through the parliament and into the general election

---

[35] Emily Gosden, 'Labour Energy Price Freeze "Preventing £130 Bill Cuts"', *Daily Telegraph*, 16 January 2015, http://www.telegraph.co.uk/news/earth/energy/11351710/Labour-energy-price-freeze-preventing-130-bill-cuts.html, accessed 11 August 2015.
[36] Patrick Wintour, 'Ed Miliband Makes Election Pledge to Tackle the Country's Deficit', *The Guardian*, 11 December 2014, http://www.theguardian.com/politics/2014/dec/11/ed-miliband-labour-pledges-deficit-nhs, accessed 10 August 2015.

campaign as a reason for having abandoned the party and as an argument not merely for leaving the party but for seeking its humiliation. Its importance came not merely from the contribution of student support to the party's success in 2010, which was much exaggerated[37]: more damagingly, it was an unarguable instance of a clear manifesto pledge being directly reneged upon. As such, for many of their former supporters it symbolised the descent of the Liberal Democrats to the level of the other political parties against whose faults they had been voting.

It was also a self-inflicted wound, although Nick Clegg and other senior members of the party would no doubt argue it was in fact evidence that they were less rather than more cynical — having concluded that their stance on the issue had been wrong, they chose to admit it and vote in line with their new convictions rather than quietly allowing the Conservatives to do their dirty work and pretending to have been compelled to comply. In their manifesto, the Liberal Democrats had promised that tuition fees for all students taking their first degree would be phased out completely within six years[38], and all of their successful candidates had signed a National Union of Students (NUS) pledge "to vote against any increase in fees in the next parliament and to pressure the government to introduce a fairer alternative."

After the election, the Browne Review of Higher Education and Student Finance reported, recommending among other things that the cap on tuition fees should be removed completely. The Conservatives decided not to implement the recommendations in their entirety, but did accept proposals to raise the fee cap to £9,000 a year for undergraduate degrees, from the existing level of only just over £3,000. Nick Clegg signalled his

---

[37] Analysis by the Higher Education Policy Institute makes some convincing and revealing points about the influence of the student vote. In a December 2014 report they rejected an NUS claim that "Students could swing almost 200 seats at the General Election", putting their likely influence instead at between 5 and 12 seats. In a post-election re-assessment they concluded that in the Liberal Democrat constituencies with large numbers of students, on which so much attention had been centred, the collapse of the Liberal Democrat vote was such that most of them would have lost however the students voted, and also pointed out that Lib Dem MPs who had voted against the fee increase fared no better than those who voted in favour. See Nick Hillman, *Students and the 2015 General Election: Did They Make a Difference?*, HEPI Report 78 (Oxford: HEPI, October 2015).
[38] Liberal Democrats, *Liberal Democrat Manifesto 2010* (London, 2010), 39,
http://www.politicsresources.net/area/uk/ge10/man/parties/libdem_manifesto_2010.pdf,
accessed 29 October 2015.

support for this and, when the issue came up before the Commons on 9 December 2010, he, all other Liberal Democrat ministers, and half his parliamentary party, voted in favour (although 21 voted against, including two parliamentary private secretaries (PPSs) who resigned to be free to do so).

Despite being in government with the Conservatives, there was no compulsion on the Liberal Democrats to vote for the tuition fees increase: the Coalition Agreement had explicitly stated that "If the response of the Government to Lord Browne's report is one that Liberal Democrats cannot accept, then arrangements will be made to enable Liberal Democrat MPs to abstain in any vote." But Liberal Democrat abstentions *en masse* would not have prevented the proposals from going through, and would not have met the pre-election pledge to vote against any increase.

Nick Clegg explained that he was wrong to have signed the pledge, saying "You need to be careful. I should have been more careful perhaps in signing that pledge at the time. At the time I thought we could do it."[39]. He also dismissed the issue as one of the compromises that inevitably must be made by a party joining a coalition government. His problem was that those who had voted for the Liberal Democrats proved to be less prepared to accept such compromises. Immediately after the party entered government, three-quarters of those who had voted Liberal Democrat said they thought Nick Clegg had been right to form a coalition with the Conservatives and only one in five that he had been wrong[40]; but a year later, asked how they thought parties should work together in coalition, 60% of those who had voted Liberal Democrat said that "The parties should stand up for the policies they believe in, even if this makes it more difficult to make decisions", rather than that "The parties should work together to reach agreement, even if this means giving up on policies they promised and taking on new policies". This is plainly not a state of mind that made it easy for the party to satisfy their own supporters.

---

[39] 'Nick Clegg Regrets Signing Anti-Tuition Fees Pledge', *BBC News*, 11 November 2010, http://www.bbc.co.uk/news/uk-politics-11732787, accessed 12 August 2015.
[40] Ipsos MORI interviewed 1,023 British adults aged 18+ (including 323 who said they had voted for the Liberal Democrats) by telephone on 12-13 May 2010. The survey was conducted for the *News of the World*.

Despite the symbolic importance of the tuition fees U-turn, there is no clear evidence that it was in any sense a watershed moment in Liberal Democrat support. Our polls showed an immediate post-election plunge from the 24% they had achieved at the ballot boxes in May to 19% in June and 14% by the end of July 2010. The tuition fees vote was in December, but their support stayed fairly steady until February the following year, when they were still at 13%. From that point onwards there were regular fluctuations, with periods of several months at a time when their support stood at 12%-13%, and other periods when it dropped into single figures, but it was a constant that from within a couple of months of joining the coalition they never looked, at best, as if they could count on much more than half the support they had achieved in 2010. For the last year before the election, they remained steady within the margin of error at just a third of their 2010 vote (and that proved to be what they finally received).

The tuition fees issue was not the only self-inflicted wound. In the pre-election debates, Nick Clegg had been eager to point out that no Liberal Democrats had been accused of exploiting loopholes to profit from expenses claims for a second home, yet within three weeks of the election David Laws was forced to resign from the Cabinet for outright breaches of those same regulations. Chris Huhne resigned from the Cabinet in 2012 over charges of perverting the course of justice in a motoring case, and from Parliament the following year when he was convicted and received an eight-month prison sentence. Thus two of the four other Liberal Democrats Nick Clegg initially chose to serve with him in the coalition cabinet had departed in disgrace in less than two years. However, there is no evidence that either incident did any serious damage to the reputation of the party. There may well have been sympathy for Laws, who argued that his motivation had not been dishonesty but to keep details of his sexuality private; and the Liberal Democrats retained Huhne's Eastleigh seat in the by-election following his resignation, one of their most heartening electoral performances of the entire parliament.

Much of the criticism of the Liberal Democrats was personalised as attacks on Nick Clegg, rather as the bubble in their support during the 2010 election campaign had been personalised around support for him, and this led some discontented Liberal Democrats to attempt a coup against his leadership in 2014 in a desperate last-ditch attempt to salvage something for the general election. Private polling was commissioned in a number of key constituencies by a Liberal Democrat peer, Lord Oakeshott, and a backbench MP, John Pugh, began collecting names of MPs who would join him in demanding Clegg's resignation. But with no alternative leader lined up to take over if the coup succeeded (Vince Cable was apparently bullied out of making a commitment by the threat that he would be revealed in the press as one of the conspirators before the success or failure of the attempt was known), and with no evidence of grassroots support, Pugh's backers melted away once he went public. Nothing came of the attempt beyond some mild embarrassment to the party and to Cable.[41] It now appears that Clegg was already considering resigning as leader at the time of the attempted coup and was talked out of it by his predecessor Paddy Ashdown and his eventual successor Tim Farron[42]; Oakeshott's clumsy attempt to supplant him with Cable may have strengthened rather than weakened his determination to stay on.

How far was Nick Clegg's leadership a liability to the Liberal Democrats? It is difficult to be certain because the personalisation of issues that are not fundamentally personal can hide more serious problems. If Clegg had been ousted, it might well have been that the burden of unpopularity would simply have been transferred to his successor's shoulders. Nevertheless, we found over the course of the parliament that almost half (48%) of those who told us that they voted Liberal Democrat in 2010 and did not intend to do so again said that they liked the party but did not like Nick Clegg, while only one in five of them disliked both and just 7% liked Clegg but not the party.[43] Moreover, Clegg's monthly satisfaction scores (rating the way he was doing his job as deputy PM) were consistently dreadful, and almost always significantly worse than Ed Miliband's. On the face of it, installing a new leader whose honeymoon period had not run out by the time of the election might have muted some of the hostility towards the

---

[41] Patrick Wintour and Nicholas Watt, 'The Clegg Catastrophe', *The Guardian*, 24 June 2015, http://www.theguardian.com/politics/2015/jun/24/the-nick-clegg-catastrophe, accessed 3 July 2015.

[42] Patrick Wintour and Nicholas Watt, 'Nick Clegg Offered to Resign as Lib Dem Leader a Year before 2015 Election', *The Guardian*, 24 June 2015, http://www.theguardian.com/politics/2015/jun/24/nick-clegg-offered-to-resign-as-lib-dem-leader-a-year-before-2015-election, accessed 12 August 2015.

[43] Data was aggregated from polls in January 2011, October 2012, August 2013, September 2014 and March 2015. In total, Ipsos MORI interviewed 366 GB adults aged 18+ who said that they had voted Liberal Democrat in 2010 but who did not intend to vote Liberal Democrat at the time of interview.

Liberal Democrats and perhaps saved some of their votes and seats. But because this is precisely the sort of situation where the voters are least able to anticipate their future attitudes under changing circumstances, no polling of the "what if" description could give a definitive answer.

The freedom of the press

A good deal of the political debate during the 2010-15 parliament was taken up with what eventually proved to be side issues, and while it was not necessarily a mistake for Labour to pursue them in the interests of good government, they had little impact on the political agenda.

The ramifications arising from the misbehaviour of tabloid journalists were perhaps the most prominent example of this. The question was not at bottom a party-political one, but became one because of Conservative links with some of the newspapers involved. However, as no evidence of impropriety in these links on the Tories' behalf was ever proved or even seriously advanced, the entire matter was so far as the political agenda was concerned a damp squib. The wider implications were certainly of legitimate public concern and as such a problem that the government had to solve, but one on which the Conservatives and Labour essentially ended up seeing eye-to-eye.

The first intimations of the scandal to follow came during the previous parliament, when a *News of the World* journalist was convicted of 'phone hacking' (illegally accessing voicemails) in pursuit of a scoop. But the newspaper's management was adamant that it was an isolated case, and although doubts were widely expressed nobody produced any evidence to prove otherwise. However, when Andy Coulson, who had been *News of the World*'s editor at the time, was hired by David Cameron as his communications director before the 2010 election, it was plain that the matter would become a party-political one should Coulson's assurances that he had known nothing of the matter subsequently be brought into doubt. Nevertheless, after the election Cameron appointed Coulson as the government Communications Director in Number Ten. The *Guardian* and other media were by this time running stories alleging that phone hacking was much more widespread at the *News of the World* and other newspapers than had thus far been proved, and that Coulson and other senior figures were fully implicated.

Speculation and allegations about Coulson's role continued to surface, and he felt compelled to resign in January 2011 as this was making it impossible for him to do his job effectively. A few days later the Metropolitan Police announced that it was opening a new investigation into illegal phone hacking by journalists. Coulson was arrested in connection with this investigation on 8 July 2011, and the opposition began to make political capital out of the affair, notably raising questions about Coulson's vetting and security clearance.

By this stage, however, the phone hacking issue had escalated into a major scandal. On 4 July, the *Guardian* broke the story of the *News of the World's* reporting of the disappearance in 2002 of Milly Dowler, a schoolgirl who had gone missing and was later found to have been abducted and murdered. The *Guardian* noted that, in fact, the *News of the World* had not at the time concealed from either its readers or the police force investigating the disappearance that it had accessed her voicemail[44]; nevertheless, this revival of the case in 2011 – pointing out as the *News of the World* had not that such practices are illegal – sparked a public and political outcry. (The reaction was almost certainly intensified by the *Guardian's* further allegation that journalists had deleted voicemails from her mailbox, giving friends and relatives false hope that she might still be alive; but this later turned out to be entirely untrue.[45]) Further allegations of hacking on other sensitive stories quickly followed, and a string of major companies announced that they were withdrawing their advertisements from the *News of the World*. On 7 July, its owner News Corporation announced that it had decided to close the newspaper and on 10 July, less than a week after the *Guardian's* story, the *News of the World* published its last ever edition.

The Coulson story in itself amounted as a political issue to no more than an embarrassing reflection on the Prime Minister's good judgment in

---

[44] Nick Davies and Amelia Hill, 'Missing Milly Dowler's Voicemail Was Hacked by News of the World', *The Guardian*, 5 July 2011, http://www.theguardian.com/uk/2011/jul/04/milly-dowler-voicemail-hacked-news-of-world, accessed 13 August 2015.
[45] Nick Davies and David Leigh, 'Police Logs Raise Questions over Deletion of Milly Dowler Voicemails', *The Guardian*, 10 December 2011, http://www.theguardian.com/media/2011/dec/09/milly-dowler-voicemails-police-logs-inquiry, accessed 13 August 2015; Rebecca Camber and Vanessa Allen, 'News of the World Staff "Did NOT Delete Milly Dowler's Voicemails after Hacking Her Phone as Guardian Claimed", *Mail Online*, 5 November 2013, http://www.dailymail.co.uk/news/article-2487372/News-World-staff-did-NOT-delete-Milly-Dowlers-voicemails-hacking-phone.html, accessed 13 August 2015.

having hired him, and perhaps reinforced public impressions of Cameron's 'arrogance' as he obstinately refused to listen to criticisms of Coulson until very late in the day. However, the escalation of the story into one involving other News International editors and journalists potentially raised wider issues about links between the Conservatives and Rupert Murdoch's News Corporation (of which News International was the British arm). Rebekah Brooks (who had been editor of the *News of the World* at the time of the Milly Dowler story[46] and was by 2011 chief executive of News International) was a friend and neighbour of David Cameron, and reportedly a regular guest at his constituency home. Cameron had met other senior executives of the company on many occasions while Prime Minister. Murdoch's newspapers had all endorsed the Conservatives at the 2010 election, the *Sun* and the *News of the World* having both switched from being enthusiastic supporters of Labour between 1997 and 2005. It was suggested that Murdoch was particularly keen to gain government backing for his bid to gain full ownership of BSkyB (in which he held the largest minority holding) and to affect government policy on the BBC to his own company's competitive advantage.

Ed Miliband chose to make the Murdoch bid for BSkyB the subject of the Opposition Day motion in the Commons on 13 July 2011, but Labour gained no political leverage from the affair. Murdoch withdrew his bid before the Commons debate, at which Conservative MPs joined other parties in attacking him, and the motion was passed *nem con*. On the same day, David Cameron announced the setting up of a public enquiry chaired by Lord Justice Leveson into the culture, practices and ethics of the press (accusations of journalistic misbehaviour were already spreading beyond Murdoch's titles to encompass other newspapers).

Leveson reported in November 2012, recommending strict statutory control of the press. Labour called for full implementation of the report and the Liberal Democrats expressed sympathy, but the Conservatives were initially more cautious, citing concerns about freedom of the press so that, unusually, they were taking a more liberal position than either of the

---

[46] She had been on holiday at the time the story had run, and was thus not responsible for that edition of the paper; she denied any knowledge of phone hacking, and was acquitted of all charges at the subsequent trial.

other two parties. There might conceivably have been an opportunity for Labour to make political capital here since, almost certainly, public opinion would have backed the most stringent measures to control and restrain the press[47], but it was probably a responsible decision not to do so. The parties subsequently hammered out a compromise behind closed doors, a Royal Charter to which almost the whole of the press has refused to accede; instead, most newspapers have subscribed to an 'Independent Press Standards Organisation' (IPSO) set up by themselves. The ultimate outcome is still unresolved.

The whole Coulson/Leveson saga illustrates an important lesson on the difference between politics in the 'Westminster bubble' and in the real world where votes are cast. For many of the commentators and the politicians themselves, this was an issue of real substance, seeming to pose a genuine danger that David Cameron could be significantly damaged by his association with Murdoch, smearing him with possible appearances of naive incompetence or cynically corrupt collusion with Murdoch's business interests. But to make an impact on the public as a whole, the evidence has to be far more compelling, the alleged misconduct far more blatant and the accusations sustained in the public eye for a far longer period.

This is not to suggest that the public were unaware of the issue, but their reaction to it was not the same as that of the seasoned Westminster watcher. With allegations that were rarely raised above the level of innuendo, most people took their cues from their existing preconceptions, rather than having their view of the world radically changed. Those who already distrusted David Cameron no doubt drew the grimmest conclusions in this case as well, but those who had previously supported him continued to do so, seeing nothing in the stories that came out to shake their faith. Solid proof of dishonesty or corruption might have been

---

[47] A YouGov poll in March 2013 found 63% of the public saying that the press needed "much tougher independent regulation with fines for newspapers that behave badly", and when told that "Some people have claimed that giving the state a role in press regulation is a major change to the relationship between the state and the press whereas others believe that it will actually make very little difference at all", 21% felt it would be a major and worrying change but 24% a major and welcome change. The poll also suggested that the majority of the public took a cynical view of Cameron's motives for resisting state regulation. (YouGov interviewed 1,684 GB adults online on 10-11 March 2013: https://yougov.co.uk/news/2013/03/15/support-leveson-softening/, accessed 22 September 2015.)

a different kettle of fish, but nothing of the sort emerged; without that it remained entirely peripheral to the real issues that the average voters believed mattered to them. This was no Watergate moment.

Managing the economy

The Conservatives, meanwhile, concentrated on their primary pre-election aim of securing economic recovery, or at least sufficient progress to justify keeping them in office.

Figure 4: Economic optimism and Conservative support 2007–15

Q. Do you think that the general economic condition of the country will improve, stay the same, or get worse over the next 12 months?

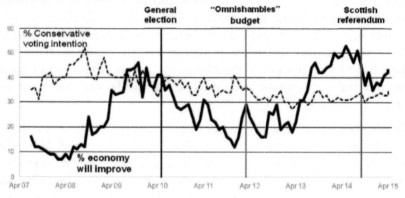

Base: c. 1,000 GB adults aged 18+ each month
Source: Ipsos MORI Political Monitor

Our tracking of the public's economic optimism (Figure 4) shows some distinct changes in fortune. From the trough of early 2008, following directly on the financial crisis, confidence had steadily risen towards the 2010 election but, despite an enthusiastic reception for George Osborne's first budget, it shifted to a distinct downturn thereafter. By the start of 2012 it was almost as low as four years previously, with barely one in ten of the public expecting things to get better within a year. After this, a brief revival was reversed abruptly at the time of the 2012 budget, which Ed

Miliband memorably characterised as an "Omnishambles" (borrowing the terminology of fictional spin-doctor Malcolm Tucker[48]).

Many of the budget proposals were immediately unpopular, notably increasing taxes for pensioners to find more money to help lower-paid workers, cutting the top rate of income tax and confirming a planned rise in fuel duty of 3p a litre.[49] Worse, the budget seemed poorly planned, with U-turns within weeks and memorable if trivial gaffes in the arguments over the details. (One of the new measures was cleverly christened by the press as a 'Pasty Tax' and when George Osborne admitted he had no idea when he had last eaten a Cornish pasty, he was derided as being out of touch with ordinary people! David Cameron then incautiously tried to retrieve the situation by recalling a "delicious" pasty he had recently eaten at Leeds railway station, but the *Sun* reported that there were no pasty outlets at Leeds station at the time he claimed to have done so.)

An issue of more substance was the 'bedroom tax' (officially the 'under-occupancy penalty'), actually a restriction on housing benefits to prevent them from being used to rent houses bigger than the recipient needed. This was introduced as part of the 2012 Welfare Reform Act, and came into force in April 2013. As an example of the potency of successful spin, and one of the few issues on which the opposition undoubtedly scored public opinion points against the government, it is perhaps worthy of detailed consideration. Polls showed that in general the public backed the government's clamp-down on benefit payments. Indeed, it was one of the strongest and most widely supported elements in the package of cuts. But by successfully applying a damaging though misleading nickname to the under-occupancy penalty, the opposition succeeded in giving themselves a

---

[48] As played by Peter Capaldi in the satirical TV comedy *The Thick Of It*. After Miliband's initial use of the term, it was so widely adopted and reused, both to describe the budget and for other criticisms of the government, that the Oxford English Dictionary chose "omnishambles" as its "word of the year" in November 2012. It may be worth remarking that "omnishambles" is one of the few Malcolm Tucker catchphrases that can be repeated in polite society.

[49] ICM's post budget poll for the *Sunday Telegraph* found 63% opposing "measures ... for pensioners to pay more in tax as a result of lowering their tax-free allowance to help cut taxes for lower-paid workers", 56% against cutting the top rate of income tax from 50p to 45p in the pound and 88% against going ahead with the planned rise in fuel duty. (ICM interviewed 1,000 GB adults aged 18+ by telephone on 22-23 March 2012: http://www.icmunlimited.com/media-centre/polls/post-budget-poll-for-sunday-telegraph-1, accessed 5 November 2015.)

rallying call and in using the policy to discredit the government – such is the power of framing.

In fact, in an August 2013 survey by Ipsos MORI for the Department of Work and Pensions (Table 13), in which questions were put in the context of more general consideration of reform to welfare benefits, we found more support than opposition for the principle of the under-occupancy restriction[50]. Opinions differed dramatically by the respondent's own housing tenure, but even among those who rented there was significant minority support for the policy.

Table 13: The 'bedroom tax'

Q. In principle, do you support or oppose the reduction in the amount of Housing Benefit for those of working age and living in social housing (rented from a council or housing association) if they have more bedrooms than the Government thinks they need?

	All	Owner-occupiers	Private renters	Social renters
	%	%	%	%
Strongly support	18	22	12	10
Tend to support	31	36	23	18
Neither support nor oppose	15	14	19	17
Tend to oppose	16	15	21	18
Strongly oppose	17	10	23	35
Don't know	3	3	3	1
Support	49	58	35	29
Oppose	33	25	44	53

Base: 2,021 British adults aged 18–75 interviewed online, 23–28 August 2013
Source: Ipsos MORI/DWP

But ComRes polls for the *Sunday People* in February and April 2013, asking about the measure under the name 'bedroom tax' (with no further explanation offered) found the balance of opinion in each case was in favour of abandoning the policy. In the later of the two, 55% also agreed that "The 'Bedroom Tax' shows how out of touch the Government is with the lives of real people". Here as on so many other issues there was a dramatic difference in opinions by party loyalty, meaning that the potential to swing votes may have been limited, but 22% agreement even among

---

[50] And the poll probably understated the overall level of support as it was an online poll excluding those aged 75+, generally the most Conservative group.

those intending to vote Conservative that a flagship policy showed their party as 'out of touch' suggests at least that the issue had more potential than most.[51]

Economic optimism fluctuated between April 2012 and April 2013, but thereafter began a dramatic and sustained rise for a year and a half. In the same period, the objective economic indicators also began to look distinctly healthier. By July 2014, official figures showed that the size of the economy had now surpassed its pre-recession peak[52].

Table 14: Blame for cuts

Q. From what you know, who do you think is most to blame for the level of cuts to public services?

	March 2011			January 2013		
		Reported 2010 vote			Reported 2010 vote	
	All	**Conser-vative**	**Labour**	**All**	**Conser-vative**	**Labour**
	%	%	%	%	%	%
The previous Labour government	31	65	11	26	57	6
Banks	29	15	41	23	13	31
The state of the global economy	18	12	19	21	20	24
The Coalition government	10	1	22	21	4	33
Local councils	5	4	2	4	3	3
None of these	2	0	2	1	1	1
Don't know	6	2	3	4	2	2

Base: 498 British adults 18+, 11–13 March 2011; 1,015 British adults 18+, 12–14 January 2013
Source: Ipsos MORI Political Monitor

Yet, to the surprise of many, Conservative voting support remained almost entirely steady through these fluctuations in economic perceptions, neither collapsing as prospects seemed to be worsening nor burgeoning as things improved and Mr Osborne could plausibly claim to have been proved right. We consider the explanation for this in more detail in a later chapter, but the basis is simple and unsurprising, even if going somewhat against

---

[51] ComRes interviewed 2,002 British adults online on 13-14 February 2013 and 2,059 on 3-5 April 2013. In the April survey, 51% agreed that "David Cameron should abandon the 'Bedroom Tax' entirely and think of other ways to save money". (http://comres.co.uk/polls/the-people-bedroom-tax-poll/; http://comres.co.uk/polls/the-sunday-people-bedroom-tax-poll/, accessed 14 August 2015.)

[52] Maria Tadeo, 'UK Economy Bounces Back to Pre-Recession Levels', *The Independent*, 25 July 2014, http://www.independent.co.uk/news/business/news/uk-economy-bounces-back-to-prerecession-levels-9628045.html, accessed 12 November 2015.

precedent. In the opening years of the parliament, Conservatives stood firm and gave the government the benefit of the doubt – they had not expected nor been promised a swift economic miracle, and most blamed the previous Labour government for the depth of the crisis rather than the new government for taking time to build a way out of it. (Table 14).

Labour supporters, of course, saw their worst fears confirmed and even though many accepted the case for cuts in spending, they had little sympathy for the details of the policies that were implemented. Those who had voted Liberal Democrat – the majority of whom within a year were recanting that decision – were hardly more reconciled to it. But Conservative voters mostly felt the right decisions had been made – it would take time and persistent failure to shake their faith, if it could be done at all.[53]

Table 15: Satisfaction with government decisions on cuts, 2011

Q. From what you know, do you think the government has on the whole made the right decisions or the wrong decisions about where spending cuts should be made?

| | | Reported vote in 2010 | | |
	All	Conser-vative	Labour	Liberal Democrat
	%	%	%	%
Right decisions	35	69	15	28
Wrong decisions	55	23	78	64
Don't know	10	9	7	9

Base: 1,000 British adults 18+, 11–13 March 2011
Source: Ipsos MORI Political Monitor

When recovery came, however, the boot was on the other foot. Conservatives saw themselves justified, any doubts resolved. Those Liberal Democrats who had stayed with the party were equally happy but gave credit to their own contribution to the Coalition rather than seeing any reason to swing to the Conservatives. Labour supporters persisted in giving greater weight to the damaging effects of the austerity than to any economic improvements – which were in any case sufficiently ambiguous for sceptics to doubt them – and noted that consumer standards of living had prospered far less from the upturn than had corporate profits.

---

[53] Ipsos MORI interviewed 1,000 British adults aged 18+ by telephone on 11-13 March 2011.

In fact, perceptions of an upturn were in any case stronger among Conservative supporters, no doubt partly because they relied strongly on which spokesman the individual voter found most convincing. Cameron and Osborne were trusted and believed by Conservatives, but most Labour voters found Miliband and Balls more credible judges of the average family's wellbeing than the former denizens of the Bullingdon Club.

No matter. Chancellor Osborne may not have driven a dramatic personal vote *to* the Tories, but he had come to the country's economic rescue before the patience of his own voters had run out, and this in effect secured the second victory.

Nevertheless, not all voters were convinced by either the Conservatives or Labour. Coincidentally or not – probably not – the palpable impression of chaos that briefly hung around the government at the time of the Omnishambles budget coincided with the dramatic arrival of the UK Independence Party (UKIP) as serious players on the electoral chess board.

At the 2010 general election, they secured only 3% of the vote, concentrating mainly on the European Union issue, which is in itself of limited interest to most voters. But by linking the European issue to one of wider concern, immigration, they gave themselves much more traction. Nevertheless, the surge in their support was very sudden: up to November 2012 in our polls, they never scored above 6%; from March 2013 onwards, there were only two polls where their support was not in double figures. Probably they were already building support before the budget, but that certainly marked the point at which they became permanently established at this new, higher level.

Undoubtedly a crucial element in UKIP's accumulation of support was the appeal of their leader, Nigel Farage, who immediately gave sympathisers an impression of competence and forced his way into the public's attention as more than merely the leader of a fringe party. On 2 April 2014, he appeared on a head-to-head BBC2 debate on Britain's future in Europe with the Deputy Prime Minister, Nick Clegg (who had made his own breakthrough into the public consciousness by his performance in the election leaders' debate four years earlier); Farage wiped the floor with him. An ICM poll of viewers immediately afterwards found 64% felt

Farage had won, only 28% that Clegg had done so; even 40% of Lib Dems gave the verdict to Farage.[54]

UKIP had already partially confirmed that the increase in their support was more than a mere polling mirage with local election successes, and set any lingering doubts to rest in the 2014 European election, a few weeks after the Farage-Clegg debate (Table 16).

Table 16: British elections to the European Parliament, 2009 and 2014

Party	2009 votes %	2014 votes %	Change	2009 Seats	2014 Seats	Change
Conservative	27.7	23.9	–3.8	25	19	–6
Labour	15.7	25.4	+9.7	13	20	+7
Liberal Democrats	13.7	6.9	–6.8	11	1	–10
UKIP	16.5	27.5	+11.0	13	24	+11
Scottish National Party	2.1	2.5	+0.4	2	2	0
Plaid Cymru	0.8	0.7	–0.1	1	1	0
Green Party	8.6	7.9	–0.7	2	3	+1
BNP	6.2	1.1	–5.1	2	0	–2
Others	8.5	4.1	–4.4	0	0	0
Total	100	100		69	70	+1

Source: Results given in House of Commons Library Research Paper 14/32
Note: Figures apply only to Great Britain, not Northern Ireland

UKIP won the popular vote across Great Britain, polling 4.4 million votes. Their 27.5% vote share was an 11-point increase on their performance five years earlier, and about nine times the size of their vote share at the 2010 general election.[55] Of course, the proportional representation system used in the Euro-elections is far friendlier to UKIP, and other middling-sized parties such as the Greens, than is the First-Past- the-Post system used in general elections: there, UKIP can only win seats if it can concentrate its vote in particular constituencies, and many voters will be deterred from supporting them by the fear that their votes will be wasted. Moreover, turnout is low in European elections and even 4.4 million votes amount to

---

[54] Poll for *The Guardian*. ICM interviewed 1,458 debate viewers aged 18+ online on 2 April 2014: http://www.icmunlimited.com/media-centre/polls/over-two-thirds-vote-farage-in-eu-debate, accessed 5 November 2015.

[55] Oliver Hawkins and Vaughne Miller, *European Parliament Elections 2014*, House of Commons Library Research Paper (London: House of Commons Library, 11 June 2014), http://www.parliament.uk/business/publications/research/briefing-papers/RP14-32/european-parliament-elections-2014, accessed 29 October 2015.

considerably less than 27% of a general election turnout. So it was no surprise that UKIP's performance in the European election outstripped their continuing ratings in the polls which asked people how they would vote if there were a general election tomorrow.

But even at half their European election share of the vote, UKIP's presence radically changed the political calculations. As a party of the right, they had far more natural appeal to Conservative than Labour voters, although they certainly drew some support from both parties. Polling showed that their support was coming more from the Conservatives than from Labour, with immigration the touchstone issue. If the Tories leaked more votes to UKIP than did Labour in marginal seats, they risked losing those seats to Labour by default.

Worse, in the autumn of 2012 the Conservatives lost two seats directly to UKIP by the defection of sitting Conservative MPs and, embarrassingly, came nowhere near to dislodging either when both voluntarily called by-elections. Douglas Carswell at Clacton won 60% of the vote, Mark Reckless at Rochester & Strood a less-unprecedented but still impressive 42%. Might there be more defectors? Might UKIP even win other seats at the general election from a standing start? Suddenly the threat to the Conservatives on their right looked far more potent than the threat on the left.

Nor was it just voters that the Conservatives were losing to UKIP. The support of a widely-read national newspaper might be considered to be one of the clearest distinguishing marks of a major party in Britain, and UKIP won the backing of the *Daily Express* (only once previously since the War had that newspaper failed to support the Conservatives), and our polling suggests that a third of *Express* readers who voted did so for UKIP, considerably higher than for any other paper, although UKIP did comparatively well among readers of all the Fleet Street popular tabloids. (See Table 9 above, p. 39.) The *Sunday Express* also backed UKIP, but Richard Desmond's other morning paper, the *Daily Star*, remained true to its usual election policy of carrying little political news, and did not endorse any party[56]. Perhaps surprisingly, or perhaps demonstrating the

---

[56] Dominic Ponsford and William Turvill, 'UK Daily Newspaper Market Backs Tories over Labour by a Margin of Five to One', *Press Gazette*, 6 May 2015, http://www.pressgazette.co.uk/uk-daily-newspaper-market-backs-tories-over-labour-margin-five-one, accessed 7 September 2015.

potency of a newspaper's active support for a party, *Star* readers were less likely to vote for UKIP than readers of any of the other red-top or mid-market dailies, giving the party less than half the support that *Express* readers did.

Who was it that was swinging to UKIP? The *Daily Express* clearly thought it knew: echoing its more routine, non-election obsessions, it was keen to record that "A vote Ukip poster has been spotted in the grounds of Buckingham Palace, according to reports",[57] although as it went on to refer to "The bright yellow and purple poster, *which normally* [our italics] display the slogan 'I'm voting Ukip' in large bold letters", there seems to have been some element of doubt. And what, exactly, should one draw from the reporter's further observation that "Although the Queen, who has met Nigel Farage, does not vote herself, members of her household are allowed to"? Our polls do not have a separate social class category for members of the Royal Household, but they found that UKIP support came more from the working class than the middle class, especially from C2 men, and – as the Tories had feared – more from people who had voted Conservative in 2010 than from those who had voted Labour.

Changing the rules

The Fixed-term Parliaments Act, already mentioned, was a constitutional novelty, but there were several other attempts to make changes to the electoral ground rules whose practical effects would have been even more radical – a referendum to change the electoral system, the bill to reduce the number of MPs to 600 and equalise constituency electorates in the process, another referendum to take Scotland out of the UK – each of these could have rendered the election unrecognisably different, but in each case the status quo emerged victorious. Individual electoral registration did replace household registration, potentially as dramatic a change with profound party consequences, but transitional measures were adopted to delay the full introduction of the new register until after the

---

[57] Scott Campbell, 'Does the QUEEN Want out of the EU? Vote Ukip Poster Spotted in Buckingham Palace', *Express*, 15 April 2015, http://www.express.co.uk/news/politics/570547/Queen-Ukip-Nigel-Farage-Buckingham-Palace-Elizabeth-II-Royal-family-London, accessed 24 September 2015.

general election, and if the diluted change had any meaningful impact on the result, nobody seemed to have been talking about it by the time the election arrived.

The referendum on the electoral system

The referendum on changing the electoral system was an object lesson in how not to persuade the public to endorse a new idea, which was perhaps precisely the intention of some of those responsible for the arrangements. It was not even as if it was an idea to which the public were naturally hostile: on the contrary, an ICM poll immediately after the 2010 election found public support for the change at 56% and those preferring to keep the existing system only 35%.[58] But that was before the public had had a chance to think about it, and before opponents of the proposal had had a chance to put their case.

The referendum sprang from the Coalition Agreement, the Conservatives committed to allowing a vote on the issue but not to supporting the change. The system which was proposed, AV (the alternative vote), was wanted by almost no-one: most Liberal Democrats and other reformers would have preferred a much more proportional system, most Conservatives (and some Labour traditionalists) did not want to change the system at all. Therefore, the most obvious virtue of AV, that it represented a relatively small change from the familiar system, commended it to almost nobody. Reformers had difficulty arguing for it, because it lacked most of the benefits for which they could make out a principled case. Above all, it could not guarantee greater proportionality of seats to votes.

Moreover, while AV seemed to be a complicated system, in most respects it could hardly be simpler. (Its consequences are anything but simple, but that is another matter entirely.) Yet the advocates of AV proved entirely unable to explain it simply. Their opponents may have engaged in deliberate obfuscation to make it seem even more complicated than it is, but that is uncertain; it is not impossible that they didn't understand it either. An infamous *Today* programme argument between David Cameron

---

[58] Survey for the *Sunday Telegraph*. ICM interviewed 1,004 GB adults aged 18+ by telephone on 12-13 May 2010 (http://www.icmunlimited.com/media-centre/polls/con-lib-coalition-poll-for-sunday-telegraph, accessed 29 October 2015).

and John Humphrys, in which both seemed to show that they did not understand what the other – or perhaps even they themselves – were saying, was not a great advert for politicians or broadcasters, and can hardly have enlightened the voters.[59]

Probably most decisive, however, was the No campaign's cost argument, reminiscent of the equally-successful 'White Elephant' campaign used in the devolution referendum of 2004 in the North East of England, and successful for the same reason. Having failed to put across either what the change entailed or why it was a good idea, AV's proponents were helpless against the complaint that what they were proposing was a waste of money. The projected costs raised in these arguments were outrageously inflated, and the presentation of the point far overstepped the bounds of normally acceptable political rhetoric in Britain. (One poster showed the head of a soldier with the caption "He needs bulletproof vests not an alternative voting system: Say NO to spending £250m on AV".)[60] But it was an open goal in any case.

On 5 May 2011, the UK voted by two-to-one on a 42% turnout to keep the existing electoral system. The Liberal Democrats, to whom the change would probably have been worth dozens of seats, had forced their Conservative 'allies' to concede a vote on this issue of fundamental principle for them, and were then able to produce barely six million votes in its support, less than had turned out for them in the previous year's general election. They fumed at the frustration of the hopes raised when the commitment to the referendum was included in the Coalition Agreement. It would not take much more to provoke them into a temper tantrum; and it did not.

---

[59] Daily Mail Reporter, '"Go back to School": The Moment David Cameron Blasted BBC's John Humphrys over the AV Voting System', *Mail Online*, 4 May 2011, http://www.dailymail.co.uk/news/article-1383137/AV-referendum-David-Cameron-blasts-John-Humphrys-voting-system.html, accessed 28 September 2015; 'Humphrys Could Have Been "Clearer" over AV Says BBC', *BBC News*, 3 May 2011, http://www.bbc.co.uk/news/uk-politics-13272353, accessed 28 September 2015.

[60] This estimate of £250m apparently included the £82m cost of the referendum itself, which would of course be spent whatever the outcome, and an estimated £130m for electronic vote counting systems, which would be entirely unnecessary. Educating voters about the system was expected to cost £26m. See James Chapman, 'A Good Reason to Choose No? Switch to New Voting System "Will Cost Us All £250m"', *Mail Online*, 15 February 2011, http://www.dailymail.co.uk/news/article-1357038/New-voting-switch-cost-250m.html, accessed 28 September 2015.

The boundary review

The second abortive attempt to change the ground rules was the review of parliamentary constituency boundaries, which together with the AV referendum provisions was provided for by the Parliamentary Voting System and Constituencies Act 2011. The Conservatives came into government in 2010 despite a bias against them in the operation of the electoral system, and were committed to correcting it by a redistribution of seats under new rules that would guarantee much stricter numerical equality in constituency electorates. The hopes they placed on this measure reflected two misunderstandings: the inequality in electorates, although real and to the Conservatives' disadvantage, was only a minor cause of the electoral bias; and the discretion over constituency sizes which the old rules gave to the Boundary Commissions was only a minor cause of the difference between the parties in the average size of their constituency electorates.

It is true that Conservative constituencies have higher electorates than Labour or Liberal Democrat ones: in 2010, the average electorate in Conservative-won constituencies was about 72,000, and in Labour-won constituencies about 68,500. But although the Boundary Commissions under the old rules had considerable latitude to vary constituency sizes from the norm, this was not the main reason for this imbalance. Much more significant is that boundaries are only revised every so often and the Conservatives tend to be stronger in the sort of areas which are growing in population (rural areas and suburbs) than those which are shrinking (inner cities), so outdated boundaries normally hurt the Conservatives and help Labour. The Conservatives are also weak in Wales, which under the old rules has systematically smaller constituencies than the rest of the UK. The revised rules embodied in the 2011 Act dealt with both of these situations, setting a common electoral quota for all four countries of the UK, so removing the over-representation of Wales, and providing for more frequent boundary reviews (once in every five-year parliament, in fact) which would have prevented the boundaries becoming too out of date.

However, the difference in constituency electorates is not the main reason for the bias in the electoral system – as was pointed out to the government consistently before the whole process started[61]. Two more important factors contribute to the bias, turnout and the distribution of votes. Turnouts are on average lower in Labour-held seats, so Labour needs a smaller number of votes to get the same vote share in its constituencies as the Conservatives get in theirs. The Conservatives also get many more votes in seats they can't realistically hope to win than Labour does – there are many constituencies where the Conservatives and Liberal Democrats are the two strongest parties and Labour is very weak indeed. In 2010, there were only 74 constituencies where the Conservatives had less than 15% of the vote, but there were 142 where Labour fell below that level, so far more Conservative votes are "wasted", being cast where they cannot help the party win seats. Moreover, up to 2010 Labour was winning almost all the constituencies where the Conservatives were placed third or lower, while the Conservatives were losing many of the seats where Labour was placed third, to the Liberal Democrats. (It was the reversal of this position, the Conservatives winning back most of these seats from the Liberal Democrats while Labour lost a raft of Scottish seats to the SNP, that was in the end responsible for the electoral bias reversing in 2015, even without any equalisation of constituency electorates through boundary review.)

To their determination to equalise the electorates the Conservatives added a second aim, reducing the number of seats from 650 to 600. A 600-seat House is not inherently better or worse for the Conservatives than a 550-seat or 650-seat House. It is true that for Liberal Democrats in particular, so reliant on establishing relationships between sitting MPs and their constituents so as to build a personal vote, any radical disruption to the constituency framework is a threat, but it cannot be reasonably blocked on those grounds – if that objection were taken to its logical conclusion, Old Sarum would still have two MPs. (In any case, when the election came few Liberal Democrat MPs were saved by their personal votes even on

---

[61] Galina Borisyuk, Colin Rallings, Michael Thrasher, and Ron Johnston, 'Parliamentary Constituency Boundary Reviews and Electoral Bias: How Important Are Variations in Constituency Size?', *Parliamentary Affairs* 63 (2010): 4–21; Ron Johnston, Iain McLean, Charles Pattie, and David Rossiter, 'Can the Boundary Commissions Help the Conservative Party? Constituency Size and Electoral Bias in the United Kingdom', *The Political Quarterly* 80 (2009): 479–494; Robert M. Worcester, Roger Mortimore, Paul Baines, and Mark Gill, *Explaining Cameron's Coalition: How It Came about - an Analysis of the 2010 British General Election* (London: Biteback, 2011), 264–269.

unchanged boundaries.) But the number of seats as such is not an issue of party advantage: for Labour to attempt to portray this part of the policy as gerrymandering, as they did, was nonsense, and presumably a deliberately cynical smokescreen to hide the fact that their real objection was to the removal of a manifestly-unfair advantage which they enjoyed from representing smaller constituencies.

For in fact the benefit for the Conservatives, more modest than they probably supposed, would have come entirely from the equalisation of constituency electorates. To this Labour had a more reasonable objection, that not everybody who should be is on the electoral register, and the shortfall is biggest in the sort of constituencies Labour wins: lower registration of underprivileged voters systematically disadvantages Labour areas, ensuring that they will have fewer seats than would be the case if eligible population rather than electorate were the yardstick.

The case for moving to constituencies based on population rather than electorate size is a viable, perhaps even a compelling one; nevertheless, as electorates have invariably been used as the standard since the 19th century, it was once again dishonest of Labour to accuse the Conservatives of gerrymandering by adhering to it, especially as Labour had made no attempt to reform the system in their own 13 years in government.

The legislation was enacted in 2011, and the Boundary Commissions set to work devising a revised set of boundaries under the new rules. The government had ignored clear warnings of how radical the resulting changes to the character of the system were likely to be. The reduction in the number of seats ensured that few existing constituencies were large enough to survive, and even those that were would often have to be dismembered to allow neighbouring constituencies to be brought up to size. Moreover, the strict size limits made it almost impossible to continue the tradition of observing the local government boundaries.[62] The result

---

[62] For example, Cornwall (including the Isles of Scilly) had 418,865 electors. But five constituencies of the maximum size could only have 402,365 between them, and the minimum number for six constituencies was 436,860. So it was literally impossible for Cornwall to have a whole number of constituencies, and at least one constituency must cross the boundary between Cornwall and Devon. The practice of insisting that constituencies in England should consist of whole wards also reduced the flexibility to find sensible solutions, necessitating for example taking the ward which included Gloucester Cathedral and the city's shopping centre and docks, separating it from the rest

was a new constituency map that was almost unrecognisable, and would have been a massive culture shock in its near-abandoning of the tradition that most constituencies should represent recognisable communities.

But the boundary changes were never implemented. In 2012, after the Conservatives dropped the House of Lords Reform Bill, Nick Clegg retaliated by stating that he would instruct his MPs to vote against the boundary revisions.[63] Subsequently, Liberal Democrat peers joined Labour in the House of Lords to block them by inserting an amendment into the Electoral Registration and Administration Bill to postpone any boundary changes until at least 2018.

The constitutional propriety of this expedient was, at the least, dubious. Of its political propriety it is difficult to mount any defence. Labour could at least hope to gain naked party advantage, the Liberal Democrats only revenge. Both were blocking a measure that would provide for greater equality in the value of votes. It is difficult not to reach the conclusion that it was Labour, not the Conservatives, who can most justly be accused of gerrymandering. The Liberal Democrats claimed to be justified in breaching the Coalition Agreement on the grounds that Conservative failure to implement House of Lords reform was an equal breach. But as the Conservatives pointed out, the Coalition Agreement explicitly linked Liberal Democrat support for the boundary changes to Conservative support for holding the AV referendum (and made nothing conditional on the outcome of the referendum). Perhaps neither side was entirely in the right, since the Conservatives had still failed to deliver House of Lords reform. But for a party with the reforming self-righteousness of the Liberal Democrats to protest against failure to democratise the Lords by using their votes there to block a measure which would have made elections to the Commons more democratic, and to justify this by arguing, in effect, that the failure to replace the Commons electoral system with one they preferred absolved them of any duty to help make the existing system fairer, opened the Lib Dems up to accusations of hypocrisy.

---

of the city and joining it instead to the Forest of Dean; but this practice was not a statutory requirement and was relaxed in the Commission's revised proposals.

[63] Tim Shipman, '"Traitor" Clegg Sparks Civil War in Coalition: Tory Fury as He Accuses Them of Breaking Deal on Lords Reform', *Mail Online*, 6 August 2012, http://www.dailymail.co.uk/news/article-2184431/Nick-Clegg-Lords-Reform-Tory-fury-Lib-Dem-leader-delivers-crushing-blow.html, accessed 3 September 2015.

The immediate result was that the 2015 general election was fought on the old boundaries; the whirlwind to be reaped may come in 2020 with new boundaries, perhaps redrawn after further revisions to the rules imposed by the current majority Conservative government, and certainly based on an electoral register purged by the introduction of individual registration.

Electoral registration reform

The introduction of individual electoral registration (IER) was less controversial in principle than either of the two previously considered measures. This was a change initiated by the previous Labour government, and a long overdue reform to an archaic system in which the responsibility for registration to vote rested with the head of household. But, in practice, the old system generally worked: while non-registration (which is, in theory, illegal) had reached a disappointing level of 14%,[64] it was expected to increase considerably under IER (as had been the case when IER was introduced in Northern Ireland some years earlier). The most notable virtue of the reform was the increased scope it offered to crack down on fraudulent registration and, to facilitate this, inclusion on the new register was to depend on proof of identity. This was a new bureaucratic hurdle which was likely to depress registration levels even further. While these aims were unimpeachable, the practical result would be to the Conservatives' advantage.

The Electoral Commission was naturally concerned with minimizing the level of inadvertent deregistration, of existing validly-qualified electors dropping off the register by failing to understand the demands of the new system or to correctly complete the administrative process of re-registration. A process was therefore introduced using automated record matching – in essence, verifying the credentials of current electors, where possible, from other government sources such as National Insurance records, and carrying over their names automatically to the new register. This would, presumably, significantly reduce the incidence of deregistration by incompetence or inaction; but, since the legitimate voters who were least likely to be on the records with which the register was

---

[64] Electoral Commission, *The Quality of the 2014 Electoral Registers in Great Britain: Research into the Last Registers Produced under the Household Registration System*, July 2014, http://www.electoralcommission.org.uk/__data/assets/pdf_file/0005/169889/Completeness-and-accuracy-of-the-2014-electoral-registers-in-Great-Britain.pdf, accessed 3 September 2015.

being matched were those without stable addresses or jobs, it might well have increased rather than reduced the consequent advantage which the Conservatives would derive.

There was, unsurprisingly, a good deal of opposition agitation about the effects of IER, but this seemed to died away as the election approached, probably as it became clear that the effect would not be immediate. Sensibly, the government included in the reform provisions a transitional arrangement by which the removal of any elector from the register under the new rules would not take effect until after the general election. But it has happened now, and will affect voting at the next round of local elections, for the Mayor of London and in the forthcoming referendum on European Union membership. The purged register will also be the basis for any new boundary revisions.

Scotland

All of these possible changes were very small beer compared to the prospect of Scotland leaving the UK. Scottish nationalism has been a vocal and persistent presence on the political agenda for decades, but there has never previously been a majority who indicated they would vote for independence, or anything close to it. Devolution with powers repatriated from Westminster to a Scottish Parliament was introduced by Labour after their general election victory in 1997, and was supposed to dull any appetite for outright separation. The SNP won a respectable vote in Scottish Parliament ('Holyrood') elections, but many of their supporters voted for unionist parties when it came to Westminster elections. However, the SNP's support grew, steadily, until in 2011 a majority SNP government took power in Edinburgh and demanded a referendum on independence. David Cameron's government agreed to this: it was under no constitutional or legal obligation to do so, but refusal would have been politically difficult and, arguably, undemocratic; besides, nobody seems to have contemplated any outcome except a clear rejection of independence.

By the final weeks before the vote, things looked very different: the nationalists had run much the more convincing campaign, the unionists had failed to put across any convincing case for Scotland staying part of the UK, and two polls had put the 'Yes' campaign ahead (although they were outliers and most polls gave 'No' a narrow lead).

Figure 5: Scottish support for independence 1978-2014

*Q. Should Scotland be an independent country?**

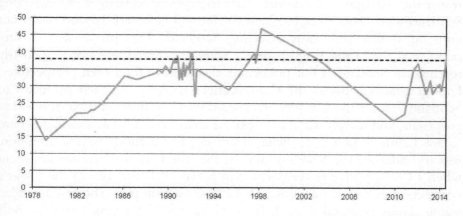

*Question wording has varied

Base: c. 1,000 Scottish adults in each survey
Source: Ipsos MORI Scotland

Much of the substance of the pro-independence campaign was explicitly anti-Conservative, and made the argument that separation was the only way to prevent Scotland being ruled by Conservative governments based on English votes. It was on Labour, as the biggest unionist party, that the task of countering this argument fell. Meanwhile, the Conservatives were potentially torn between their own unionist principles and the possibility of the permanent abolition of forty or more Labour seats if Scotland ceased to be represented at Westminster. (At this stage the idea that Labour might in any case lose all their seats to the SNP had crossed nobody's minds.) To their credit, Cameron and his colleagues stuck to their principles and fought for the Union, but the intervention of Gordon Brown in the final few days – still respected in Scotland despite being soundly defeated in England – was more weighty and possibly more effective. In a state of near panic, all the leaders at Westminster promised a new package of devolved powers provided Scotland voted 'No', and Scotland did vote 'No', by 55% to 45%.

But in terms of the general election, the referendum proved not an end but a beginning. Immediately after the referendum, the fragile truce between unionist parties was shattered when the Conservatives linked their proposals to implement further devolution for Scotland with moves towards 'English Votes for English Laws' (EVEL), in other words restricting the rights of Scottish MPs to vote on legislation not affecting Scotland when MPs from England, Wales and Northern Ireland could not vote on similar laws only affecting Scotland. This proposal was very popular as far as the English public were concerned and not particularly resented in Scotland[65]; but politicians always have their own perspectives. Labour attacked this as the Conservatives reneging on their promises to Scotland.[66] Since the Conservatives were standing firm on their devolution proposals, and merely using it an excuse to bring in EVEL *as well*, it is hard to see Labour's point. But what it did do, for anybody paying attention, was to underline the SNP's argument that the Labour Party are impotent when a Conservative government is in power. Whether or not there was a connection, it was at this juncture that the opinion polls showed a sudden swing across Scotland from Labour to the SNP of a scale normally only seen in by-elections.

Of course, that was only the opinion polls. Could it happen in practice? Despite the scepticism of the pundits it was soon plain that Labour in Scotland was taking the threat very seriously indeed and, worse, seemed to be admitting in private that it had no solution.

The revolution in Scottish party politics had a long incubation period, its causes stretching back far beyond the current parliament. Because the nationalists' near-miss in the referendum apparently came – at least, as viewed from England – out of the blue, and Labour's collapse in voting support came only after the referendum and was possibly caused by it, the temptation is to look entirely for short-term causes and to blame Ed Miliband or Johanna Lamont (the party's leader in Scotland at the time of the referendum). But this would be a mistake.

---

[65] After the general election, we found that if the public were reminded that Scotland had its own parliament "which makes decisions about issues such as health and education", people in England would support Scottish MPs not being allowed to vote "on issues that have no direct impact on people in Scotland" by 53% to 30%, and even those in Scotland split 44% to 35% in favour. Support was even stronger in England, but weaker in Scotland, when the proposal was put in terms of a "veto" for English MPs. (Ipsos MORI interviewed 1,026 British adults aged 18+ by telephone on 18-20 July 2015.)

[66] And since the general election, the SNP have also attacked EVEL arguing that English MPs voting on English matters might still affect Scottish funding.

Taking a slightly over-provocative stance, it could be argued that the Labour Party laid the foundations of its inevitable eventual eclipse in Scotland when it elected John Smith as its leader in 1992. Smith committed to the idea of establishing a Scottish Parliament, which was firmly adopted as Labour policy. It was understandable that the Labour Party were reluctant after Smith's death to jettison a policy with which he was so personally associated, but this ensured that devolution remained in New Labour's programme, to be implemented after the election victory in 1997 by a leadership that had little interest in it and no ideological commitment to it. Tony Blair has recently admitted that his government made a mistake in not paying enough attention to nurturing the Union once devolution had been implemented.[67]

Devolution created the institutional structure that allowed the SNP to build a power base, and devolution emphasised the hollowness of Labour's claims to represent Scotland's interests as the party's centre of gravity remained entirely London-centric, even under a Scottish Prime Minister between 2007 and 2010. Supposed to be the magic solution to Scottish separatism which would cause nationalism to wither on the vine, it instead enflamed nationalist feeling. Although the prospect of Labour's annihilation north of the border seemed to spring to life quite abruptly after the independence referendum, in truth it was the natural and probably inevitable outcome of a much longer process, of which the very establishment of the referendum was also a part. Certainly, the referendum acted as a trigger, but it is now plain that Labour was, unnoticed, standing on a precipice long before that.

By 1997, Labour had established a virtual one-party state in Scotland apart from a few dusty corners where the Liberal Democrats clung on to their parliamentary seats. Labour had 56 of Scotland's 72 MPs (the Conservatives had not a single one), and 613 local councillors out of 1,159. They had controlled Glasgow and Aberdeen City Councils since 1980, and

---

[67] Simon Johnson, 'Tony Blair Admits Mistake over Scottish Devolution', *The Telegraph*, 2 September 2015, http://www.telegraph.co.uk/news/politics/tony-blair/11839841/Tony-Blair-admits-mistake-over-Scottish-devolution.html, accessed 7 September 2015.

had finally (1995) retaken Edinburgh, after which they were the majority party in 20 of Scotland's 32 unitary districts – the other 12 were all hung.[68]

But Labour's reforms after the 1997 election established proportional representation for the European Parliament elections, as well as a PR-variant for electing the Scottish Parliament; and Labour's share of the vote in the Scotland-wide elections that followed, with the exception of the first-past-the-post Westminster elections, looked a great deal less dominant than this record might suggest. Proportional representation in local government elections came next, and this allowed the SNP to gain a foothold in councils across Scotland where they had previously won no seats, probably invigorating their local party organisations by giving them something attainable to fight for.

Figure 6: Labour share of the vote in Scotland since devolution

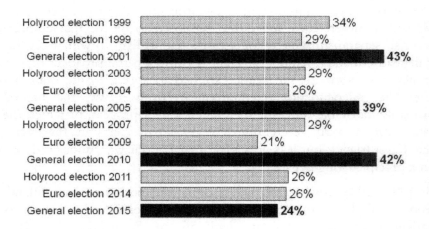

Source: Results reported in House of Commons Library Research Papers RP04-50, RP05-33, RP12-43, RP14-32 and Briefing Paper CBP-7186

In fact, in the four European Parliament elections between 1999 and 2014, Labour did not pass 30% of the vote once, and fell as low as 21% in 2009. The party list vote for Holyrood, at first a worrying 34%, fell to 29%, 29%

---

[68] David Butler and Gareth Butler, *British Political Facts*, 10th ed. (Basingstoke: Macmillan, 2011), 273, 510–11, 515.

again and finally 26%, as a result of which Labour passed from being the dominant party in the ruling coalition to onlookers under an SNP majority in 2011, so opening the door to a demand for an Independence Referendum. That a Conservative government in London should concede that demand was unpredictable, but entirely beyond Labour's control. Since it was obviously always a likely risk that Labour weakness at Holyrood would coincide with Labour weakness at Westminster, the election of an SNP majority in the Scottish Parliament would almost inevitably be the point at which Labour lost any say in Scotland's destiny – but, everybody was assured, an SNP majority was impossible. It was exactly what the electoral system was chosen to prevent; and the independence referendum condemned Labour to defending the possibility of Scotland being periodically ruled by Tories in Westminster. The plunge in Labour's Westminster support which the polls began to find in the autumn of 2014, although something that had been avoided up to that point, does not look in the least unlikely when taken in the context of their performance in other contests. The referendum looks like the catalyst of the change rather than its main cause.

This change injected a new element into the wider electoral equation. Of the 40 seats Labour won in Scotland in 2010, the SNP were second in 18, but in only one of those was the margin less than 15% of the vote, meaning that under normal circumstances all of them would be regarded as safe seats. However, if the SNP vote were to move ahead of Labour in Scotland, which would require an 11% swing, then many more seats begin to look vulnerable. On a 13% swing from Labour, the SNP could make 10 gains (including some from the Liberal Democrats and some where they were placed third last time); on a 15% swing, 18 gains; on a 17% swing, 22 gains; if the swing got as high as 25%, as some of the polls were suggesting, in theory it might leave the SNP with 56 of the 59 seats. This had implications for Westminster as well as for Scotland. The Conservatives now had the prospect of reaping all the short term electoral benefits of independence without losing the Union – Labour might lose so many seats in Scotland that it was no longer a credible contender for majority power. On the other hand, the SNP were suddenly likely to win enough seats to have serious influence in any post-election coalition negotiations, a prospect which was to play a prominent part in the election campaign.

Implications of an unchanged agenda

These various aspects of the course of events between 2010 and 2015 all had some formative influence on the context in which the election was eventually fought, but none were so important as what did not happen: nothing emerged to jolt the political debate out of the rut into which it had settled, and ensure that the 2015 election would be fought on a fundamentally different division between the two main parties from that which had prevailed in 2010.

With no realignment of the issues, for a voter to switch their preference from Conservative to Labour during the course of the 2010-15 parliament, or *vice versa*, would be an admission that they had made the wrong decision in 2010. How could Labour, defeated in 2010 and so needing to gain votes to win, convince some of those who voted Conservative in 2010 that they had been wrong to do so and that they should therefore switch their loyalties? In theory, that might come from shifting the emphasis that was put on different aspects of the issue – if voters who sympathised with the Conservative view of the deficit but with Labour's preference for more spending on the NHS could be made to prioritise the latter over the former, then a Labour vote this time would make more sense to them than another Conservative one. But the problem was that voters whose loyalties were divided in this way were thin on the ground. As we shall see, most voters who accepted the Conservative arguments on economic issues also accepted their arguments on the public service and social issues where Labour felt stronger. Public opinion had become polarised.

There may be a number of interconnected reasons for this. Since the parties try to put forward a coherent and comprehensive case for their policies on each issue, we should expect that many voters' views on the different issues are not independent of each other – people who accept the Conservative view of the state of the economy and the remedies that it needs may naturally find that affects their view on what is the best course for the future of the NHS, for example. But that to some extent assumes a reasonably sophisticated and policy-knowledgeable electorate, which suggests it can only be at best part of the explanation.

There is also the likelihood that many voters' policy preferences are driven by their party choice, rather than vice versa. In other words, voters who trust David Cameron more than they trust Ed Miliband, or who generally feel closer to the Conservatives than to Labour in ideology or values, may prefer some policies which they know the Conservatives support because (consciously or unconsciously) they think their party or leader is more likely to be right. We discuss this in more detail below.

But probably equally important are voters' feelings of political identity. This may encompass factors such as loyalty to a party or regard for its leaders, but may also involve wider feelings of belonging or of exclusion which while not in themselves party-political in nature nevertheless have party-political consequences. Towards the end of the parliament we see this clearly exemplified in the way that feelings of Scottish national identity combined with a shared feeling of victimhood from Westminster drove support first for a vote for independence and then for an SNP vote at the general election. Similarly, the power of xenophobia and distrust for the political establishment's approach to immigration in communities that felt under threat from an influx of foreign workers was one important factor in UKIP's support. In each case, the key development is the voter's perception of a world divided into 'them' and 'us', and the party that for the moment succeeds in becoming identified with defending the interests of 'us' can rest assured of a powerful loyalty that will probably affect the understanding of all other political issues.

To the extent that the Conservatives or Labour manage to become identified with defending the interests of particular groups, communities or industries, they too can profit from it, although such identification is weaker than it used to be. To those who have identified themselves with a party in this way, the political campaigning of their opponents is not viewed as a potential argument for switching their vote but as an attack upon them as well as upon the party. (Indeed, the more convincing it appears, the more dangerous the attack may seem and the stronger the resistance it evokes.)

It is not clear how far the polarisation of voters before the 2015 election was one of party identity rather than built around the simple policy divide, pro- or anti-austerity. But this did not affect the consequences. Labour could only undermine the support of Conservative voters for the party they had supported in 2010 by challenging their entire political world view. Their vote in 2010 would only come to seem a mistake if they believed that the Conservatives' policies had failed in their objectives, which in most cases would amount to a verdict that the government had not sufficiently revived the economy. The government's perceived success or failure in their economic policy, therefore, was of paramount importance to Labour's chances.

This is not to say that either party's supporters had fully bought into their own side's economic arguments, or that those who had voted for them could be relied upon to parrot the party line. On the contrary, many of those on each side stated support for arguments that entirely undermined their own party's case. Shortly after the 2010 election, as many as 44% of Labour voters agreed that the debt necessitated cuts in spending on public services. (Table 17). However, 51% also agreed that all the necessary savings could be achieved through greater efficiency without damaging services, rejecting Labour's analysis of the situation but at least explaining how they could rationally support the need for cuts while still being Labour voters.

Support for the need for cuts was still 41% among Labour voters in November 2010, but down to 30% by February 2011 and then levelled out, at 32% in June 2012. Agreement that there was still a need for cuts had also fallen over the same period among those who had voted Conservative, but still stood at 67%.

Table 17: The need for cuts

Q. How strongly do you agree or disagree with the following statement? "There is a real need to cut spending on public services in order to pay off the very high national debt we now have"

	June 2010			June 2012		
		Reported 2010 vote			Reported 2010 vote	
	All	Conser-vative	Labour	All	Conser-vative	Labour
	%	%	%	%	%	%
Strongly agree	30	49	20	21	39	10
Tend to agree	27	32	24	25	37	22
Neither / nor	6	5	3	7	4	5
Tend to disagree	14	5	18	20	15	21
Strongly disagree	22	8	34	24	11	37
Don't know	1	1	1	3	3	5
Agree	57	81	44	45	67	32
Disagree	35	13	52	44	26	58

Base: 1,002 British adults 18+, 18-20 June 2010; 1,016 British adults 18+, 9-11 June 2012
Source: Ipsos MORI Political Monitor

Similarly, many Conservative supporters were prepared to express doubts about the speed with which cuts were being implemented. Shortly after the 2010 election and again in March 2011, we found almost half of those who had voted Conservative saying that spending should be cut slowly, to reduce the impact on services and the economy, far from the government's policy and very close to Labour's. (Table 18).

Table 18: Cut fast or cut slow?

Q. And which of these comes closest to your opinion about how the government goes about reducing the deficit?

| | June 2010 | | | March 2011 | | |
| | | Reported 2010 vote | | | Reported 2010 vote | |
	All	Conser-vative	Labour	All	Conser-vative	Labour
	%	%	%	%	%	%
It is important to cut spending quickly even if this means immediate job losses, because it will be better for the economy in the long term	25	47	10	25	52	9
It is better to cut spending more slowly, to reduce the impact on public services and the economy	69	47	83	71	45	88
Neither	3	4	3	2	1	1
Don't know	2	2	3	2	1	2

Base: 1,002 British adults 18+, 18-20 June 2010; 1,000 British adults 18+, 11-13 March 2011
Source: Ipsos MORI Political Monitor

However, there was much less evidence of sympathy for the other side's arguments when a question was asked in explicitly partisan terms. Asked which party had the best policies for managing the economy, 66% of those who had voted Labour said they thought Labour was best in October 2010, and this rose to a peak of 72% in May 2012; and perhaps more to the point, only 11% felt the Tories had the best policies in the first poll and 5% in the second. Similarly, 83% of those who had voted Conservative endorsed Tory economic policies in October 2010, and 72% in May 2012 (when criticism of the 'omnishambles' budget was at its height); 3% in each case thought Labour's policies were better.

It is clear that dissenting from a party's line on specific details of policy, even vital principles of policies central to the whole argument such as the need for cuts in public spending, were not strong indicators of either past vote or of future voting intention. This may be for a combination of reasons. Simple ignorance of policy, misunderstanding of its importance and implications or an inability to reason from political cause to effect probably accounts for some cases.

But it is plain, too, that 'doublethink' as defined by Orwell[69] is part of the normal psyche of many voters. They are entirely able to hold many formally-contradictory beliefs simultaneously, and perhaps even to act in accordance with those different beliefs on different occasions.

In studying public opinion, we have always found it useful to distinguish between three ways in which an individual can hold a view: **opinions**, **attitudes** and **values**.[70] We have sometimes described these by analogy: opinions as ripples on the surface of the water, attitudes as more powerful currents and values as deep tides in the ocean of public opinion; but we have also drawn the distinction informally in terms of the intensity with which these views are held and the power that they have to drive behaviour.

But these categories correspond roughly to a more fundamental distinction of quality and function. Opinions are instant reactions to stimuli, as typified by responses to opinion poll questions on which the respondent has not previously deliberated. They may be easily affected by context, and, not being based on any deep process of decision, are probably of little importance to the person and are also unlikely to influence his or her behaviour on anything important (or, at least, that he or she thinks is important). A person's opinions can easily be contradictory, since no conscious effort has been made to ensure that they are not, and they may be a very poor guide to the stance that person will take if they ever give the matter deeper consideration.

---

[69] "The power of holding two contradictory beliefs in one's mind simultaneously, and accepting both of them." – George Orwell, *Nineteen Eighty-Four* (Harmondsworth: Penguin, 1987), 172.
[70] For a more thorough exposition, see Robert M. Worcester, 'Why Do We Do What We Do?', *International Journal of Public Opinion Research* 9 (1997): 2–16.

At the other end of the scale are values, often learned early and held for life, hard-wired into somebody's world view. They are not susceptible to rational argument because they are not held on that basis: the person knows what side they are on, and that is final. For ideological voters (such as those whose party preference is based on left-or-right considerations), support for their political party may come into this category, although they are probably fewer than was once the case.

In between these two are attitudes, and they are in many ways the most interesting. Typically, attitudes are rational: they are based on beliefs or evidence of some sort, and are thus susceptible to change if the belief is no longer held or the evidence is seen to be wrong.

We are most interested in the kind of attitude that directly drives behaviour – voting intention is, for most voters, an attitude of this type. These attitudes reflect values: they are in fact a judgment of the course of action that will best achieve the goals that one's values dictate. But they also reflect one's knowledge or beliefs, and one's other attitudes and values: these are what feed the judgment. If the facts change, naturally this may change one's chosen course of action – a different choice may now seem to fit one's values better. But vaguer impressions, even those only on the level of opinions, perhaps emotional as well as rational, may play a part too.

For example, one may hold as a value that one should vote in the way best calculated to benefit one's family, and hold as reasoned attitudes that austerity policies will be better for one's family than the high-spending alternative and that voting Conservative is the best way to ensure the next government pursues such policies. But what if one also, as an opinion, dislikes and distrusts David Cameron? That view may be less securely held, on grounds that cannot be argued at all; but that is no guarantee that its intensity is any less than that of the thought-out attitudes. Either may triumph in determining the eventual attitude that drives voting behaviour.

Considering behaviour in this way helps highlight the different tasks involved in swaying somebody's vote. It may depend on the purely rational and deliberative, making the voters better informed about the details or consequences of policies. It may involve challenging their reasoning, so as to change their minds about which of their attitudes and opinions are relevant to meeting their values, or as to which of their values should be invoked by their decision on how to vote. Or it may involve influencing their opinions, much more fluid and liable to change, perhaps intensifying the influence they bring to bear on the voting decision. It is not simply a matter of 'winning the argument'; the argument is likely to be different for each different voter.

Trench warfare:
the stalemate in public opinion

The elements of the voting equation

So far we have considered the political events that may have affected voters' opinions, and discussed the way some of those opinions may have interacted, but we also need to look more systematically at the state of public opinion at the time the election campaign was fought.

The traditional view is that elections are, or at least ought to be, settled on the issues. ("This has been a good fight... concentrated on issues of political importance, and there has been no personalities, no horseplay nor anything of that kind" as Clement Attlee once complacently described the election in his constituency[71].) Certainly the issues were prominent enough in 2015. Labour fought the election mainly on the need for greater public spending to protect services, especially the NHS. The Conservatives trumpeted their economic management (with little concession to allowing their Lib Dem coalition partners any share of the credit), and charged Labour with irresponsibility in its past record and its future plans which would wreck the recovery and leave everybody poorer. Meanwhile UKIP accused both the bigger parties of failing the country on immigration. Was the election won and lost on voters weighing up these arguments against each other?

We know that voters' values can sometimes trump the arguments on the specific issues, and there was no shortage of scope for this in 2015. There were intensely powerful forces such as national identities (of Scots feeling Scottish or feeling that to be Scottish is also to be British, of Britons feeling European or not European, and how that shaped their reactions to the European Union and to immigration), religious convictions (Christians, Muslims, Jews and indeed agnostics outraged by the stand of one party or another on Syria or gay marriage, as examples), animal rights (activists fearing a Conservative government might legalise hunting again),

---

[71] Proposing the vote of thanks after the declaration of the result at Walthamstow West in 1950, recorded as part of the BBC TV coverage of the election
(https://www.youtube.com/watch?v=yTmt5Rz-DTA, at 9:08, accessed 31 August 2015).

environmental convictions (with worries over global warming or fracking, and the equally fervent views of opponents dismissing these fears as unscientific). And, as always, there was the simple commitment of some voters to their party or to the ideology they believed it should stand for, whether socialist, liberal, libertarian or conservative.

Then, of course, there were the leaders. To judge from the tone of much of the media coverage, the furore over the attempts of the parties to mould the format of the televised debates to their own advantage and, indeed, much of the party campaigning during the last weeks before the election, little else was of much concern. A foreigner coming ignorant to Britain, seeing the coverage, the campaign and the result would surely conclude that things happened as they did because David Cameron was tolerated for his competence (if not much liked), Ed Miliband dismissed as a candidate for power because he could not even be trusted to eat a bacon sandwich properly, and Nicola Sturgeon feared by most people outside Scotland. Could this be true and explain everything?

There were certainly enough signs of political volatility in the public's uncertainty about their voting intentions: on 12-15 April, almost two in five (38%) of those who expressed a voting intention still said they had not yet definitely decided how to vote – and of these three in ten said they had voted in 2010 and were currently intending to vote for a different party to the one they backed then. Even on the eve of the election, one in five (21%) said they might still change their minds. Many of these switchers were cancelling each other out, it is true, so that the net effect was very small, but if they could be taken at their word the potential for a bigger, decisive shift was real, and perhaps the stimulus needed to achieve it might have been very small.

Let us consider the various strands of opinion that might make up, and might change, the voters' view of the electoral choice that was before them.

The political triangle

There are many different elements to each party's election campaign, and the voters can take them in many different ways, but we have found that generally the factors on which most voters make their decisions can be usefully divided into four categories:

- what voters think of the parties;

- what voters think of the party leaders;

- what voters think about the key issues in the election (which ones they feel are important and which parties have the best policies to deal with those issues); and

- what voters think of the candidates in their local constituency.

Of these four, the last is usually held to be the least important, and by its nature it is local, with only limited scope for the national campaign organisers to affect it and with little that can be reliably inferred about it from the national opinion polls. This we therefore place to one side and the remaining elements – parties, leaders and issues – make up what we call the "Political Triangle".

Ever since MORI began political research at the start of the 1970s, we have made the interplay between the three 'sides' of this triangle one of the key foundations on which our polling is built, and by investigating each we believe we can account for almost all the major factors that will determine how – and whether – each elector will vote, once we allow for the values that he or she brings to bear on the decision. Some remain loyal to a party they have always supported or choose a party that seems to stand for the values in which they believe; some vote for the party they feel has the best policy on the issue most important to them, some for the most appealing cocktail of policies across a wide range of issues; some prefer to opt for the leader they believe will make the best Prime Minister, some vote to keep a leader they dislike or distrust out of Number Ten. For some, two or more of these prompts may be influential.

The traditional account of how elections ought be fought tends to concentrate on the issues element of the triangle – parties try to change voters' perceptions of the relative importance of different issues, moving the emphasis towards issues where they think they are at an advantage, or they try to make ground on a particular issue, either by making the case more effectively for their existing policies or by adopting new policies that they believe will be more popular. All of these factors we can track in our polling, and all can also be explored by the parties in their own polls or focus groups, testing the attractiveness of their proposed policies and the effectiveness of their messages. (The parties, of course, unlike those of us conducting polls for publication in the media, know which groups of voters they are targeting or considering targeting, and can design their own polling accordingly. A campaign stance that seems misconceived or puzzling when viewed from a national perspective may make more sense when seen from the point of view of attracting the support of a particular group of voters.)

But parties can also aim at changing their own image or that of their leader, although this is usually a longer-term project than changing where they are seen to stand on the issues. 'Image' in this case is not about trivialities, the cut of a politician's suit or the shade of colour used on a party's leaflets. We are talking here about the entire impression that a party or leader makes on voters, the factors that inspire real loyalty and trust, that mark out one party or candidate from another, that if fully established can be so powerful as to influence the way the voter interprets new information in the future.

Nor is the overall structure of the political triangle a static one: the relative importance of the three factors changes over time, and this has just as much potential to swing votes, and perhaps swing elections, as changes in the images of the parties and leaders or the popularity of their policies. Again this is fully within the scope of what the party campaigners might aim at affecting during the campaign, and it sometimes makes sense for them to do so. In 2015 there was much more widespread public goodwill towards the Labour Party than to the Conservatives, who have never quite succeeded in shaking off their image as the 'nasty party'. On the other hand, David Cameron was more widely liked than Ed Miliband, and was felt by far more voters to be a capable leader. (Two-thirds of the public thought Miliband was *not* "ready to be Prime Minister".) So Labour had every incentive to push voters towards giving more weight to what they thought of the parties in making their decisions, whereas the Conservatives would prefer voters to focus much more on the choice of a Prime Minister for the next five years.

What was the relative importance of the three elements in 2015, and how similar or different was that to other recent elections? At every election since 1987, we have asked the public to tell us how important they thought issues, leaders and parties had each been in persuading them how to vote. Each participant in the survey has ten points to divide between the three elements, and we convert their average scores into percentages. Very few, we find, say that their decision depends entirely on just one of the three factors: in April 2015, just 2% of those with a voting intention said they were attracted solely by the policies of the party they had chosen, 2% by what they thought about the party as a whole and 1% by the party's leaders; the remaining 95%, apart from a handful of don't knows, credited at least two of the three factors with contributing to their decision. On the other hand, more substantial numbers denied the influence of one of the three factors: 11% felt it was all about policies and the party as a whole, nothing to do with the leader, while 9% didn't feel they had been affected by the party as a whole and 5% thought their choice had nothing to do with policies.[72] Nevertheless, that still leaves around seven voters in ten feeling that all three factors have had at least some effect on them.

Which of the three do the voters feel is most influential? For five elections in a row, from 1987 to 2005, the order of priority was the same and the scores were fairly stable:

- policies were always judged most influential, but less so than the other two factors combined, scoring between 41% and 47%;

- leaders came second, with between 31% and 35%; while

- identifying with the party as a whole was felt to be the least important, garnering between 20% and 24%.

However, in the run-up to the 2010 election we found a dramatic change (see Figure 7). In August 2008 and again in February 2010, we found the voters rating the importance of the leaders as highly as that of policies in determining their votes (they were tied on 38% each in the 2010 poll, with party image trailing on 22%). And certainly the 2010 election will be remembered as one when the image of the leaders seemed to play an important part in the campaign, although that really became most evident – the leaders' debates, the unprecedented sight of Conservative and Labour campaign posters each featuring pictures of the opposing leader – after our poll had shown that the voters already rated them as more influential than in the past.

In the 2015 election, the picture changed again. Surveys in December 2013 and in February and April 2015 all showed that the perceived importance

---

[72] Ipsos MORI interviewed 1,000 GB adults aged 18+ by telephone on 12-15 April 2015.

of the party leaders had plummeted to third place whilst the attraction of 'the party as a whole' had risen, but policies were once more the clear primary influence: in the last of these three polls, conducted during the heat of the campaign, policies were accorded 43% of the influence, parties 30% and leaders only 26%.

Figure 7: The Political Triangle: trends

Q I want you to think about what it is that most attracted you to the ... party. ... If you had a total of ten points to allocate according to how important each of these was to you, how many points would you allocate to the leaders of the party you intend voting for, how many to its policies, and how many to the party as a whole?

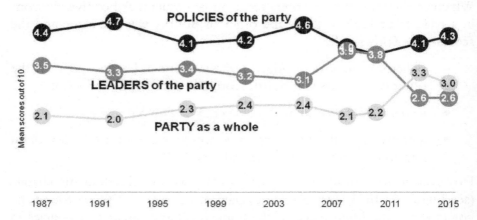

Base: c.800/1,600 British adults aged 18+ and giving a voting intention in each survey.
Source: Ipsos MORI

There was some variation in these answers by party, as might be expected (Table 19). 'Party as a whole' was the weakest influence on Conservatives – in fact the attraction of leaders was a whisker ahead in their case – while it was much more important, and leaders correspondingly less so, to those intending to vote Labour. This is in line with the general impressions that the media conveyed of public reactions to the parties, and of the evidence from a range of other polling questions: Ed Miliband was weak as an attraction to voting Labour and, indeed, potentially a liability, while David Cameron was less of a deterrent to voters but his party's overall image remained weak. As we shall see, these impressions are also borne out in the more detailed polling data.

Table 19: Reasons voters were attracted to their parties, 2015

Q. I want you to think about what it is that most attracted you to the ... party. ... If you had a total of ten points to allocate according to how important each of these was to you, how many points would you allocate to the leaders of the party you intend voting for, how many to its policies, and how many to the party as a whole?

			Current voting intention		
	All	Conser-vative	Labour	Liberal Demo-crat	UKIP
	%	%	%	%	%
Policies of the party	4.3	4.4	4.3	4.2	3.9
Leaders of the party	2.6	2.8	2.3	2.6	3.3
Party as a whole	3.0	2.7	3.4	3.0	2.8

Base: 879 British adults 18+ and declaring a voting intention, 12-15 April 2015. Figures shown are mean scores for each answer (excluding don't knows).
Source: Ipsos MORI Political Monitor

Perhaps as interesting, however, is that there was no difference between supporters of any of the traditional three main parties in the average number of points out of ten they assigned to the importance of policies, all within 0.1 of the overall 4.3 average. Only UKIP was slightly out of line, with the somewhat higher score for the importance of the leader reflecting the centrality of Nigel Farage to his party's appeal and the positive reaction that he elicited from like-minded voters.

Two further observations are necessary at this point. Because this question dwells on the positives rather than the negatives, it measures only one half of the voting equation: it asks voters to think about what attracted them to the party they currently support, not about anything that may have driven them away from supporting other parties. It will therefore tend to indicate each party's strengths, but may reflect its weaknesses only indirectly. This may be of particular importance in judging the relative importance of the three sides of our triangle in determining the election result. The leadership factor may appear to be a weak one in attracting voters, but that might be misleading because it ignores the possible strength of negative influences. For example, how many were driven to or confirmed in their support of the Conservatives by fear or dislike of Ed Miliband or, at a later stage in the campaign, of Nicola Sturgeon?

Secondly, and even more importantly, bear in mind that these answers represent only the voters' own impressions of what is driving their voting decisions. Those impressions may be neither accurate nor entirely candid. We shall return to this point below.

Nevertheless, the dominance of policy issues in the Political Triangle might seem to suggest that the party which stands out best on whichever issues are most widely-recognised as important would enter the election in the box seat, and that their opponents' primary tactic would need to be either to break their stranglehold on that issue or to promote the importance of a different one where the public rate the parties differently.

Issues and policies

'Weaponising' the NHS

In 2015, the issue named by most of the public as important to their vote was healthcare or the NHS. In each of our five polls between the turn of the year and the end of April, we asked people to say which issues, if any, would be *very* important in helping them decide which party to vote for[73] (and they could name as few or as many issues as they thought appropriate).

Figure 8: Reported issue salience in the 2015 election

Q. Looking ahead to the next general election, which, if any issues do you think will be very important to you in helping you decide which party to vote for?

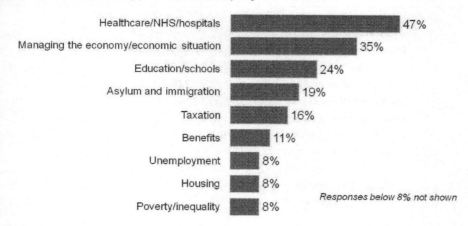

Base: 1,000 British adults 18+, 12-15 April 2015
Source: Ipsos MORI Political Monitor

In the start-of-campaign poll, on 12-15 April, we also asked which party (if any) they felt had the best policies on each of 16 issues which had been scoring highly on the importance scale in the previous polls. By matching

---

[73] All responses were spontaneous, unprompted by any list of suggested answers, but were categorised by the interviewer according to a list not seen by or read out to the respondent. Any answers which did not clearly match an existing category were recorded verbatim as well as being counted in the "other" category.

up the issues each respondent thought were important with their choice of best party on that issue we were able to form a clear picture of each party's strengths and weaknesses on the various issues and their relative importance to the overall picture. Almost half the public named healthcare as an issue that would be *very* important to them, well ahead of any other issue, and the Labour Party had a clear lead as the party whose healthcare policies were most widely preferred.

The importance that voters accord to the NHS is nothing new. It occupies a strong and long-established place in Britain's sense of national identity.

Figure 9: What makes people proud to be British

Q. Overall, which two or three of the following would you say makes you most proud to be British?

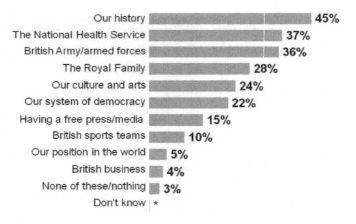

Base: 931 British adults aged 15+ living in GB, 27 January-5 February 2012
Source: Ipsos MORI/Channel 4

In a survey we conducted at the start of 2012 (Figure 9), with the upcoming Diamond Jubilee and London Olympic Games on people's minds, we found the NHS level with Britain's armed forces and only trailing "our history" as a source of national pride – even The Royal Family was well behind, and British sports teams barely on the scale. Danny Boyle rightly chose to include a sequence celebrating the NHS in the pageant depicting Britishness that he designed for the Olympic opening ceremony, however strange this seemed to some foreign eyes and notwithstanding dissenting voices in the *Daily Mail*.

Small wonder, then, that the Labour Party felt the future of the NHS to be their strongest campaigning suit, and although one might take exception to the phraseology, nobody can have been much surprised when it was revealed that Ed Miliband intended to 'weaponise' it.[74]

Figure 10: Party with best policies on healthcare 1988-2015

Q. Which party do you think has the best policies on healthcare: the Conservatives, Labour, Liberal Democrats or some other party?

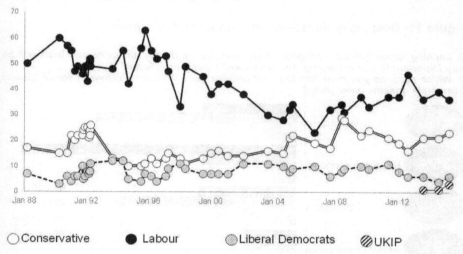

Base: c. 1,000 British adults 18+ in each survey
Source: Ipsos MORI Political Monitor

The NHS has been traditionally an issue where the Labour Party has felt strong, and one where there seems to be lasting public distrust of the intentions of the Conservatives' plans for it. In all of our frequent polls since 1983 asking voters which party they thought had the best policies on healthcare (Figure 10), Labour has never failed to come out on top[75] and the gap is usually wide (although it had narrowed to only five points at the

---

[74] Steven Swinford, 'Ed Miliband Said He Wanted to "Weaponise" NHS in Secret Meeting with BBC Executives', *The Telegraph*, 11 January 2015, http://www.telegraph.co.uk/news/politics/ed-miliband/11338695/Ed-Miliband-said-he-wanted-to-weaponise-NHS-in-secret-meeting-with-BBC-executives.html, accessed 10 August 2015.

[75] The Conservatives did lead in a single poll in August 1978 as having the best policy on healthcare by 38% to 33%, but have never done so since then.

time of the 2010 election, and even when it re-opened it was not on the scale of the advantage Labour had through the 1990s). Five years of the Coalition government, despite its ring-fencing of NHS budgets to protect it from the cuts being applied in almost every other area of public spending, did nothing to diminish this. In the opening weeks of the 2015 campaign (in a poll on 12-15 April), 36% picked Labour as having the best healthcare policies, 23% picked the Conservatives, and 6% the Liberal Democrats (though 22% said they didn't know or that no party was best.)

Figure 11: Best party on issues very important to voters

Q. Looking forward to the next general election, which, if any, issues do you think will be very important to you in helping you decide which party to vote for?
Q. Which party do you think has the best policies on... the Conservatives, Labour, Liberal Democrats or some other party?

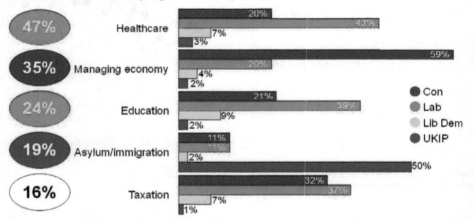

Base: 1,000 British adults 18+, 12-15 April 2015
Source: Ipsos MORI Political Monitor

Moreover, Labour's lead is strengthened when we consider only those who say they consider healthcare or the NHS to be an important election issue: among these, the voters who might realistically be swayed by their preferences on health policy, Labour's lead over the Tories was 43% to 20%. Labour was also seen to be the party with the best policies on education (the third-most salient issue) by most of those who felt *that* was an important issue, again one which has generally been thought of as a strong issue for Labour since the days when Tony Blair put "education, education, education" at the heart of his first successful campaign in 1997, but on which the Conservatives and Labour were in fact neck-and-neck in 2010.

The pocket-book voter

However, the Conservatives also had their strong issue – that of managing the economy, sitting in second place in the league table of issues. Of the 35% who judged this a very important issue in deciding their vote, three in five felt that Conservative policies were the best, giving the Tories a three-to-one lead over Labour, even more convincing than Labour's advantage of roughly two-to-one on its own two strongest issues. This, too, was an issue on which a gap had opened over the course of the parliament: in 2010 the Conservatives had a lead over Labour on economic policies, but only narrowly by 31% to 28%.

There is a long tradition in political commentary of regarding the economic issue as one that trumps all others in prompting voting behaviour. This theory of the 'pocket-book voter' is well-embedded in both British and American political analysis, and often surfaces as an assertion that all other indicators are misleading. Especially when, as in 2015, the polls are seen as having mis-predicted the election, the theory is floated that the pollsters "should have known that the polls were wrong" because the party that eventually won had a clear lead on the economic issue. But this is a fallacy. It is simply not the case that the party with a lead on the economic issue always wins the election – see Figure 12. At the time of the 1997 election, the Conservatives had a convincing lead as best on economic policies, by 33% to 26% among the public as a whole and by 45% to 23% among those who rated the issue as important; it only became a strong issue for Labour a few months after the election, once the voters had seen their policies in practice. Yet in 1997 the Conservatives went down to their worst defeat since before the First World War. Why? Because the economy was simply not an important issue to many voters in 1997: 68% said that health care and 61% that education were among the issues that would be very important to them in deciding how to vote, but managing the economy was picked by only 30%, relegating it to seventh place. It is not therefore the issue itself that is important in determining the vote but the salience of the issue for most voters at any particular election.

Figure 12: Best party on managing the economy 1990-2015

Q. Which party do you think has the best policies on managing the economy: the Conservatives, Labour, Liberal Democrats or some other party?

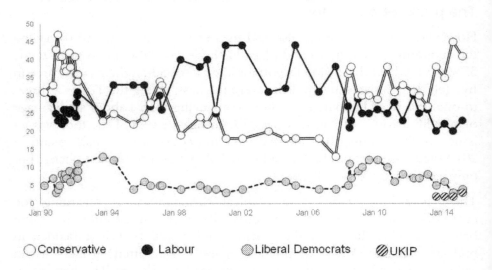

Base: c. 1,000 British adults 18+ in each survey
Source: Ipsos MORI Political Monitor

What makes issues important to voting?

There are those who would like to reduce the determinants of voting behaviour to a simple equation based upon a very small number of key indicators that predict the election result every time. Experience consistently shows that real life decision-making is much more complicated than that. There is no 'magic bullet' issue that catches all the voters every time. Without understanding, or at least allowing for, the psychology of the voter no formula is likely to capture the relationship between the political situation at election time and the result of the election. The economic issue is a case in point. It is argued, convincingly, that for the vast majority of voters in any modern Western democracy no issue is more important than the economic security and comfort of themselves and their families, and that very few will vote, even for the most-pressing altruistic reasons, against their own interests[76]. Therefore it might seem that virtually all voters will support whichever party is seen as having the soundest economic policies, and the party favoured by most voters will always win. But this assumes that the voter feels capable of judging between the parties' policies, finds one that she feels is clearly superior and will make a material difference, and the party promising it can be trusted to implement it competently. Above all, it assumes that the voter is holding the economic issue in mind at all.

In fact, most people's minds do not work this way. It may seem irrational to the observer who is trying to predict voter behaviour with a mechanistic equation, but the average voter tends to stop worrying about the economy when things are going well, and to give more weight to other issues, even if deep down there is no more important consideration than maintaining the economic position. For this reason, governments do not always get as much credit as they may feel they deserve for successes in managing – or indeed improving – the economy. For that matter, the same is true in any other field. Many voters equate "most important" with "most urgent" or "causing most concern at the moment", and there will tend to be more votes in offering solutions to problems than in preventing problems from arising in the first place.

At the same time, the rational voter tends to concentrate more on the future than the past: the question to be decided at the ballot box is who should rule the country for the next five years, not to pass a verdict on the previous five years. In contrast, the irrational (or emotional) voter might tend to concentrate more on the party or its leaders' past record or personality (either positively as indicated by her own party or negatively as implied by the opposition).

The issues that the public say will be most important to their vote vary from election to election, and they are not always the same as the ones that

---

[76] Mark Textor, an Australian pollster and business partner of Lynton Crosby (the Conservatives' polling and strategy advisor), suggested that the 2015 vote was won by the 'mercenary voter', voting purely on the basis of their own economic security. So whilst a voter might identify politically as Labour or Lib Dem, they voted Conservative because they wanted a Conservative government as an outcome in order to ensure economic security. (See Lenore Taylor, '"Mercenary Voters" Decided UK Election, Says Pollster Who Predicted Tory Victory', *The Guardian*, 5 August 2015, http://www.theguardian.com/politics/2015/aug/05/mercenary-voters-decided-uk-election-says-pollster-who-predicted-tory-victory, accessed 26 October 2015.)

they mention as the "most important issues facing the country" in our separate monthly Issues Index poll. Why not? Because no matter how important an issue may be, it can't swing votes if the public don't see one party's policies to deal with it as being better than another's or if they don't trust any of the parties to find, or implement, the right solution. In 2010, race/immigration was generally the second most-frequently named important issue facing the country (after the economic crisis), but it was far down the list of important election issues, well behind healthcare and education, probably because the voters did not much trust any of the parties on immigration. For that matter, even though managing the economy was seen as the most influential election issue, most of the voters did not much like the prescriptions being offered by any of the parties. This, no doubt, was part of the reason why, as we have seen (Figure 7), they felt policies as a whole had had less effect on their vote choice in 2010 than at any previous election we had measured.

In fact, all these considerations merely illustrate the general rule that we have always put forward[77] for understanding the 'issues' element of the voting decision. If an issue is to move a voter, it must jump the following four separate hurdles:

- the voter must care about the issue (and it must be top-of-the-mind, not merely an underlying preference that will be forgotten on election day);

- she must see a difference between the parties on the issue, so that she is able to form a clear preference for one over the other;

- she must believe that the party she prefers is able to make a difference on the issue; and

- she must believe that if the party she votes for wins power the party will be able to, and will, implement its policy on that issue.

For most voters, very few issues tick all of these boxes.

In our early April poll, when we included the best-party-on-key-issues questions, we found that on average people named only 2.3 issues they

---

[77] We discuss this in more detail in Robert M. Worcester and Roger Mortimore, *Explaining Labour's Landslide* (London: Politico's, 1999), 46–48.

considered important to their vote, although around one in five named three and one in five more than three (and one of our 1,000 respondents came up with 21, including all 14 that we had earmarked for follow-up questions, despite not being prompted with a list of any sort. She was a Labour voter in the South of England, incidentally, who read the *Daily Mirror* and said she was only "fairly interested" in politics!) But one in seven (13%) failed to name a single issue that was important to them, and a further 21% picked only one important issue. Yet three-quarters of those who did not name any issues as important still knew how they intended to vote. Not everybody's voting behaviour therefore is dictated by what they think of the parties' policies.

Leader image

Studying the issues can only take us so far. We need also to consider what the public thought about the parties as a whole and what they thought about their leaders. Even if the voters thought that these were less influential than the parties' policies on the important issues, party and leader image are not negligible – and, as we shall see, the reality is probably that they are considerably more influential than voters realise or are prepared to admit.

The natural place to start in assessing views of the party leaders is, perhaps, the simplest and best-known of our polling measures, which are also the most regularly asked and the longest-standing of all our political data series apart from the raw voting intentions.

Figure 13: Satisfaction with David Cameron as Prime Minister, 2010-15

Are you satisfied or dissatisfied with the way David Cameron is doing his job as Prime Minister?

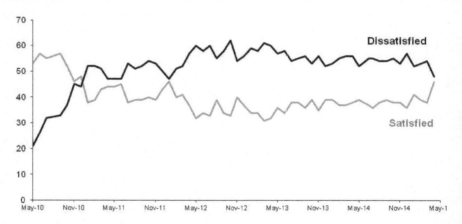

Base: c. 1,000 British adults 18+ in each monthly survey
Source: Ipsos MORI Political Monitor

We first asked the public whether they were satisfied or dissatisfied with the job that the Prime Minister and Leader of the Opposition were doing in the mid-1970s, and for most of the time since then we have been repeating these measurements once a month. This gives us a very long series of historical comparisons to help us put the current political situation into context.[78]

As Figure 13 shows, David Cameron's satisfaction rating as Prime Minister between the start of 2011 and the start of 2015 ranged from a high of 46% satisfied to a low of 31%, and even allowing for some don't knows those who were dissatisfied outnumbered those who were satisfied in every poll.

To those unfamiliar with the history of British satisfaction ratings, and perhaps assuming that 50% satisfied should be regarded as the par score, this might appear to be overall a poor record. But in fact, unlike presidential approval scores in some countries where regularly achieving a 50% positive rating is indeed generally a pre-requisite to a hope of re-election, British prime ministerial ratings are generally lower. The public are more grudging in allowing themselves to be satisfied – and it must also be remembered that presidents will generally need 50% of the vote, or close to it, to be re-elected while a much lower share is sufficient in a multi-party parliamentary system such as Britain's. Except in the immediate post-election honeymoon period, satisfaction scores of over 50% are very rare. (In fact David Cameron topped 50% in the first four polls after the 2010 election, and was still at 48% in December of that year, but could not touch those heights subsequently and this is very much the normal pattern.) Tony Blair in his first term as Prime Minister was an exception to this, remaining above a 60% satisfaction threshold for his first 18 months in office. But Cameron's scores compare well with those of Margaret Thatcher, for example, in both her first and second parliaments as Prime Minister, after each of which she won re-election comfortably.

In fact, Cameron's average monthly rating as Prime Minister over his five years in office (39.7%) is identical to Margaret Thatcher's average, both just a whisker above the long-term average of the more-than-400 of these polls we have conducted since 1977 (39.4%.) Of the six premiers over that

---

[78] Indeed, to some extent we can take the comparisons back even further than this. When MORI was founded in 1969, Gallup had already been polling in Britain for more than thirty years, and had first asked a very similar question to the one that we adopted in October 1938, although they then used a significantly different wording for most of the period between 1939 and 1955. For details and the findings, see Anthony King and Robert Wybrow, *British Political Opinion 1937-2000: The Gallup Polls* (London: Politico's, 2001), 183–204.

period, Jim Callaghan (48.3%) and Tony Blair (44.9%) did significantly better than the average, while John Major (32.6%) and Gordon Brown (31.1%) did significantly worse.

Moreover, if we compare Cameron's score to those of his predecessors across a single parliament, his 39.7% is the same as that of Mrs Thatcher in the 1979-83 parliament, slightly better than her 39.4% in 1983-7, and also better than the 38.9% on which Tony Blair was re-elected in 2005.

Table 20: Satisfaction with Prime Ministers and opposition leaders

Q Are you satisfied or dissatisfied with the way ... is doing his/her job as Prime Minister?
Q Are you satisfied or dissatisfied with the way ... is doing his/her job as leader of the ... Party?

Period	P.M.	% satisfied with PM (average monthly score)	Oppn leader	% satisfied with oppn leader (average monthly score)	Election winner
1977-9	Callaghan	48	Thatcher	43	Thatcher
1979-80	Thatcher	40	Callaghan	42	n/a
1980-3	Thatcher	40	Foot	21	Thatcher
1983-7	Thatcher	38	Kinnock	34	Thatcher
1987-90	Thatcher	40	Kinnock	37	n/a
1990-92	Major	53	Kinnock	38	Major
1992-94	Major	26	Smith	36	n/a
1994-97	Major	26	Blair	47	Blair
1997-2001	Blair	56	Hague	24	Blair
2001-3	Blair	42	Duncan Smith	22	n/a
2003-5	Blair	32	Howard	26	Blair
2006-7	Blair	30	Cameron	30	n/a
2007-10	Brown	31	Cameron	43	Cameron
2010-15	Cameron	39	Miliband	33	Cameron

Base: c. 1,000-2,000 British adults 18+ in each monthly poll
(Ratings are only averaged for those polls in which both named leaders were rated)
Source: Ipsos MORI Political Monitor

Nevertheless, we would not expect the Prime Minister's ratings on their own to indicate the likelihood of re-election – just as relevant must be how well the leader of the opposition is regarded. Margaret Thatcher and Tony Blair were both re-elected with better satisfaction ratings over the parliament than that of their opponent. Not since Mrs Thatcher's defeat of Mr Callaghan in 1979 has the lower-rated leader defeated the higher-rated one. (Table 20). This was a further good omen for David Cameron, since his average score over the parliament was several points ahead of Ed Miliband's.[79]

Figure 14: Ed Miliband versus David Cameron (satisfaction ratings)

Q Are you satisfied or dissatisfied with the way David Cameron is doing his job as Prime Minister? Are you satisfied or dissatisfied with the way Ed Miliband is doing his job as leader of the Labour Party?

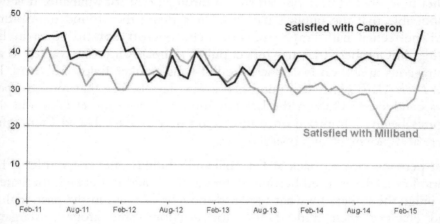

Base: c. 1,000 British adults 18+ in each monthly survey
Source: Ipsos MORI Political Monitor

Nevertheless, this advantage for David Cameron was not one that could necessarily have been taken as a foregone conclusion at an earlier stage in the parliament. There was a period of just over a year, roughly running from the reaction to the 2012 'Omnishambles' budget until the following summer, when Cameron's ratings and Miliband's were very close to each other (Figure 14) – indeed, more often than not it was Mr Miliband who was fractionally ahead. Curiously, perhaps, this was during a period that included the London Olympics and the Queen's Diamond Jubilee, exactly the sort of events that past Prime Ministers have often been able to exploit to create a feel-good factor that reflected positively on themselves, and the failure of the Prime Minister and government to achieve any substantial

[79] Cameron's average satisfaction score in the polls in which he was rated against Miliband, 38.6%, is a little lower than his overall 39.7% average, since his best scores were in his 'honeymoon' period before Miliband had been chosen as Labour's leader and after his re-election in 2015 when Miliband had resigned.

uptick in their ratings as a result could reasonably have been read at the time as a bad omen for his re-election hopes. But this proved the lowest ebb of his fortunes, and his ratings began to rise again from the middle of 2013 while, at the same time, Ed Miliband's fell away badly (although with more fluctuation in the trend).

It is not immediately obvious why the Spring of 2013, rather than any other time, should have proved such a turning point for Miliband. It is not impossible that the public's patience for a figure they found uninspiring and ineffectual had simply run out. (The one-off upward spike in his ratings in October 2013 may reflect public sympathy after he reacted to an outrageous attack on his father, the left-wing thinker Ralph Miliband, by the *Daily Mail*, which was published a few days before that month's poll was conducted.) Only in the last few months before the election did the figures begin to improve once more, and by this stage David Cameron's were also moving in an upward direction.

But perhaps looking back at Ed Miliband's ratings over the whole of his period as leader is a red herring. After all, we would not expect the voters to judge the leaders by what they had thought of them in the past, if they had changed their mind before the election came around. Margaret Thatcher's apparently surprising defeat of Jim Callaghan came at the end of a parliament in which his ratings had generally been better than hers, but she had turned the tables on him by the start of 1979, and had a higher satisfaction rating than he did in all four of the polls we carried out after the turn of the year. So let us consider, instead, what the public thought about Mr Miliband as election year began – which was, however, no more comforting a message for him than the longer-run figures.

Since MORI started polling on satisfaction with the party leaders in the late 1970s, no leader has become Prime Minister with a satisfaction rating at the start of election year as low as Ed Miliband's 26% in January 2015. The lowest January rating for a winning PM has been Tony Blair's 33% satisfied in 2005, and he was pitted against Michael Howard on a 22% score; David Cameron's January 2015 rating was 41% satisfied. The leader with a higher January satisfaction rating has won every general election in which we have polled (although that was not much of a guide in January 1987, when Margaret Thatcher and Neil Kinnock were tied on 37% satisfied, and Mr Kinnock's net score was better than Mrs Thatcher's as fewer were dissatisfied with him – Mrs Thatcher won the election easily).

Likeability

The satisfaction scores are the simplest of our measures of attitudes towards the leaders, and perhaps offer the best overall assessment, but every now and then we also explore the public's thoughts in more detail, considering some of the impressions that might be contributing to that overall image. An obvious place to start is whether the voters feel they like each of the leaders or not.

Table 21: Like him/her? Like his/her party?

Q Which of these statements comes closest to your views of ... and the ... Party?

	David Cameron & Con	Ed Miliband & Lab	Nick Clegg & LD	Nigel Farage & UKIP	Nicola Sturgeon & SNP	Natalie Bennett & Greens
	%	%	%	%	%	%
I like [leader] and I like [party]	25	22	19	18	17	24
I like [leader] but I do not like [party]	14	8	12	12	9	4
I do not like [leader] but I like [party]	8	30	21	7	4	12
I do not like [leader] and I do not like [party]	46	32	36	52	34	23
Don't know	7	8	12	10	36	36
Like the party	33	52	40	25	21	36
Do not like the party	60	40	48	64	43	27
Like the leader	39	30	31	30	26	28
Do not like the leader	54	62	57	59	38	35
Asset/liability (like leader minus like party)	+6	-22	-9	+5	+5	-8

Base: 518 British adults 18+, 8-11 March 2015
Source: Ipsos MORI Political Monitor

Ipsos MORI regularly ask the public whether they like each of the leaders and whether they like his party and/or his policies[80]. While this is definitely not an infallible guide to how people will vote, it does at least give some indication of which leaders are an asset to their party and which may be a liability – or equally, if you believe voters think more in 'presidential' terms

---

[80] Similarly, product marketers have long asked in advertising research whether people 'like' the brand being advertised or not, believing it to be correlated with persuasiveness and hence advertising effectiveness. See David Walker and Tony M. Dubitsky, 'Why Liking Matters', *Journal of Advertising Research* 34 (1994): 9–18.

rather than along party lines these days, which potential Prime Ministers are helped by their association with their party and which are hindered by it.

When we polled on this in March 2015 (Table 21), we found that both Ed Miliband and Nick Clegg were considerably less popular than their parties; David Cameron and Nigel Farage, on the other hand, were slightly more liked than their parties. None of these figures showed much movement from previous polls in 2013 or 2014, except that both David Cameron and the Conservatives had lost a degree of popularity in the six months before the election. (We also asked, for the first time, about the SNP leader Nicola Sturgeon and the Green leader Natalie Bennett, both in the public eye because of the seven-leader TV debate in which they took part shortly before our poll. Nicola Sturgeon proved more popular than her party and Natalie Bennett less so, but both questions elicited far more don't knows than those about the other four, illustrating their relative obscurity to many voters.)

Despite the drop in his ratings in the election run-up, David Cameron was still the best-liked of the four leaders – or perhaps it would be more accurate to say he was the least disliked. In his case, 39% of the public said they liked him and 54% that they did not. (In September 2014, they were evenly split – 48% liked him and 49% didn't.) This is significantly better than the 31% who liked Nick Clegg, the 30% who liked Nigel Farage or the 31% who liked Ed Miliband. However, likeability is not all that matters to voters: Margaret Thatcher won three elections despite always being more widely disliked than liked in our polls, and 51% said they liked John Major in January 1997, shortly before he led the Conservatives into their most comprehensive defeat since the First World War.

We can learn a little more about attitudes to David Cameron and Ed Miliband if we look separately at the responses of those who say they voted Conservative and Labour at the 2010 election (Table 22), although we must treat the figures with caution as the sub-sample sizes are small. In each case we see that their asset/liability figure is worse among those who voted for their party than among the public as a whole – in other words if a party's supporters did not like both the party *and* the leader, it was more likely to be the leader than the party that they disliked, which perhaps is not very surprising. But even so 18% of those who had voted

Conservative and 9% of those who had voted Labour were by the end of the parliament saying they did not (any more) like the party.

Table 22: Like him? Like his party?

Q Which of these statements comes closest to your views of David Cameron/Ed Miliband and the Conservative/Labour Party?

| | Voted Conservative in 2010 | | Voted Labour in 2010 | | Did neither in 2010 | |
	David Cameron & Con	Ed Miliband & Lab	David Cameron & Con	Ed Miliband & Lab	David Cameron & Con	Ed Miliband & Lab
	%	%	%	%	%	%
I like [him] and I like [his party]	61	5	4	43	16	18
I like [him] but I do not like [his party]	10	9	13	7	17	7
I do not like [him] but I like [his party]	16	18	4	45	5	29
I do not like [him] and I do not like [his party]	8	67	77	2	49	30
Don't know	4	1	2	3	12	15
Like the party	77	23	8	88	21	47
Do not like the party	18	76	90	9	66	37
Like the leader	71	14	17	50	33	25
Do not like the leader	24	85	81	47	54	59
Asset/liability (like leader minus like party)	-6	-9	+9	-38	+12	-22

Base: 518 British adults 18+, 8-11 March 2015
Source: Ipsos MORI Political Monitor

More striking, though, is how bad both leaders' scores were among supporters of their own party. David Cameron, of course, had been leader in 2010, so anybody who voted Conservative in that year had voted for him as Prime Minister; to find that a quarter of those were saying by 2015 that they did not like him suggests either that he suffered a substantial reverse in his reputation during the period he was Prime Minister (which is not obvious in the other polling evidence) or that the influence of leadership factors on the result of the 2010 election may have been somewhat exaggerated. For Ed Miliband the situation is different, since he became leader only after the election, but it seems plain that either his party made the wrong choice or he antagonised a lot of people during his time as leader, since almost half of those who had voted Labour said they didn't like him.

Naturally enough, both Cameron and the Conservatives were widely disliked by Labour voters and, equally, Labour and Miliband got short shrift from Conservatives. If there were to be any shifting of floating votes between the two major parties, the Conservatives looked more vulnerable than Labour, with almost a quarter of Conservative supporters admitting that they liked the Labour party. (Many of these may have been former Labour voters, who swung to the Tories in 2010.)

More relevant, however, were the views of those who voted for neither major party in 2010, the battleground where both would hope to be able to pick up support. Here again, it is clear that David Cameron was an asset while Ed Miliband was a liability. If these voters were to be motivated purely by what they thought of the parties, then Labour was very clearly better placed, as more than twice as many of this group said they liked the Labour Party as liked the Conservatives. But if leaders were to come into the equation, then we see that one in three of them liked Cameron and only one in four liked Miliband; or, put another way, 29% were being deterred from switching to Labour because although they liked the party they did not like its leader. With Labour having lost in 2010 and therefore needing to attract new votes to have any hope of winning, this was not a comfortable position to be in.

Ready to be Prime Minister?

Perhaps the clearest single indicator of an opposition leader's real vote-winning potential is his credibility as a potential premier. We have been asking the public whether they think the leader of the opposition is ready to be Prime Minister at intervals since the 1990s. Ed Miliband's score in November 2014, when 13% agreed that he was ready, was the lowest we have ever found, beating Iain Duncan Smith's record of 16% in 2003. By February 2015, Mr Miliband's rating had improved somewhat, with 21% thinking he was ready for office. But that still left him with a lot of ground to make up if he was to catch the scores of the last two successful opposition candidates for Number Ten: in the month before they were elected, 53% said Tony Blair and 51% said David Cameron were ready to be Prime Minister. Even Michael Howard, who lost convincingly in 2005, was seen as ready to be PM by 40% (a good many more than voted for him!).

This is clearly a perception that matters. It does not matter too much to a party leader if he can't convince those people who are not going to vote for him of his merits, but he needs to be taken seriously by his own voters – however well-disposed they may be towards him, his party or his policies, most are surely going to think twice before voting for him if they don't think he is up to the job. If any single poll finding in the run-up to the election was a warning that the neck-and-neck voting intentions might be misleading, this was surely it. When almost two in five of those who said they were certain to vote and would vote Labour also said – just three months before the election – that they disagreed that "Ed Miliband is ready to be Prime Minister", this was plainly a sign that the Labour vote was probably softer than it looked. (Table 23). True, it was not entirely possible that such doubts might be put to rest during the course of the campaign – hence, no doubt, the reluctance of David Cameron to risk a head-to-head TV debate giving Ed Miliband a platform where he had the chance to look Prime Ministerial. But that was obviously a very faint hope indeed – negative public impressions are much harder to shake off than to acquire.

Table 23: Ed Miliband – up to the job?

Q On balance, do you agree or disagree with the following statement – "Ed Miliband is ready to be Prime Minister?"

	All	Conservative	Labour	Liberal Democrat	UKIP	Green
	%	%	%	%	%	%
Strongly agree	9	1	23	5	0	2
Tend to agree	13	3	27	13	3	16
Neither agree nor disagree	7	1	10	4	2	19
Tend to disagree	20	14	21	26	23	28
Strongly disagree	49	79	18	52	72	35
Total agree	22	4	50	18	3	18
Total disagree	69	93	39	78	95	63
Don't know	2	2	2	0	0	0

Base: 1,010 British adults 18+, 8-10 February 2015
Source: Ipsos MORI Political Monitor

Meanwhile, Conservative supporters were entirely clear what they thought: four in five *strongly* disagreed that Mr Miliband was ready for Number Ten, and 93% at least tended to disagree. More significantly for the election, UKIP supporters were as negative as the Tories (although no surprise there, and they also tended to be just as negative about David Cameron as Labour supporters); Liberal Democrats were hardly more positive about him, and even Greens split more than three-to-one against Miliband. And this, remember, was in February, well before the Conservative campaign got fully underway in articulating doubts about the Labour leader. The effect of the campaign was therefore to underline the existing beliefs of Conservative supporters, and to undermine the determination of anti-Conservatives to vote Labour by reminding them of those same already-present doubts, rather than to plant new ideas that might swing floating voters.

But why could voters not see Ed Miliband as Prime Minister? To gain some insight into their thinking about him, and about the other leaders, we need to look at our more detailed image questions, which ask about characteristics voters like to see, or do not like to see, in a party leader and in a Prime Minister. We have refined these questions over the years, and the version we included in our April 2015 poll asked respondents to consider nine separate descriptions, telling us whether each fitted their impression of David Cameron, Ed Miliband, Nick Clegg and Nigel Farage.[81] They could apply as many or as few of these descriptions as they liked to each leader, and of course could match the same description to more than one leader if that seemed appropriate. (Table 24).

---

[81] Loyal readers of the previous books in this series may perhaps notice that these questions are similar but not identical to the batteries of leader image questions which we asked at previous elections: the number of descriptions tested for each leader is smaller, and as well as dropping some of the descriptions used in the past we have introduced one or two new ones. This is a consequence of having switched most of our election polling from face-to-face interviews to interviews by telephone. In the face-to-face interviews, we showed our respondents a printed list of all the descriptions and asked them to pick the ones that fitted. With telephone interviewing, of course, this is not possible: instead, the interviewer has to read out each description in turn and get a yes-or-no response before moving on to the next. Naturally, this affects the way that the respondent answers and although we believe that both provide an accurate picture of the way the public feels about the leaders the responses are not directly comparable to each other. (In particular, with the read out method the tendency is for all the figures to be higher.)

Table 24: Leader image, 2015

Q I am going to read out some things both favourable and unfavourable that have been said about various politicians. Which of these, if any, do you think apply to...?

	David Cameron	Ed Miliband	Nick Clegg	Nigel Farage
	%	%	%	%
Capable leader	57	33	31	26
Has a clear vision for Britain	56	45	31	43
Good in a crisis	51	24	24	17
Understands the problems facing Britain	47	50	46	33
Has sound judgment	44	35	33	19
Has got a lot of personality	40	20	34	64
Average positive	**49**	**35**	**33**	**34**
Looks after some sections of society more than others	75	58	41	62
Out of touch with ordinary people	65	42	41	42
More style than substance	44	30	38	55
Average negative	**61**	**43**	**40**	**53**
Net positive	**−12**	**−8**	**−7**	**−19**
None of these	2	3	4	5
Don't know	3	5	8	5

Base: 1,000 British adults 18+, 12-15 April 2015 (on Clegg, 507; on Farage, 493)
Source: Ipsos MORI Political Monitor

Looking at each leader in isolation, this gives us a fairly clear view of what the voters saw as their strong and weak points. David Cameron scored more strongly on competence than empathy, with three-quarters thinking he "Looks after some sections of society more than others". This is also the most frequently applied description for Ed Miliband, but "Understands the problems facing Britain" is in second place for him, while the second-widest impression of Mr Cameron was that he is out of touch. However, on the two impressions which perhaps above all others define what voters look for first in a Prime Minister, being a "Capable leader" and "Good in a crisis", Mr Cameron was rated far ahead of Mr Miliband. Taking the average percentage applying each positive and negative description to the two, David Cameron had the worse net score, being viewed negatively by three-fifths of voters and positively by only a half. But while Ed Miliband's −8 was better than David Cameron's −12, it was a deceptive advantage – the deterrent represented by his lower scores on those key positive attributes may weigh much more heavily with the voters than the attractions signified by his lower scores on the negative ones. Indeed, that is precisely what his low overall ratings – on satisfaction with his performance as leader, on his readiness to be Prime Minister – would seem to suggest.

What of Nick Clegg and Nigel Farage? Neither could realistically hope to become Prime Minister after the election, but there is no reason why their public image should not be assessed against the same yardstick. Clegg, too, had a slightly negative net rating overall, but the single clearest impression of him was a positive one: 46% felt he understood the problems facing Britain. On the other hand, his lowest score was for being "good in a crisis". That is also true of Nigel Farage who, to compound it, had almost as few people feeling he had sound judgment; but the most widespread impression of the UKIP leader was that he had "a lot of personality", although this was offset by his also having a strikingly high score on having "more style than substance".

But quite apart from what the voters think of the leaders of the smaller parties as a matter of interest in itself, it provides extra context for understanding what they think of David Cameron and Ed Miliband. Clegg's overall ratings were very similar to Miliband's, just a couple of points lower on both positives and negatives. Nevertheless, there are clear distinctions: Miliband is much likelier than Clegg to be seen as having "a clear vision for Britain" – perhaps understandably as the leader of one of the two major parties, responsible for setting out the programme of government that he hopes to be given power to implement by the voters – but, on the other hand, Clegg is far ahead of Miliband on having "a lot of personality". In fact Clegg's score on this attribute is only a disappointing 34%, far behind Nigel Farage and even David Cameron, a sad comedown for the TV star of the 2010 election; but he still completely eclipses Miliband, on 20%. In short, most of the voters feel Ed Miliband lacks charisma. In theory, of course, this should not matter, and when we ask the voters they usually tell us that they think that having a lot of personality is one of the least important factors in deciding which way they will vote.[82] But in reality it is usually the power of that personality that gives a leader the opportunity to put their message across and to convince

---

[82] At the 2001 election, when we were using a somewhat different list of descriptions to test leader image, the public rated "has a lot of personality" 14th out of 14 in importance; "understands the problems facing Britain", "capable" and "good in a crisis" were almost inseparable in the top three places.

the voters of their other positive qualities. In all the elections we have polled, only John Major in 1992 succeeded in overcoming the handicap of an inferior personality rating to win the election.

There is one problem with using these image profiles to compare leaders, however: some leaders are much better known than others, and many more of the voters therefore have clear impressions of what they think about them. This can mean when we try to compare one leader or one party with another, simply comparing the numbers who apply each description can give a very misleading impression.

Take David Cameron and Ed Miliband. For almost all the positive descriptions in our poll, many more people felt they applied to Mr Cameron than to Mr Miliband. But Mr Cameron also got more people applying the negative descriptions – it is simply that people tend to have a clearer picture of what they think about the Prime Minister than about the Leader of the Opposition (and that's almost always true, it is not unique to this election).

Fortunately, there is a solution. Using a statistical technique called Correspondence Analysis, we are able to compensate for the public's different levels of knowledge. This analysis produces an output in graphical form, an easily comprehensible and accessible visual format called a perceptual map.

Conceptually, a perceptual map is a diagram of image space based on differences between perceptions of the leaders or parties. It produces a picture of relative image – which descriptions are seen as best fitting each leader (whether he has made a strong or weak impression) and the leader to which each description best applies (whether or not it seems to describe any of them particularly well). It gives a view of how the leaders are viewed in comparison with each other, and to which leader particular attributes are most strongly seen as applying or not applying. In essence, it finds the most distinctive features even of a very weak image, and assigns even rarely chosen descriptions to those leaders that they are most nearly seen as fitting.

The perceptual map of leader image is shown in Figure 15. Very roughly speaking, the nearer a description is to a leader, the more strongly that description applies to that leader. (The dotted ovals around each party leader are not part of the statistical output but are added to aid the interpretation.) Take, for example, having a "clear vision for Britain": this is plotted right at the centre or origin of the graph (where the axes cross), indicating that it applies almost equally to all four leaders and is not a distinctive part of the image of any of them. There are plenty of other differences to look at, however.

Figure 15: Leader image 2015 – perceptual map

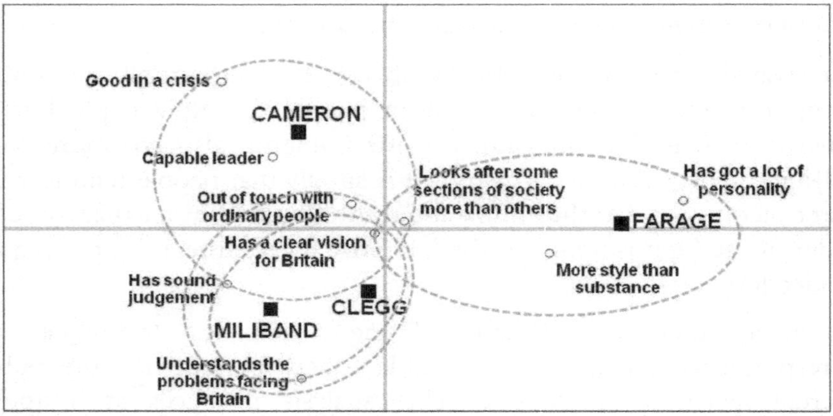

Base: 1,000 British adults 18+,12-15 April 2015
Source: Ipsos MORI Political Monitor

The most fundamental distinction is between Nigel Farage and the others: the dividing line is that Mr Farage is seen as the leader with "a lot of personality", but with this also being interpreted as "more style than substance". Fundamentally, he seems to have achieved the perception of being a mould-breaking outsider to the existing political establishment (something he had clearly aimed to do).

The three other leaders are more like each other, but Mr Cameron scores on competence issues, Mr Miliband on understanding the problems facing the voters and also on having sound judgment (and Mr Cameron is also seen as being the leader who is particularly out of touch, although this is not a very strong distinction – symbolised by that description being quite close to the origin). Mr Clegg is in the shadow of Mr Miliband, seen a little less clearly as being a polar opposite of Nigel Farage, but generally felt to display the same positive attributes as Mr Miliband although to a lesser

130

degree, and also distinctly inferior to Mr Cameron on being a capable leader and good in a crisis (as Mr Miliband also is).

Finally, we find some fairly important attributes so close to the origin that they are failing to distinguish between the competitors: if the voters want to vote for the leader who has the clearest vision for Britain, or who is least likely to look after the interests of some sections of society more than others, they are going to be stuck.

Party image

As we consider the image of the leaders, so we can also look at the image of the parties. As we have seen (p. 104), the public are reluctant to admit that what they think of the parties is particularly influential on their vote. But the factor is pervasive, not least because some impressions of the parties are longer standing and harder to shift than either party leaders or policy detail. After all, David Cameron, the longest-standing of the party leaders, has been in office less than ten years and few party policies have remained unchanged even for that long; but all three of the major parties are more than a century old[83], so there is a natural historical context and a continuity to party image.

Parties are not widely respected these days, and party membership was at a historic low in 2015[84], so party loyalty is perhaps an unfashionable motivation to which to admit. But voting *against* parties is certainly alive and well. Party image remains a factor of importance, and the campaign teams accord it due respect.

We measure party image with a similar question to the one used for leader image, although the descriptions from which our interviewees choose are different. What they thought of the parties in the month before the election is shown in Table 25. The public saw good as well as bad in all three of the traditional major parties, but with different virtues in different cases. The Conservatives, Labour and the Liberal Democrats all scored on average slightly higher on the negative than on the positive descriptions, without much to choose between the net scores. UKIP, however, was more widely disliked. (We class "different to the other parties" as a neutral description, since it may clearly be viewed as either an advantage or a disadvantage.)

---

[83] That assumes, of course, that we take the Liberal Democrats as being a continuation of the old Liberal Party, which most voters surely do.

[84] Membership of the three main parties, Labour, Conservative and Liberal Democrats, was at 1.0% of the electorate in 2015, down from 3.8% in 1983; see Richard Keen, *Membership of UK Political Parties*, House of Commons Library Standard Note (London: House of Commons Library, 11 August 2015), http://researchbriefings.parliament.uk/ResearchBriefing/Summary/SN05125, accessed 29 October 2015.

Table 25: Party image, 2015

Q I am going to read out some things both favourable and unfavourable that have been said about various political parties. Which of these, if any, do you think apply to...?

	Conserv-atives	Labour	Liberal Demo-crats	UKIP
	%	%	%	%
Fit to govern	50	40	23	9
Understands the problems facing Britain	45	52	44	31
Has a good team of leaders	44	28	29	17
Looks after the interests of people like me	33	43	38	20
Keeps its promises	23	24	17	13
Average positive	**39**	**37**	**30**	**18**
Will promise anything to win votes	63	63	57	55
Out of date	44	36	33	41
Divided	43	43	43	39
Extreme	23	14	10	65
Average negative	**43**	**39**	**36**	**50**
Net positive	**–4**	**–2**	**–6**	**–32**
Different to the other parties	42	39	40	71
None of these	3	2	3	6
Don't know	4	4	7	3

Base: 1,000 British adults 18+, 12-15 April 2015 (on Lib Dems, 507; on UKIP, 493)
Source: Ipsos MORI Political Monitor

Once again, we can reduce this table of results to a more digestible perceptual map. The perceptual map of party image has obvious strong similarities with the leader image map. The party image map shows that each of the parties has a distinctive image, with a clear division between virtues of 'head' and 'heart':

- the Conservatives put across an impression of competence, being "fit to govern" and having "a good team of leaders";

- Labour is more empathetic, seen as better at understanding the problems facing Britain and looking after the interests of people like me.

Both apparently gain some credibility for tending to keep their promises, but this is only because the impression of their not doing so is weaker than for UKIP. This is a good illustration of the difference between this comparative measurement of party image and the absolute measurement taken from the raw figures, which shows that only a small minority trust the promises of any of the four parties: the public may distrust them all, but it is a less prominent part of their impression of the Conservatives or Labour than of UKIP, about which they know less.

Figure 16: Party image 2015 – perceptual map

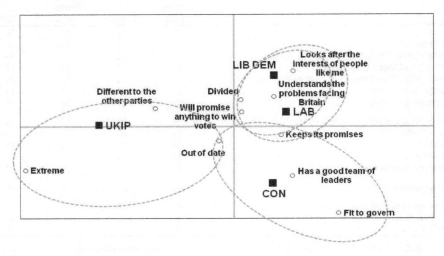

Base: 1,000 British adults 18+, 12-15 April 2015
Source: Ipsos MORI Political Monitor

- UKIP was distinctive in being seen as extreme, but also (which will be more to their liking) as being different from the other parties, although this impression is weaker (which the perceptual map shows by putting the "different to the other parties" marker nearer the centre).

- The Liberal Democrats, intriguingly, made a very similar impression to Labour. This was, perhaps, not an asset in an election where so much of the emphasis was on the danger of wasted votes, and the smaller parties may have been reliant on establishing a distinctiveness as justification for voting for them rather than for one of the contenders for government.

The descriptions closest to the centre – "divided", "will promise anything to win votes" and "out of date" are those that distinguish least well between the four parties, unfortunately because the public felt there was truth in all of them as applied to all four competitors.

As we have already noted, David Cameron was seen by most of the public to be a more capable Prime Minister than Ed Miliband, and outscored him in the public's perceptions on almost every measure. But it should not be supposed that Mr Miliband was Labour's sole weakness, and that every other front-bencher far surpassed him in the voters' assessment. Both the perceptual map and the raw figures show the Conservatives having a clear lead over Labour as the party with "a good team of leaders", and this was borne out when we explored people's views in more detail. In our poll conducted with just over a week to go to election day[85], we found that 52% of the public thought David Cameron would make the most capable Prime Minister of the two, with 31% opting for Ed Miliband. But George Osborne also led Ed Balls as most capable Chancellor by 47% to 34% and Theresa May led Yvette Cooper as most capable Home Secretary by 45% to 36%. Only Douglas Alexander had a slight lead over his opponent, Philip Hammond – as most capable Foreign Secretary – by 36% to 32%.[86] (Probably Hammond and Alexander were both less well-known than the other three from their party, as suggested by the lower total who opted for either of them.)

---

[85] Ipsos MORI interviewed 1,010 British adults aged 18+ by telephone on 26-29 April 2015.
[86] We also tested views of Harriet Harman, but as she was pitted against Nick Clegg as "most capable deputy Prime Minister", the findings tell us less about the relative standing of Conservatives and Labour. In the event that contest was a near-tie, Mr Clegg preferred to Ms Harman by 41% to 39%.

Beyond the Political Triangle

So far, we have taken for granted that we can rely on asking the voters what factors most influenced their decisions. But, it is not really as simple as that. The three sides of the Political Triangle cannot be viewed in isolation, because they are constantly impinging on each other. How accurately can the voters really judge the influences on their decisions? When they tell us, for example, that they are most influenced by the parties' policies, are they taking into account, or are they even aware of, the way in which what they already think about the party and its leader have affected what they think about those policies in the first place? We think it is unlikely that many are consciously self-aware in this way.

Moreover, even setting these complications aside, there may be a bias in the answers. The idea that voters 'ought' to vote on the issues rather than 'trivial' factors such as the image of the leaders, and 'ought' to keep an open mind before each election rather than voting loyally and unthinkingly for the same party that they always support, is consistently argued or implied by politicians themselves, by the media, and is probably broadly supported in theory by most of the public. It seems inevitable that respondents will feel pressure to give more weight in their explanations to issues than they truly achieve, reluctant to admit to the interviewer quite how much they have taken into account factors which they feel might show them in a bad light[87]; and this pressure may act unconsciously as well as consciously, so as to deceive the voters themselves – when they are affected by influences that they consider 'less respectable' reasons for coming to a decision. They may subconsciously downplay the impact that such, often emotional, decision-making has on their thinking. We cannot only rely on what the voters tell us about why they have come to a particular conclusion.

But, on the other hand, nor should we go to the other extreme. One of the reviewers of *Explaining Cameron's Coalition* entirely dismissed our evidence about voters' reports of the surprisingly low salience of the economy as an explanation of their voting in the 2010 election, on the grounds that other

---

[87] This is an example of "social desirability bias", where some respondents tell the interviewer what they think the interviewer wants to hear, and has a distorting influence that is well known in various forms of survey research on many topics. See pages 242-244.

survey evidence showed a close correlation between voting behaviour and preferred party on economic policy.[88] (So, for that matter, did our polls.) He argued, in effect, that the voters' reports of their own reasoning were entirely worthless, and only the statistical demonstration of a significant causal effect between one opinion or behaviour and another had any validity.

But this runs into the problem posed by almost all survey evidence, that proof of correlation is not a proof of a causal connection and, even if a causal connection can be logically inferred, the direction in which it runs cannot[89]. There probably was a strong causal connection between how people voted in 2010 and which party they thought had the best policies on the economy. But was this because what they thought about the economy was a powerful influence on their voting decision? Or was it, equally possibly, that party choice, already made for other reasons – for example, whether they trusted David Cameron or Gordon Brown as honest and competent – had a powerful effect in forming their reactions to the economic policies that the parties put forward? The survey data cannot tell us, because the statistical relationship would be the same in either case.

So why not ask the people who might know, the voters themselves? We might have to treat the answers with a little caution, but they certainly should not be dismissed outright. In the 2010 case, we tend to the opinion that what they were telling us was broadly reliable, and that for many voters the economic alignment in 2010 was more a consequence of their attitudes to the parties than a cause of it, and that their impressions of the party leaders played an unusually large role.

Nevertheless, the decision-making process is complex, and voting decisions are as subject to the vagaries of the human mind as any others. Political psychology is a distinct and active academic discipline, but while some of its insights are widely recognised and incorporated into the

---

[88] Paul Whiteley, 'Explaining Cameron's Coalition: How It Came About - An Analysis of the 2010 British General Election', *Times Higher Education*, 1 September 2011, http://www.timeshighereducation.co.uk/books/explaining-camerons-coalition-how-it-came-about-an-analysis-of-the-2010-british-general-election/417314.article, accessed 19 August 2014.

[89] Those statistically minded who want to know more about how to prove causality should look up the definitive paper on the topic: see Austin Bradford Hill, 'The Environment and Disease: Association or Causation?', *Proceedings of the Royal Society of Medicine* 58 (1965): 295–300.

thinking of both political scientists and political marketers, it would probably be fair to say that they are less well known either to politicians or to the general public. Two American books in recent years have explored important elements of this work on a level accessible to the general reader, and although they consider mainly examples from American politics the lessons they teach about how voters' minds work are relevant in Britain. Nevertheless, neither should be particularly surprising in their message, their value being in explaining the reasons behind processes whose presence common sense should already have revealed.

Drew Westen's *The Political Brain*[90] was briefly flavour-of-the-month in political circles during the last parliament, and probes the role of emotion in political decision-making. More recently, Weeden and Kurzban's 2014 study *The Hidden Agenda of the Political Mind* digs into the psychology behind voting behaviour that aligns with self-interest, sometimes on an unconscious as well as a conscious level.[91] This latter phenomenon is closely allied to another that has been much studied in recent years, 'motivated reasoning', in which a voter's existing opinions and predispositions affect the way she evaluates evidence and reasons from it towards new conclusions, so that – it is suggested – deliberation on new issues will tend to reinforce a voter's partisan or ideological identification rather than undermine it.[92]

A distinct but closely-related idea has become popular among political scientists in recent years. This arises from the concept of 'valence issues', those where there is little difference in aims or ideological approach between the parties, and where the voters are therefore forced to choose between them on the basis of competence. A commonly-given example of

---

[90] Drew Westen, *The Political Brain: The Role of Emotion in Deciding the Fate of the Nation* (New York: Public Affairs, 2007).

[91] Jason Weeden and Robert Kurzban, *The Hidden Agenda of the Political Mind: How Self-Interest Shapes Our Opinions and Why We Won't Admit It* (Princeton, N. J.: Princeton University Press, 2014); see also Daniel Finkelstein, 'Left and Right Are Dead in Our Social Revolution', *The Times*, 1 July 2015.

[92] For a thorough survey of recent theoretical and empirical work on this subject, see Thomas J. Leeper and Rune Slothuus, 'Political Parties, Motivated Reasoning, and Public Opinion Formation', *Advances in Political Psychology* 35 (2014): 129–156; also Matthew J. Lebo and Daniel Cassino, 'The Aggregated Consequences of Motivated Reasoning and the Dynamics of Partisan Presidential Approval', *Political Psychology* 28 (2007): 719–746; Charles S. Taber and Milton Lodge, 'Motivated Skepticism in the Evaluation of Political Beliefs', *American Journal of Political Science* 50 (2006): 755–769.

a valence issue is crime – the main aim of all parties is to minimise it.[93] The theory of valence issues allows political scientists to reconcile their established issue-based models of voting with emerging evidence of the importance of what the voters think about the party leaders. In terms of the individual voter's decision-making process, they argue that these factors operate through 'heuristic cues' (mental short cuts): for example, having already concluded that they trust David Cameron, voters will tend to accept his verdict on a new policy proposal rather than evaluating it from first principles. Again, there is plenty of evidence that people's minds do, in fact, operate in this sort of way, even if they may not themselves be fully aware of the process.

Emotional as well as deliberative reasoning, mental short cuts, unconscious prejudice in interpreting the evidence needed to evaluate new ideas or policies, all these suggest than any notion of the voter as approaching an election with a clean slate and weighing up the policy offers of the various parties from a neutral perspective is entirely misconceived. Add to this the convincing evidence that the vast majority of voters have very little knowledge of the parties' programmes and limited understanding of many of the basic political, social and economic facts with which the government they choose is tasked to deal, and it should be obvious that simply having superior policies to the other parties is insufficient to win elections.

Nor should this be very revolutionary: this new work helps us understand the process better and illuminate some of the details, but politicians and political parties have long understood that factors such as attachment to party, assessments of the party leaders and other leading figures, and group

---

[93] But as an example it may only demonstrate that valence is a temporary rather than a permanent characteristic of an issue. At many points in the past there has been the potential, perhaps not fully realised, for very substantial differences of ideology and policy to arise between the parties in their approach to crime. Labour, especially in its more left-wing phases, would tend to put more emphasis on the social causes of crime, on reformative rather than retributive justice, in ways that a traditionalist Tory would regard as "soft on crime, soft on the causes of crime". Labour has abolished capital punishment and the birch; Conservatives have stood for election on policies of Putting Bobbies Back on the Beat and increasing spending on prisons. In fact, given that the images of the two major parties on the issue are probably fixed and distinct even if their substantive policies may have moved closer together, it does not seem unreasonable to wonder whether any significant proportion of those votes swung by the crime issue have ever done so on a valence basis rather than on a real (if perhaps outdated) ideological distinction.

dynamics whether of class or locality, all affect voters' decisions as well as manifesto details[94]. They are also fully aware that a promise to voters is worthless unless the voters believe it, and that in judging a party's approach to any issue voters are likely to take into account past record as well as their judgments of a proposed future policy.

Lest they be missed, there are two unifying themes behind all these explanations. First, every one of these factors is a subjective one – elections are not, and cannot be, fought on objective fact but rather on the voters' perceptions. Second, none of these factors acts in isolation: on the contrary, they are constantly interacting with each other.

A voter's existing impressions of a party and its leaders affect how they view that party's policies and their view of the policies affects their future impressions of party and leader. What a voter thinks about a party's leader is likely to influence what she thinks of the party – after all, the party chose the leader. Perhaps less obviously, their impressions of the party also affect their impressions of its leader, especially those all-important first impressions when a newly-chosen leader is still widely unfamiliar to the public. When William Hague became Conservative leader in 1997, research found that many of the public assumed he must be a Southerner educated at a public school, because their prejudices about the Conservative Party told them that that is what Conservative leaders are like. (And they thought that even though at that time the Conservatives had not had a public school educated leader for more than 30 years).

Moreover, both party and leader image have an effect on how policy pledges are viewed. This is not just because the public discount policy pledges when they don't trust parties or leaders to keep their promises, although that is a problem in itself. The very fact of who is advocating a policy can raise or lower its acceptability. Whenever we ask a polling question about a policy, we know that it can affect the answers we will get if the question reminds the respondents whose policy it is. And, probably, many other voters have already taken into account the association between

---

[94] Academics studying public choice distinguish between expressions of voting to support a party and preferences over what outcomes the voter would like to see achieved in an election. Voting to support a party is known as "expressive voting", and includes considerations between sentiment and rational interests. For more details, see Geoffrey Brennan and James Buchanan, 'Voter Choice: Evaluating Political Alternatives', *American Behavioral Scientist* 28 (1984): 185–201.

the policy and the party or leader that supports it so that their opinions are affected even if they are not reminded of it in the poll question.

Because opinions on all three sides of the Political Triangle are so interdependent, even complex multivariate statistical analysis may be insufficient to isolate them properly. The conventional approach in political science is, rather than asking the voters what influenced their vote, to use statistical techniques such as regression to test how closely their other opinions are associated with their voting behaviour – which factors are the best predictors of their votes? But when the factors in question are not causally independent of each other – when attitudes to policies cause attitudes to parties but attitudes to parties also cause attitudes to policies – this approach breaks down and it may be impossible satisfactorily to resolve the question. Perhaps all we can say is that all three factors have some significant influence.

The uncompetitive centre

The classic idea of a British election, and the role of the Political Triangle within it, centres on the 'floating voter'. In this scenario, the Conservatives and Labour compete for the same voters, who are described as floating voters because they are attracted to one party on some criteria and to the other party on others. Whichever party best persuades these voters to give more weight to the issues on which it is strongest, or best persuades them to change their minds on the issues where they preferred the other side, will gain most of their votes. This then might translate into a swing in the marginal seats which will determine the election outcome.

But the floating voter concept rests on two assumptions. It assumes that they occupy the ideological centre ground, so that the choices between which they are wavering are a Conservative vote and a Labour vote, and it also assumes that they are torn between these choices because they are being driven between conflicting arguments – they see the advantage of voting Conservative on some grounds but of voting Labour on others.

However, in 2015 this classic floating vote was very small indeed: support for the parties was highly polarised, at least between left and right, with few of the public seeing the Conservatives as best on some aspect they judged important and Labour as best in some other relevant regard. We can see this most obviously with policy issues. Of the two issues most widely regarded as important, Labour had a big lead as the best party on the NHS, the Conservatives on managing the economy. Here we might expect to find conflicted voters. The NHS is considered to be an important issue even by a lot of Conservatives, so surely here was a vulnerability on which some Conservative voters might be pulled away towards supporting Labour?

But, although it is true that more people thought Labour had the best NHS policies than any other party, not everybody thought that. In fact, most Conservative supporters begged to differ. Two-thirds of those who intended to vote Conservative, 65%, thought that it was Conservative policies on the NHS that were best – only 13% found Labour's policies more appealing.

Figure 17: Best party on healthcare – by 2010 vote

Q. Which party do you think has the best policies on healthcare: the Conservatives, Labour, Liberal Democrats or some other party?

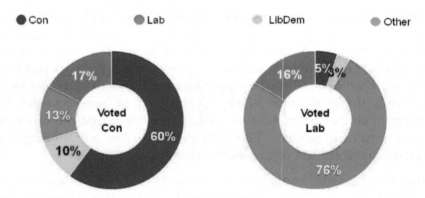

Base: 259 reported Conservative voters and 231 reported Labour voters, 12-15 April 2015
Source: Ipsos MORI Political Monitor

And those figures were almost identical whether you looked at all Conservative voters, or just the ones who said that the NHS was an important consideration in their voting. Nor was it simply because those Conservatives who were convinced by Labour's arguments on the NHS had already switched their support to Labour. If we break down opinions instead by 2010 vote (Figure 17), which is perhaps the most relevant comparison since it gives us in effect the pre-campaign starting point, the conclusion is the same.

For all Labour's overall advantage on the NHS, it gave them very little leverage in weakening the loyalty of those who had voted Conservative at the previous election. And very much the same was true in reverse on the policy where the Conservatives were strongest – the Tories had a huge lead overall as the party most trusted to manage the economy, but not among Labour voters, who mostly thought that Ed Miliband and Ed Balls had the best policies for the job.

Figure 18: Best party on managing the economy – by 2010 vote

Q. Which party do you think has the best policies on managing the economy: the Conservatives, Labour, Liberal Democrats or some other party?

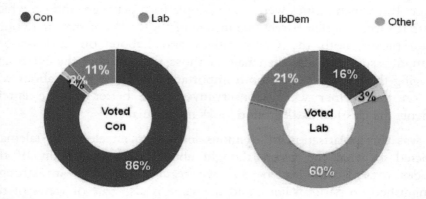

Base: 259 reported Conservative voters and 231 reported Labour voters, 12-15 April 2015
Source: Ipsos MORI Political Monitor

The upshot of all of this is that a good many voters find that their policy preferences gave them a very clear pointer on which way to vote, because they thought the same party was best on every single policy which they considered to be important, or because there was only one issue that they considered important at all. More than half the public, 55%, picked at least one important issue but said that the same party was best on every issue they thought was important (for 19% that was the Conservatives, 22% Labour, 2% the Liberal Democrats and 12% some other party).

And – reasonably enough – these preferences seem to be a pretty good guide to voting intentions. The vast majority (90%) of those who thought

Labour had the best policy on every important issue intended to vote Labour, and 89% of those favouring the Tories on every important issue intended to vote Conservative.

If we add to these the quarter of the public (26%) who were getting no guidance from the issues at all – either they didn't think any of the issues were important or didn't consider any of the parties had the best policies on the issues they thought were important – that left only one in five (19%) who might in theory have had conflicting prompts to their voting intention, thinking one party is best on one important issue but another better on some other important issue.

At first glance, one voter in five does not seem too low an estimate of the floating vote, even though it is much lower than the numbers who were claiming at that point not to have finally made up their minds which way to vote. But which parties were these people torn between, and on which issues? It turns out that barely one in five of these (4% of the total voting public) picked both the Conservatives and Labour on at least one important issue (and less than half of those thought that the NHS and managing the economy were both important issues and that Labour was best on the former while Conservatives were better on the latter). Suddenly the classical battleground looks much smaller.

Nor was this polarisation of opinions leading to an electoral stalemate restricted to what the voters thought about the issues. Many of the attitudes towards the leaders that we regularly measure are strongly distinguished on partisan lines, and the same is also true of views of the parties themselves. Take, for example, the bank of questions that we asked in the final weeks of the campaign about whether the Conservative or Labour candidate was most capable of filling each of the major ministerial offices. Considering all voters, David Cameron, George Osborne and Theresa May each had a healthy but not overwhelming lead over Ed Miliband, Ed Balls and Yvette Cooper for their respective posts. But if we look only at those who were certain to vote and intended to vote Conservative, 99% preferred Cameron, 94% Osborne and 88% May; of those certain to vote and intending to vote Labour, 82% opted for Miliband, 77% for Balls and 80% for Cooper.

In a sense these Labour loyalty figures, especially the 82% considering Miliband to be the more capable PM, are even more impressive than the

Conservative ones, given the apparent depth of the doubts about his capacity as conveyed by the media. The figures are less impressive if we compare the views of those who (say they) voted Conservative and Labour in 2010 (Figure 19): only 61% of Labour's 2010 voters preferred Miliband, and 25% opted for Cameron instead. The contrast between the two emphasises that it was those with doubts about Miliband who had either defected from Labour by this point, or who were no longer sure they would vote. Nevertheless, very few had gone the whole hog and switched to the Tories – and it must be emphasised, once again, that we do not know whether it was doubts about Mr Miliband that caused these voters to lose their loyalty to Labour, or the loss of that loyalty that prompted them also to think less well of Labour's leader and many other aspects of the party.

Figure 19: Most capable Prime Minister – by 2010 vote

Q. Who do you think would make the most capable Prime Minister, the Conservatives' David Cameron, or Labour's Ed Miliband?

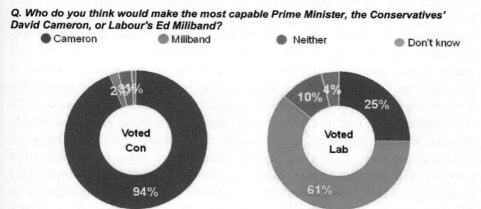

Base: 259 reported Conservative voters and 231 reported Labour voters, 12-15 April 2015
Source: Ipsos MORI Political Monitor

In addition, many of those not opting for their parties' candidates were don't knows rather than preferring their opponent: in fact not a single Conservative-voting respondent in our poll thought Ed Miliband was more capable than David Cameron, and only 2% preferred Balls and 4% Cooper to their Tory counterparts. On the other side, 11% of Labour voters thought Cameron the better PM, 11% Osborne the better Chancellor and 15% May the better Home Secretary. There was only very limited scope here for either party to work on the doubts of those intending to vote for their opponents, simply because very few of them had doubts.

Based on a slightly more advanced statistical analysis, we can probe into this in a little more detail. Our poll in the first half of April 2015 included our detailed leader image and party image questions as well as the questions on important election issues and the party judged to have the best policy on each. All the questions were asked of the same members of the public, as well their voting intentions. It is therefore possible to combine all these factors together in a single multivariate analysis, and to find which attitudes are the best predictors of how somebody (says they) will vote.

This kind of analysis (using a technique called logistic regression) is sometimes used to infer cause and effect: if the outcome, in this case vote, is shown to be closely predicted by the various attitudes that are analysed, it is assumed that these attitudes are the reason for the outcome. Of course, that is always a simplification and unless there are very strong reasons to support that theory of cause and effect, it cannot be justified purely by the statistical pattern. Just because the people who think well of party in some respect are more likely to vote for that party than those who do not, that doesn't prove that this is their reason for voting that way. In this case, we find out that people who have a favourable view of a party's policies are much more likely to vote for it than those who have an unfavourable one. But, also, people who have a favourable view of a party's leader are much more likely to vote for it; and so are people who have a favourable view of the party itself. Are all these views independent of each other? For example, are we sure that approving of a party's policies doesn't make people more favourable towards the leader, or vice-versa? Because if they are not independent, that will confuse the analysis: we can't tell which is cause and which is effect. And perhaps none of them is the real cause: if everybody always voted the same way their grandparents did, and automatically took a positive view of everything their party said and did, we would still find this correspondence between people's favourable views of the parties, leaders and policies and their voting behaviour. We might still be able to accurately predict somebody's vote from what they think about the leaders, say, even if neither attitude is the cause of the other.

146

In fact, all of these possibilities can in theory be allowed for by using much more complex analytical techniques. However, the outcome is difficult to explain to the layman and often inconclusive in any case. Those complications we will leave to the political scientists and content ourselves with the much less ambitious task of finding which attitudes are good predictors of vote, without worrying too much precisely how that comes to be the case.

Let us begin simply by considering what attitudes distinguish Conservative from Labour voters. Here we look at the 465 participants in our poll who said they were certain to vote and that they intended to vote for one or other of the two major parties. Let us begin by looking at the key issues. We took the top four of the public's list of priorities – healthcare, managing the economy, education and immigration. In each case, the voters' answers on which party they thought had the best policy were grouped into three categories, those who said that Labour was best, those who favoured the Conservatives, and everybody else (whether they picked a different party, thought no party was best or said they didn't know). And from this not very complex array of answers, just three possibilities on each of four questions, we asked the computer to find a formula that would predict whether each voter was Conservative or Labour. It did so, with startling success.

It turns out that attitudes on all four issues are helpful in predicting vote, though some more than others. Most powerful overall is the economic issue, and if all we knew about the voters was which party they thought had the best economic policies, the computer could guess correctly whether they were Conservative or Labour voters in 90% of cases. Each of the other issues adds a little further information, and using all four allows 93.9% of our voters to be correctly classified.[95]

There are no great surprises in the details of the formula: voters are much more likely to be Labour voters if they think Labour is best on healthcare

---

[95] There are various ways of testing the strength of a statistical relationship – this one, relying on the classification table, is the simplest to explain and simplest for those untrained in statistical analysis to understand, and therefore we adopt it here. In technical terms, we have run a binary logistic regression and then assigned each individual to the party for which the model predicts he or she is most likely to vote. Those better versed in these complexities would probably prefer to know that the value of Nagelkerke's pseudo-R^2 is 0.723 using only the single predictor, and 0.898 using all four; the Cox & Snell values are 0.542 and 0.674 respectively.

than if they favour neither party on that issue, and almost as strongly likely to be Conservatives if they think the Conservatives are best on that issue. Similarly on education, both parties seem to gain a benefit from being seen as best. On the economy, however, while thinking the Conservatives have the best policy is a good positive predictor of Conservative voting, there is not much difference between those who think Labour is best and those who favour neither party. (The distinction that we noted when looking only at attitudes to economic issues melts away once we bring in the other three issues – those who think Labour is best are still likely to be Labour voters but they are also likely to prefer Labour on the other issues and these turn out to be even better discriminators between Labour and non-Labour voters. This is the advantage of a multivariate analysis: we are looking at all the different factors at once, seeing what difference each makes if everything else stays constant.) Finally, policy on immigration matters, but only if voters think Labour's policies are best: these voters are much more likely to vote Labour, but there is no significant difference between people who think the Conservatives have the best policy and those who choose neither party.

Table 26: Best party on key issues as a predictor of voting intention

	B	S.E.	Signif-icance	Odds ratio
Best party on NHS (Ref. category = Other/none/DK)				
Labour	1.96	0.55	***	7.1
Conservative	-1.85	0.84	*	1 / 6.4
Best party on economy (Ref. category = Other/none/DK)				
Labour	0.48	0.89		1.6
Conservative	-2.50	0.67	***	1 / 12.2
Best party on education (Ref. category = Other/none/DK)				
Labour	1.38	0.59	*	4.0
Conservative	-2.77	0.83	**	1 / 16.1
Best party on immigration (Ref. category = Other/none/DK)				
Labour	2.11	0.79	**	8.2
Conservative	-0.35	0.66		1 / 1.4
Constant	0.62	0.54		

Base: 465 British adults 18+, certain to vote and intending to vote Conservative or Labour, 12-15 April 2015
Source: Ipsos MORI Political Monitor
Binary logistic regression of Labour v Conservative voting (positive coefficients indicate Labour vote). ***=significant at 99.9%; **=significant at 99%; *=significant at 95%.

The results of this analysis are shown in Table 26. The full nuts-and-bolts of the analysis are probably of interest to the statistically-initiated, so we include them here, but the meat of the analysis is in the right hand column, the 'odds ratios'. These tell us what we know if we compare two voters *who have answered all the other questions identically* but differ in their answers to one question – how does that affect the odds that they are Labour rather than Conservative voters. For example, in the first line we see an odds ratio of 7. This tells us the odds on voting Labour were 7 times as high for those who said that Labour had the best policies on healthcare as for those who did not choose either of the major parties (the 'reference category'). For those who chose the Conservatives instead, the odds *against* voting Labour were 6.4 times as high as those for the reference category, or, expressing it more straightforwardly, that the odds on their voting Conservative were 6.4 times as high.

It can be seen from this in fact that the single most powerful predictor in this analysis is that those who thought the Conservatives had the best education policy were likely to vote Conservative. (The two cases where the odds ratio is printed in italics indicate that the figures are not statistically significant – in other words the relationship that we found, taking into the account the sample size, was so weak that it might have arisen by chance.)

So, it's pretty clear that there is a strong relationship between thinking that one of the two major parties has the best policies on the big issues of the election and intending to vote for that party. However, we mustn't jump to the conclusion that people vote rationally on the basis that support for those policies causes people to support the party; it is not inconceivable that the opposite is the case. In other words, people vote irrationally (or emotionally, or on the basis of their values) and support a party and *then* decide to like its policies.

We can take this analysis a little further. In the traditional picture of votes being driven by support for the parties' policies, the perceived importance of the issues plays an important role: we would expect voters to give greater weight to their party preferences on issues that they think are important than on issues that they don't care about. If that is the case, then we ought to be able to improve the predictive power of our formula by adding in information about which issues each voter says are important to his or her vote. (In technical language, we add interaction terms to the model.) But it turns out that this does not work: taking into account each participant's issue importance responses does not significantly improve the predictive power.

This suggests that the correspondence between support for a party's policies on the key issues and voting intention does not arise simply from policy preferences driving vote, unless the voters are completely unable to distinguish between issues that are important to them and those that are not, which seems unlikely. This does not necessarily mean that vote is not derived from policy preferences, only that the relationship is not all one way. Suppose a voter cares passionately about the NHS and regards the other three issues as being of minor importance. Maybe she compares the parties' healthcare policies, decides on that basis which party she is going to vote for, and – now knowing which side she is on – therefore comes to take a positive view of her party's proposals on the other issues about which she does not feel strongly or know very much. That would produce exactly the pattern we find here. But, so too would a situation where none of the issues really matter and the voters are picking their parties entirely on the basis of what they think of the leaders.

What we can say, however, is the correspondence between expressed party preferences on the issues and voting intention is an extraordinarily strong one. There are very few voters with dissenting or conflicted views among supporters of either of the two major parties. Any campaigner hoping to influence the election by swaying voters from one major party to the other has almost nothing to work with – there is simply no leverage.

But this conclusion does not apply only to the election issues: we find exactly the same when we look at the image of the leaders and at the image of the parties. Suppose we try the same exercise using our leader image questions: here we use as potential predictors each voter's yes-no answers on whether 9 descriptions fit David Cameron and whether the same 9 fit Ed Miliband, 18 answers in all for each voter. We find – again restricting ourselves to those who are intending either to vote Conservative or to vote Labour – that this is sufficient for us to correctly predict how 94.8% of our sample intend to vote.[96] In fact it turns out that we don't even need all 18 questions – once we have used the most informative 11 of them, the

---

[96] The Nagelkerke pseudo-R^2 for the model is 0.884 and the Cox & Snell pseudo-R^2 is 0.663.

other 7 do not tell us anything further. The single most useful answer for predicting vote turns out to be whether the voter thinks that David Cameron "understands the problems facing Britain" – simply assuming that those who think he does will vote Conservative and those who do not will vote Labour gets the answer right 83% of the time. But adding another five answers about Mr Cameron and five about Mr Miliband makes the formula work much better. The results are shown in Table 27.

Table 27: Perceived leader attributes as a predictor of voting intention

	B	S.E.	Signif-icance	Odds ratio
Descriptions fitting David Cameron:				
Capable leader	-3.18	0.93	**	1 / 23.8
Good in a crisis	-1.85	0.66	**	1 / 6.3
Understands the problems facing Britain	-1.74	0.56	**	1 / 5.7
Out of touch	1.77	0.58	**	5.9
More style than substance	1.60	0.58	**	5.0
Looks after some sections of society more than others	1.51	0.73	*	4.5
Descriptions fitting Ed Miliband:				
Sound judgment	2.27	0.58	***	9.6
Understands the problems facing Britain	2.08	0.73	**	8.0
Has a clear vision for Britain	1.22	0.60	*	3.4
Out of touch	-1.81	0.61	**	1 / 6.1
Looks after some sections of society more than others	-2.00	0.53	***	1 / 7.4
Constant	0.61	0.60		

Base: 465 British adults 18+, certain to vote and intending to vote Conservative or Labour, 12-15 April 2015
Source: Ipsos MORI Political Monitor
Binary logistic regression of Labour v Conservative voting (positive coefficients indicate Labour vote). ***=significant at 99.9%; **=significant at 99%; *=significant at 95%.

Perhaps the most interesting finding from this analysis is that the descriptions of David Cameron that are closely related to voting are not always the same ones as the descriptions of Ed Miliband that are relevant. For example, it seems to matter a great deal whether voters think David Cameron is a capable leader and is good in a crisis or not, while knowing whether the same voter thinks Ed Miliband has those abilities does not help us predict their voting at all. It is important to understand that this is not simply about the difference between the parties, or about the positive effect of viewing somebody as a competent leader – because all the factors are simple either-or choices, the Cameron factor is just as much a measure of how far thinking that he is incompetent is reflected in a Labour vote as it is of the link between judging him competent and voting Conservative.

And by the same token, answers to these two questions about Mr Miliband would measure the link between judging him incompetent and voting Conservative as well as between judging him competent and voting Labour. Yet neither is aligned with voting intention to a statistically significant degree once the other factors have been taken into account.

This difference on competence, a significant predictor in Cameron's case but not in Miliband's, is one feature worth noting. Conversely, believing that Ed Miliband has "sound judgment" and a "clear vision for Britain" is significant, while the same attributes have no impact for David Cameron; and it also proves useful to know whether the accusation that David Cameron has "more style than substance" sticks, whereas the corresponding question about Ed Miliband gets no traction. For both leaders, however, the question of whether they are out of touch, understand the problems facing Britain and look after some sections of society more than others do seem to be related to voting behaviour.

In fact, it is not a surprise to us that different attributes seem relevant for different leaders. At the 2010 election we found very much the same thing, with different factors proving relevant to the voters' overall judgments of Gordon Brown, David Cameron and Nick Clegg.[97] In the past, some over-simplistic models of voting behaviour have assumed that these factors are symmetrical, and that any given positive impression will be equally beneficial for any leader with whom the voters associate it; but in fact it seems much likelier that voters judge different leaders by different criteria. This has important implications for political campaigning: a party's strategists must know which impressions of their leader will be helpful and which will not, and plan accordingly; and, similarly, if they intend to attack their opponent it needs to be on the ground that matters to him, not simply on the same issues where their own leader gains or loses. Perhaps the only caveat here comes when a party considers campaigning against its competitors using negative messages. It's worth in this unique case remembering the old adage that "people in glass houses should not throw stones"; by which we mean that the parties should be careful when positioning their competitors on negative issues (e.g. as having a weak

---

[97] See our paper: Roger Mortimore, Paul Baines, Ian Crawford, Robert Worcester, and Andrew Zelin, 'Asymmetry in Leader Image Effects and the Implications for Leadership Positioning in the 2010 British General Election', *International Journal of Market Research* 56 (2014): 185–205.

leader or being lax on prison policy) that they do not suffer the same problem – because if they do this is likely to be picked up as hypocritical by the news and, particularly, the online and print media.

Once again, it is important to emphasise that we can't assume that the link between impressions of the leader and voting intentions come about because leader image drives voting. It may work in the opposite direction. As we have seen, we can predict voting intentions just as successfully on the basis of attitudes to the key policy issues, without knowing what the voters think about the leaders at all. If there is a causal connection, then taking this analysis in conjunction with the perceptual map of leader image which we saw earlier (Figure 15 on p. 130) tells us some interesting things about the tactical position at the start of the campaign.

The two competence issues, which are significant predictors in Cameron's case but not Miliband's, are also perceptions on which Cameron has a strong advantage: this suggests that the belief in Cameron's competence may be an important factor in keeping people voting Conservative but, despite its prominence as a theme in the Conservative campaign, a perception of Miliband's incompetence would not be effective in deterring people from voting Labour. (But this would not necessarily invalidate the campaign since, as we shall see, the most sensible focus for the Conservative campaign was not on those people intending to vote either Conservative or Labour, the group studied in this analysis, but on those intending to do neither.)

Of the other one-way issues, no leader had much advantage on having a "clear vision", and Nigel Farage rather than either David Cameron or Ed Miliband was the one most strongly seen as having more style than substance. On having sound judgment, however, Ed Miliband had a distinct advantage in the public's perceptions. This therefore had the potential to be more a positive than a negative factor for Ed Miliband – again, assuming that these perceptions drive party loyalties rather than merely reflecting them. Perhaps even more so, however, are two issues that are relevant to both leaders, the related issues of understanding the problems facing Britain and being out of touch. Ed Miliband started the election with a meaningful lead on both of these, and equally able to exploit it by promoting his own credentials or attacking David Cameron's.

Finally, of course, we repeat the same type of analysis for the party image questions. Here we have ten descriptions of each party to play with but, to avoid any risk of blurring the boundaries, we won't include "Has a good team of leaders". It turns out that we don't need to, however: we need only to use 9 of the remaining 18 to achieve an even more powerful prediction than came from either the issues or leader image analyses. The single best predictor, whether the Conservative Party "looks after the interests of people like me", successfully predicts 86% of the voting intentions on its own, and the full array of 9 factors gets the score up to 97.7%.[98]

Table 28: Perceived party attributes as a predictor of voting intention

	B	S.E.	Signif-icance	Odds ratio
Descriptions fitting the Conservative Party:				
Understands the problems facing Britain	-2.36	0.83	**	1 / 10.6
Will promise anything to win votes	3.63	0.79	***	37.5
Looks after the interests of people like me	-3.11	0.75	***	1 / 22.2
Fit to govern	-3.13	1.05	**	1 / 22.7
Divided	-1.60	0.67	*	1 / 4.9
Descriptions fitting the Labour Party:				
Understands the problems facing Britain	2.77	1.11	*	15.9
Will promise anything to win votes	-3.20	0.76	***	1 / 24.4
Looks after the interests of people like me	2.16	0.82	**	8.7
Fit to govern	2.49	0.90	**	12.0
Constant	0.74	0.60		

Base: 465 British adults 18+, certain to vote and intending to vote Conservative or Labour, 12-15 April 2015
Source: Ipsos MORI Political Monitor
Binary logistic regression of Labour v Conservative voting (positive coefficients indicate Labour vote). ***=significant at 99.9%; **=significant at 99%; *=significant at 95%.

There is one apparently odd finding here, that Conservative voters are considerably more likely than Labour voters to describe the Conservatives as "divided", once everything else is taken into account. In fact this was the last of the nine factors that the computer added. Without knowing whether the voters thought that the Conservatives were divided we could predict the voting intentions of 96.4% correctly; including this extra piece of information gives the correct classification to another 1.3%. Perhaps on

---

[98] The Nagelkerke pseudo-R^2 is 0.929 and the Cox & Snell pseudo-R^2 is 0.697.

reflection it is not entirely inexplicable: Labour voters may prefer to see the Conservatives as one amorphous mass, all of whom they dislike, while Conservatives may be more alive to the real differences between the two wings of the party, perhaps accentuated by the need to simultaneously appeal to moderate floating voters in the centre and those on the verge of defecting to UKIP on the right. It may be one more strand of evidence that the gulf between the two parties was deeper in 2015 than at most other elections in the recent past. At any rate, it seems fairly safe to assume that considering the Conservative Party to be divided was not a positive reason for voting for it to any meaningful number of voters, even if the description seemed truer to Conservatives than to their opponents.

Let us now pause and take stock. We have found that preference between the parties in their policies on a small number of key issues is a very strong predictor of whether a person intended to vote Conservative or Labour. So too is whether they accept as valid each of about a dozen descriptions of either David Cameron or Ed Miliband. So too is whether they think a number of descriptions of the parties do or do not apply. Remember that each of these three predictive 'models' works independently, without us knowing anything of how each voter answered the other two sets of questions, and each prediction is right roughly 19 times out of 20.

In other words, any one of the three factors – preferred policies, impressions of the leaders or impressions of the parties – might be almost the sole cause of voting intention, with the other two correlations just consequent effects. For example, it might be that voting intention depended entirely on policies, and that once voters had picked a party on this basis it entirely dictated their views of the parties as a whole and of the leaders. Or leaders, or party image, might have been the sole driving factor. There is no reason to suppose that all three were working together and all were essential to the outcome.

So which was foremost? It is possible in theory to do further statistical analysis, detecting which effects are the strongest and purest, and assuming that the remainder are incidental. This is the key point for understanding the election, if we can solve it. Is there some 'prime mover', one factor from which all else flows? If so, this is where the election was really decided and the point on which the parties, if they are clever enough, should concentrate their effort. But the survey evidence is almost certainly not strong enough to tell us. When so many of the effects seem to be aligned with each other (the technical term is 'collinear'), such analysis is fraught with uncertainty. There is no guarantee that the strongest numerical relationship is the root causal one. Once we recognise that voting intention may be the cause rather than the effect in some of these relationships, the simple statistical analyses can no longer help us. Regressions cannot tell us in which direction a causal relationship works.

Sometimes, however, while conclusive statistical proof is lacking, the circumstantial evidence may nevertheless be quite compelling. In the case of the link between voting intentions and economic confidence, both of which we have measured at monthly intervals for many years, we believe there is a strong case for suspecting that party loyalties are a stronger cause of economic perceptions than *vice versa*. Of course, at the level of the individual voter, either interpretation is a simplification: no doubt some people vote on the basis of their economic views while others form their economic views in response to the cues that follow from their political loyalties; surveys can detect only the net effects. But there seems to be a case for supposing that here the influence from party to economy has outweighed the influence from economy to party, and the relationship between voting intentions and economic optimism is mainly explained by the former, not the latter.

This view is slightly heretical. Political scientists and practical political campaigners alike have tended to assume that in this relationship it is the economic perceptions that are generally the cause and the voting behaviour the effect – and, consequently, that a government that is economically competent in the eyes of the voters can expect to re-elected or at least (when other issues dominate the political scene) to draw votes for their competence.

In a paper we presented at a conference in 2014[99], we considered polling data on economic perceptions and voting intentions in Britain over a long period, 1996-2014. Beginning in 1996 has the advantage of allowing us to look at both major parties in government and to examine opinions before and after two elections at which the incumbent government was ejected.

---

[99] Robert M. Worcester, Roger Mortimore, and Mark Gill, 'The Disappearance of the "Pocket-Book Voter"? The Relationship between Economic Confidence and Party Support in Modern Britain' (presented at the WAPOR 67th Annual Conference, Nice, 2014).

We looked at the statistical relationship at the level of the individual voter between answers to the two questions.

The first thing that we found, fairly consistently over the whole period, was that supporters of the government party were more likely than average to be optimistic about the country's economic prospects and less likely to be pessimistic: when the Conservatives were in government, it was those who were intending to vote Conservative who had the highest net optimism, when Labour was in power it was those who intended to vote Labour that did. So far, no surprises. That would be the case whether it was because having a government of the party they supported gave them more confidence in the policies and competence of the relevant ministers and therefore that the economy would do well, or whether it was because having looked at the economic indicators and their own sense of wellbeing they had decided that the economy was doing well and therefore gave credit to the party in office and were motivated to vote for it as a result.

But what happens when the government changes? If, as in 2010, Labour was in power before the election and its voters were most optimistic, but after the election it was Conservatives who were more bullish as David Cameron was in Number Ten, there must have been some sort of a transition period. However, we would expect the pattern during the transition to be different depending on which opinions were causes and which were effects.

Suppose that the link with voting intention is entirely caused by economic optimists deciding to vote for the government (and pessimists against it) because they give the party in power credit or blame for the state of the economy. In that case, we would expect the transition to be gradual and to last some time. When the government changes, the effect of the previous government's policies continues to affect the economy for some time, and in the early period of a new government responsibility for the state of the economy will therefore be taken to rest with its predecessor, although the longer the new government remains in office the more responsibility will be accorded to it. We should therefore expect to find that (a) immediately after a change of government, those dissatisfied with the state of the economy will support the government (the former opposition) and vice versa; and (b) as voters increasingly consider that the new government must now be considered responsible for the state of the economy, optimists will align more with the government and pessimists against it, so that eventually the normal situation of optimism predicting support for the government is reached once more.

But if it works the other way about, and the link is because voters feel optimistic if there is a government they trust and pessimistic if there is not, then the switch ought to take place immediately; and if the election result was a long-expected one, you might even see the switch beginning to take place before the election, as supporters of the government become increasingly despondent because they expect a party they don't trust to be in charge of the piggybank in the very near future, while supporters of the opposition anticipate their side getting their hands on the levers of power.

Our data showed the latter pattern – the switch was abrupt and immediately after the election, both in 1997 and 2010. In 1997, there was a significant positive relationship between Conservative vote and economic optimism in every monthly poll before the election, a significant negative one in every poll afterwards. In 2010, there was a significant positive relationship with Labour vote every month up to the election, and a weaker negative one in every month afterwards[100]. Similarly, Labour voters were immediately positive after the 1997 election and Conservatives after the 2010 election, although in each case there was a weaker 'jumping the gun' positive relationship before the election as well.

Of course, nobody supposes that the relationship is entirely one way. For some voters, economic perceptions will drive voting intentions, for others voting intentions will drive economic perceptions. Indeed, both forces probably even affect the individual voter – once a new attitude has been adopted it may then help to reinforce existing attitudes, including the ones that caused it in the first place. But our investigation seems to suggest that, in all probability, more of the flow is from voting intention to economic perceptions than vice-versa. And that suggests, in turn, that winning votes by successful economic performance may be harder than has sometimes been supposed, and that satisfaction with the government's handling of the economy between 2010 and 2015 was not – despite appearances – the root cause of the Conservative victory. On the other hand, if what is in question is the reinforcement of existing party loyalties by successfully

---

[100] Although it was some months before the relationship became strong enough to be consistently statistically significant.

delivering the economic benefits that the government's supporters already expected, the pay-off may be more worthwhile.

But in any case there may not be a single simple answer. We cannot make the assumption that the same forces apply to all voters when the obvious probability is that they do not. Almost certainly, the overall figures arise from a combination of voters for whom policies are most powerful, others who are driven by what they think of the leaders, and still others who are shifted by party image. (And, for that matter, there may well be some other underlying or contributing factor that we have not even measured.) Whatever the structure of cause and effect, the extent to which most people's opinions were aligned so that every prompt pointed them in the same direction would seem to make the task of swaying their votes a difficult one. Agenda setting – placing emphasis on certain issues in the media – has no power if the voter will vote the same way whatever the agenda; 'priming' – changing the criteria by which the voter judges the leaders – makes no difference if the same leader will be preferred whatever criteria are used; and 'framing' also makes no difference if the voter does not listen to the argument on why a particular candidate is better on a particular issue.[101]

However, we do not need to delve so deep. Such matters are of interest to the political scientists, but contribute little to our less ambitious investigation here. For us, the key point that emerges is that all the different factors that we have in the past viewed as separate determinants of voting intention were, in 2015, marching in step together. So there were no obvious chinks in each voter's armour. The Conservatives had no leverage to pry away Labour voters, and Labour could do little to dislodge Conservatives.

Nevertheless, there were still a lot of last minute waverers in the 2015 election, although fewer than in 2005 or 2010: in our final eve-of-poll survey, conducted on the final day of campaigning, we found that one in five (21%) of those who told us which party they were intending to vote for had not yet "definitely decided" (Table 29); but 27% told us the same

---

[101] For more on framing, priming and agenda setting, and a discussion of theories of how each can sway public opinion, see Dietram A. Scheufele and David Tewksbury, 'Framing, Agenda Setting, and Priming: The Evolution of Three Media Effects Models', *Journal of Communication* 57 (2007): 9–20.

in 2005 and 30% in 2010. The two major parties had equal, and large, proportions of undecided supporters: 19% of those intending to vote Conservative and 19% of those intending to vote Labour said that there was still a chance that they might change their mind. But in most cases it was not the other major party to which they were considering defecting: when we asked them which party they might vote for instead if they did change their mind, only a handful were considering switching across the divide between the two main parties: in total, 5% of Conservatives thought they might switch to Labour and 3% of Labour supporters thought they might switch to Conservative.

Table 29: Last minute waverers, 2015

Q Have you definitely decided to vote for (party) or is there a chance you may change your mind...?
Q If you do change your mind about voting for this party, which party would you vote for instead?

	All	Conser- vative	Labour	Liberal Demo- crat	UKIP
	%	%	%	%	%
Definitely decided, and certain to vote*	69	69	72	68	62
Definitely decided, but not certain to vote	9	10	8	11	5
Might change and vote Conservative	3	n/a	3	5	11
Might change and vote Labour	4	5	n/a	9	8
Might change and vote Liberal Democrat	4	5	3	n/a	1
Might change and vote UKIP	3	4	3	1	n/a
Might change and vote Green	2	0	5	3	1
Might change, don't know how	5	5	5	4	11
Don't know whether definitely decided	1	2	0	0	0

Base: 928 British adults 18+ and declaring a voting intention, 5-6 May 2015
*Those having already voted by post were included as "definitely decided and certain to vote"
Source: Ipsos MORI Political Monitor

The campaign still had the potential to affect the result, but directly switching votes between the two governing alternatives was probably the least significant part of it. Affecting support and turnout within the right-of-centre and left-of-centre camps would have been easier; and, as we have seen, in 2015 that could still matter a lot.

The campaign

Overview

It is common among political scientists to assume that campaigns make little impact on voters' intentions but evidence from the Ipsos MORI Political Monitor survey conducted on 5-6 May suggests that fully three in ten voters had yet to decide which party to vote for, or indeed whether or not to vote at all (see Table 29). In 2015, no party had a hold on the loyalties of floating voters nationally and, so, the local election campaign was the principal battleground.

In previous elections, there has sometimes been considerable volatility in the campaign voting intention measured in the polls as loyalties have been eroded over the parliamentary cycle. In 2015, the polls were very consistent in showing Labour and the Conservatives as being neck-and-neck. In the final analysis, this turned out not to be the case, but the expectation that a hung parliament might be on the cards led to the most intense negative campaigning that the British electorate has seen since the 'demon eyes' campaign of the Tories against Tony Blair in 1997, as the Tories sought to portray Labour as beholden to the SNP to gain power, the Lib Dems encouraged voters to 'look left, look right, then cross', and Labour sought to damage public perceptions of the Tories' competence on health by 'weaponising' the NHS. This was an election where fear and negative campaigning pervaded[102].

This election was therefore one where the campaigns didn't meet in the middle. In the case of the two main parties, Conservatives and Labour, each side sought to shore up its core vote, maximise its vote share and turnout through a focus on existing voters on its own side of the austerity/spending issue divide. Consequently, there was little serious competition between the two sides for the same voters, i.e. there was therefore no real middle-ground of voters to speak of.

---

[102] Robert Shrimsley, 'General Election: Where Fear and Negative Campaigning Pervaded', *Financial Times*, 6 May 2015, http://www.ft.com/cms/s/2/a944ddf6-f3cc-11e4-99de-00144feab7de.html#axzz3c0FhGZb8, accessed 3 June 2015.

The course of events

Before we launch into considering how the parties designed and implemented their campaigns, it's worth reminding ourselves of the key events in the 2015 election (see Table 30). The year 2015 was the first time that the election was called based on a pre-set date under the Fixed-Term Parliaments Act 2011 introduced by the Coalition Government. Previously, the incumbent government faced an in-built advantage by having the choice of when to call the election. The election calendar was dominated this time around both by the different debates that were held with different party leaders and by the negotiations surrounding whether or not they would take place at all, as the Conservatives in particular sought to turn David Cameron's appearance, or rather non-appearance, at them to their advantage, even vetoing the appearance of the Lib Dem leader at the BBC debate on 16 April[103].

Other notable events included the relatively-late release of the party manifestos, which tend now to be combed over only by journalists, politics academics, and the seriously committed politico rather than the general public.

This election also contained few serious gaffes, as party leaders worked hard to avoid a 'Gillian Duffy moment' (when Gordon Brown had suffered in 2010 after referring to a Rochdale voter on the campaign trail as "that bigoted woman" to a hailstorm of media criticism afterwards). Perhaps the only moment of hilarity was when Labour unveiled its election pledges on an 8-foot lump of limestone, immediately described as likely to become his tombstone in social and news media afterwards, and – harking back to a previous Labour election disaster – dubbed the "heaviest suicide note in history"[104]. Worse, Miliband's vice-chairman, Lucy Powell, suggested on Radio 5Live that Miliband might not necessarily honour the

[103] Toby Helm, 'David Cameron "Blocked Nick Clegg from TV Debate"', *The Observer*, 21 March 2015, http://www.theguardian.com/politics/2015/mar/21/cameron-blocked-clegg-tv-debate-general-election, accessed 27 October 2015.

[104] Adam Withnall, 'Ed Miliband Unveils Stone Carved With Labour Pledges to Be Placed at Downing St If He Wins', *The Independent*, 3 May 2015, http://www.independent.co.uk/news/uk/politics/generalelection/ed-miliband-unveils-stone-carved-with-labour-pledges-to-be-placed-at-downing-st-if-he-wins-10221946.html, accessed 27 October 2015.

pledges (i.e. even though they were literally set in stone, they were 'not set in stone'!), a statement she was later forced to retract[105].

Table 30: Election campaign timeline, 30 March–8 May 2015

Date	Event
30 March	Dissolution of Parliament
31 March	Plaid Cymru launches its manifesto.
1 April	Letter to the *Telegraph* from more than 100 senior business figures warns that a Labour government would threaten jobs and investment.
2 April	ITV election debate, with 7 leaders, in Salford, moderated by Julie Etchingham.
4 April	Leak of a confidential Civil Service memo claiming Nicola Sturgeon had told the French ambassador she would prefer Cameron to win the election. Sturgeon and the ambassador both deny that the comment was made. (The leak was later traced to Alistair Carmichael, the Liberal Democrat who was Secretary of State for Scotland.)
7 April	Leaders of the four main parties in Scotland hold debate on STV.
9 April	Close of nominations
13 April	Labour publishes its manifesto.
14 April	Conservative manifesto launched.
15 April	Liberal Democrats launch their manifesto, including on Instagram.
16 April	BBC hosts debate between 5 opposition leaders, excluding David Cameron and Nick Clegg.
20 April	SNP launch their manifesto; last day on which it was possible to register to vote.
22 April	TV Cymru Wales launches debate featuring five main Welsh party leaders.
26 April	Ed Miliband rules out Labour making a 'confidence and supply' deal with the SNP in the event of a hung parliament
29 April	Comedian Russell Brand releases interview with Ed Miliband on his own YouTube channel.
30 April	David Cameron, Ed Miliband and Nick Clegg appear, separately, on BBC's *Question Time*. Miliband fails to impress after stage stumble.
3 May	Ed Miliband unveils eight-foot limestone monument containing six election pledges; in a radio discussion, Labour's campaign vice-chairman, Lucy Powell, suggests Labour might still break these pledges.
4 May	Bank Holiday
5 May	BBC Northern Ireland launches leaders' debate.
7 May	Election Day. The exit poll is released at 10pm, indicating the Tories to win with 316 seats. Alastair Campbell and Paddy Ashdown declare they will eat their kilt and hat respectively if the results are right, as they later prove to be.
8 May	Election results declared. David Cameron forms first Conservative government for 23 years, Ed Miliband, Nick Clegg, and Nigel Farage all resign their party leaderships (although Farage later withdraws his resignation).

---

[105] Matt Dathan, 'Did Labour's Campaign Chief Just Suggest Ed Miliband Could Break His Election Tombstone Pledges?', *The Independent*, 5 May 2015, http://www.independent.co.uk/news/uk/politics/generalelection/general-election-2015-did-labour-s-campaign-chief-just-suggest-ed-miliband-could-break-his-election-10226399.html, accessed 27 October 2015.

By the time of the exit poll, it had become clear that Labour had not secured a victory in the election, that the SNP had done even better than expected, that the Lib Dems were in meltdown and that the Conservatives had done considerably better than expected. Next, we turn to how effective the various parties' campaigns were.

Campaign effectiveness

Many political consultants would adopt the short-term view and argue that what matters most is not how they run their campaigns (e.g. whether or not negative campaigning was used), but whether or not their campaigns were effective in winning votes and seats as a consequence. However, for many voters, it also matters how the parties run their campaigns, the implication being that if they can run a good campaign, they might just be able to run the country well also.

When the voters were asked towards the end of the campaign which party had run the most effective campaign, a significant number of all the other parties' supporters, except UKIP's, picked the SNP's campaign as the most effective, probably evidence that this was indeed the case (see Table 31). Few Conservatives and few Labour supporters rated their main opponent's campaign: probably more evidence, if any were needed, that in neither case had that campaign been targeted at them or people like them.

Table 31: Campaign effectiveness

Q Which party, if any, do you think has the most effective election campaign so far?

| | All | Voting intention | | | | |
		Con	Lab	Lib Dem	UKIP	None
	%	%	%	%	%	%
Conservatives	17	33	8	12	11	21
Labour	15	8	38	11	4	4
Liberal Democrats	3	2	2	10	1	2
UKIP	13	12	7	10	60	5
Scottish National Party	25	22	27	30	7	14
Greens	4	*	5	2	1	3
Other	1	*	*	1	3	2
None	12	13	7	19	8	20
Don't know	10	9	6	4	5	30

Base: 1,010 British adults 18+, 26-29 April 2015
Source: Ipsos MORI Political Monitor

Tellingly, UKIP's campaign did better among Conservatives than among Labour supporters while that of the Greens was better viewed by Labour than Conservative. In each case, the evidence seems to be clear that most people were likely to see the most effective campaign as one with which they were ideologically in tune, and perhaps one putting across a message they, at least partially agreed with. This was even more dramatically illustrated by UKIP supporters, three-fifths of whom thought their own party's campaign had been best (a view shared by not very many who were not UKIP supporters, and a much stronger endorsement than any other party's adherents gave their own campaign).

For a less partial view, though, we are better advised to take the opinions of those who did not admit to supporting any party. Half of these had no opinion or thought no party's campaign had been effective. This is not surprising given this group consists of those with little interest in politics, which is why they have no voting intention in the first place. The remainder were split between thinking that the Conservatives' and the SNP's campaigns were most effective, with the other parties gaining only trickles of support.

That is a verdict we would endorse. After all, the SNP wiped out Labour in Scotland (which was the only place in which they fielded candidates), and with 4.7% of the total vote share (up 3.1% on 2010) won 56 of the 59 seats in Scotland. It didn't achieve the balance of power at Westminster, but this was always going to be outside the SNP's control since this result largely depended on what happened in England. The Conservatives can also claim to have won the election campaign because they gained a 12-seat majority in the House of Commons and formed the government, but their campaign performance was arguably less impressive (increasing their vote share by only 0.8% – although perhaps, given how rarely parties already in government increase their vote, that would be an unrealistically harsh verdict). Above all, both the Conservatives and the SNP seem to have succeeded in getting across their message to the voters at which it was aimed, making the most of the opportunities with which they came into the election.

One might also argue that UKIP's campaign was much more effective than it was given credit for, since it did manage to win the third largest share of the vote at 12.6% (up 9.5% since 2010), overtaking the Liberal Democrats, even though in the UK's first-past-the-post voting system this did not translate into parliamentary seats. They too ran a campaign that seems to have been well received by its target audience, even if – predictably – it was also especially execrated by its opponents. Despite the powerful efforts of the Conservatives and Labour to squeeze the minor party vote in the marginals, and to convince the waverers that a UKIP vote was a dangerously wasted vote, UKIP managed to draw a good many voters to them even there. They also probably picked up a good deal of the British National Party (BNP) vote, given that the BNP were only able to field 8 candidates in 2015 compared to 267 in 2010[106].

The Greens could also have claimed to have had a successful election, increasing their vote share to 3.8% (up from 2.8% in 2010), and retaining the parliamentary seat they already held though winning no others. It is less clear how much this owed to election campaign itself, which started badly with Natalie Bennett's 'brain fade' (a car crash interview with Nick Ferrari on LBC, before the formal start of the campaign, when she forgot her own party's housing policy), but proceeded more smoothly thereafter. Their vote share was perhaps slightly disappointing when compared to their poll ratings at the turn of the year; on the other hand, it was an increase on the previous general election, whereas in the 2014 European elections their vote share had marginally slipped.

Plaid Cymru's campaign however, despite increased coverage as a result of their leader Leanne Wood's participation in the TV debates, made little impact on their result and they held the same three seats they had in 2010 with virtually no change in their vote share.

But the election's biggest losers by a long shot, of course, were the hapless Liberal Democrats, who saw their seat tally drop by 49 seats to 8 and their vote share cut by two-thirds. By the time of the election they were mainly pinning their hopes on the possibility that they might save some seats by local resistance to the national tide and the personal vote of their sitting MPs. Success or failure in such a situation does probably not rest strongly on the conduct of the national campaign. But it did fail, the scale of the defeat probably beyond the party's worst fears. The minimal impact of their national campaign (which only one in ten even of their own supporters thought was the most effective) can hardly have helped.

---

[106] See Doug Bolton, 'The BNP Has Almost Vanished from British Politics', *The Independent*, 17 April 2015, http://www.independent.co.uk/news/uk/politics/generalelection/general-election-2015-the-bnp-has-almost-vanished-from-british-politics-10176194.html, accessed 29 October 2015. In our polls we found far fewer admitting in 2015 that they voted BNP in 2010 than can have been the case (the BNP took more than half a million votes in 2010), but those who did were split between intending to vote for UKIP in 2015 and not voting at all.

Positive versus negative campaigning

It could also be argued that the Conservatives managed to win the election campaign, at least partially, because they persuaded the English electorate that a vote for Labour would benefit the SNP and the SNP won the election campaign (in Scotland) because it managed to persuade the Scottish electorate that it was the only effective anti-Tory alternative. Whilst some elections can be characterised in hindsight as based more on hope appeals (e.g. Labour's 1997 campaign by Tony Blair and 'cool Britannia' which drowned out the negative approach of the Tories with their 'demon eyes' campaign), others are more characterised by the parties' appeals to fear.

Any well-designed campaign is therefore based upon an understanding of the target voter: knowing which voters it needs most to persuade and what it wants to persuade them to do. A party chooses its messages based on those that will be best received by the voters and are therefore the most persuasive.

There are some who argue that a political campaign ought to be entirely positive[107], concerning only what is good in a party's own offering and ignoring the other side(s) altogether. One argument goes: why use your own airtime to discuss the opponent? But not comparing against the competition at all is rarely realistic. There is normally a need for a comparative element to extol one's own virtues by reminding the voters of the alternative.

Nevertheless, the wholly negative campaign is rare in British politics. Even if the dangers of electing one's opponents are emphasised, this is generally coupled with some reassurance that one's own stewardship will result in peace and prosperity (or at least as much of these as it is possible to achieve).

---

[107] Theresa May argued for a positive campaign at an event during the election, see Jason Beattie, 'Even Tories Can't Stomach Smear Tactics Used by Party against Labour', *Mirror Online*, 17 April 2015, http://www.mirror.co.uk/news/uk-news/even-tories-cant-stomach-smear-5187623, accessed 29 October 2015. Another critic of the Tories' negative campaign was Lord Ashcroft: see Ian Birrell, 'I Wrote Cameron's Speech in 2010. This Campaign Is Too Narrow and Uninspiring', *The Observer*, 12 April 2015, 25.

Which message should a party lead with; positive or negative, using hope or fear appeals? Fear appeals have generated very memorable political messages in the past[108] (consider the 1979 "Labour isn't working" poster of the Conservatives). The mainly negative campaign is usually considered a risk, however, because it can alienate as many voters as it attracts when not designed properly. Negative campaigning is least effective when the aim is to change people's votes from another party to one's own. The Conservatives are unlikely to persuade many Labour voters to join them by attacking the Labour Party, for example. But for reminding voters of fears they already have, and for reinforcing their opinions rather than changing them, the negative message is excellent. It can therefore be used to depress the vote of the opposition (i.e. stop Labour or Lib Dem voters from voting at all). Nevertheless, there is a risk that it can also evoke negative affect for both the sponsor and the object of the message[109]. Negative campaigning is most evident in the US, where it is used extensively and often in a vitriolic way to smear candidates. Barack Obama was attacked by his opponents in the 2008 US Presidential election, where he was ludicrously depicted as a terrorist sympathiser and fundamentalist Muslim, despite being a committed Christian[110].

In the UK, perhaps the best recent example of an unsuccessful negative campaign was the Conservatives' infamous "New Labour, New Danger" campaign of 1997, featuring Tony Blair and the 'demon eyes', which impressed few (apart from *Campaign* magazine's awards jury, on the basis that it was said to have generated £5m worth of publicity for a spend of £125,000[111]). As a means of convincing disgruntled former Conservatives that they were wrong to be planning to vote Labour, 'demon eyes' was a

---

[108] See Suzy Bashford, 'The Fear Agenda', *Marketing*, April 2015, 40–45.

[109] Sharyne Merritt, 'Negative Political Advertising: Some Empirical Findings', *Journal of Advertising* 13 (1984): 27–38; Richard R. Lau, Lee Sigelman, Caroline Heldman, and Paul Babbitt, 'The Effects of Negative Political Advertisements: A Meta-Analytic Assessment', *American Political Science Review* (1999): 851–875.

[110] For more on the smear campaign, see Frank Rich, 'The Terrorist Barack Hussein Obama', *New York Times*, 11 October 2008, http://www.nytimes.com/2008/10/12/opinion/ 12rich.html? pagewanted=all&_r=2&, accessed 29 October 2015. Obama discusses his Christianity in Sarah Pulliam and Ted Olsen, 'Q&A: Barack Obama', *Christianity Today*, 23 January 2008, http://www.christianitytoday.com/ct/2008/januaryweb-only/104-32.0.html, accessed 29 October 2015.

[111] Andrew Culf, 'Demon Eyes Ad Wins Top Award', *The Guardian*, 10 January 1997, http://www.theguardian.com/politics/1997/jan/10/past.andrewculf, accessed 29 October 2015.

hopeless failure: it tried to convince them of a proposition that they did not find easy to believe, namely that Blair was evil and had evil intentions, and it did so in a very unpersuasive, comedy villain kind of way. By contrast, the earlier "Labour isn't working" poster did its job very effectively, because it reminded voters of what they already thought and fortified their misgivings about voting Labour again by encapsulating them in a simple and memorable image, based around an employment policy that everyone could see was ineffectual.

There are therefore two important implications for those who plan the parties' election campaign appeal, especially those working for a party in government seeking re-election. First, to gain maximum value from voter satisfaction with a government's past performance, it is important to frame it as being a demonstration of competence, so giving a reason to believe that a re-elected government can be expected to succeed in the future (i.e. hope), rather than as merely eliciting gratitude and respect which may not transfer into votes and might look like complacency and hubris.

Secondly, and perhaps more importantly, we should remember that a problem solved may be a problem forgotten. A government that succeeds too well in some field may merely kill its usefulness as an election issue. In the 2010-15 parliament, solving the economic crisis that followed the global financial crash was explicitly the first priority of the Coalition Government, and the Conservatives rested almost all of their hopes of re-election upon convincing enough of the voters that they had succeeded in this aim. They therefore continually banged the drum on their long-term economic plan[112]. But if they succeeded too well, they risked reducing its salience as an election issue and seeing the votes decided on other issues where the opposition was stronger (like the NHS, for example). To ensure that their potential supporters voted for them on economic grounds, they needed to ensure that voters were still worried about the economy. Since they naturally did not wish to weaken their appeal by talking down their own achievements, the natural consequence was that negative campaigning messages would play an important part in the most effective tactics

---

[112] For a negative consideration of the Tories' framing of economic policy, see Larry Elliott, 'Tory Long-Term Economic Plan? Not Even the Propaganda Is Working', *The Guardian*, 19 April 2015, http://www.theguardian.com/business/economics-blog/2015/apr/19/tory-long-term-economic-plan-not-even-the-propaganda-is-working, accessed 29 October 2015.

available to the Conservatives to exploit this most important issue. Rather than raising the importance of the economy in voters' minds by arguing that its state was already precarious, which could have been dangerous because they were part of the Coalition Government that had decided the previous economic policy, they therefore had to argue that it was important to vote Conservative because a Labour government would seriously damage the economic progress which was part-way through the process of solving the crisis which had arisen under the previous Labour government. M&C Saatchi therefore created an advert with the message "A recovering economy ... don't let Labour wreck it", replete with wrecking ball imagery (see Figure 18), and launched it in March in the run up to the campaign proper.

Figure 20: Negative Conservative campaigning over the economy

For the Tories to adopt a negative campaign approach was to some degree at odds with the normal assumptions about in which situations negative campaigning is most effective, those being when the message sponsor focuses on issues where they are strongest (this was the case), or is a challenger party operating against an incumbent party (which was not the case), or are trailing that party being attacked (again not the case), or where they are attacking a party or candidate perceived to be weak on personal attributes (here Miliband was perceived more negatively than positively by voters but less so than Cameron, see Table 24)[113].

However, such a dry academic assessment of when to use negative campaigning fails to consider the tumult of the campaign as parties respond to each other's initiatives with statements and rebuttals. The Conservatives had issued a briefing document to their candidates advocating negative campaigning to suggest that they should focus on highlighting how Miliband was not up to the job of Prime Minister and to point out that he had not ruled out a coalition with the SNP. Michael Fallon, the Defence Minister, led the 'attack Ed' charge pointing out that the public should not vote for a man who had "stabbed his own brother in the back"[114].

Nevertheless, there was a general feeling that the attacks on Ed Miliband's personal competence were not having the effect they were designed to have as the campaign progressed, but insight for a strategy change was said to have come when Tory candidates contacted the Conservative election strategy chief, Lynton Crosby, to explain that voters had expressed concerns about there being a Labour government in power, bolstered by the SNP[115].

Polls confirmed that voters in England were, indeed, unhappy at the prospect of the SNP having influence over the government, although Nigel Farage would have been an even more unwelcome influence. Our poll (Table 32) taken towards the end of the campaign, after the Conservative message had had time to sink in, found that almost half of adults in England, 47%, would be unhappy if Nicola Sturgeon were to have an influence and – perhaps more tellingly – the figure rose to 72%

---

[113] This topic is considered in more detail in an article written by several of the authors: see Roger Mortimore, Paul Baines, Robert Worcester, Clifford Young, and Julia Clark, 'Asymmetric Political Image Effects and the Logic of Negative Campaigning' (presented at the Academy of Marketing Science Conference, Monterey, California, 2013).

[114] Faisal Islam, 'Tory Dossier Urges Attacks On Ed Miliband', *Sky News*, 9 April 2015, http://news.sky.com/story/1461837/tory-dossier-urges-attacks-on-ed-miliband, accessed 29 October 2015.

[115] Tim Shipman, James Lyons, and Marie Woolf, 'The Decision Was Made: Destroy the Lib Dems', *Sunday Times*, 10 May 2015, 20.

among those in England intending to vote Conservative. There is little doubt, therefore, that the message was getting home where it was intended that it should. Around a third of Tories also saw Plaid Cymru's Leanne Wood and the Greens' Natalie Bennett as threats, much on a par with the DUP's Peter Robinson (who, unlike the others, had not appeared in the main televised leaders' debate).

Table 32: Scenarios for a hung parliament

Q As you may know, there has been much discussion about the possibility of another hung parliament after this election. This means that more than one party could have an influence over the government, either because they join a coalition or because a minority government relies on their support.
If there is a hung parliament, and thinking about parties other than the Conservatives and Labour, which of the following parties and their leader, if any, would you be happy to see having influence over the next government? (You may pick more than one.)
And which of the following parties and their leader, if any, would you be unhappy to see having influence over the next government? (Again, you may pick more than one.)

	Unhappy		
	All GB	England	Con voters in England
	%	%	%
The Scottish National Party and their leader Nicola Sturgeon	44	47	72
The UK Independence Party and their leader Nigel Farage	59	58	46
Plaid Cymru and their leader Leanne Wood	21	23	35
The Green Party and their leader Natalie Bennett	22	23	33
The Democratic Unionist Party and their leader Peter Robinson	28	29	29
The Liberal Democrat party and their leader Nick Clegg	21	21	17
Other	2	2	2
None of them	5	5	4
Don't know	5	5	3

Base: 1,010 British adults 18+, 26-29 April 2015
Source: Ipsos MORI Political Monitor

This theme designed to play on the fears of English voters was duly turned into election posters, revealed first by a tweet from the Prime Minister on Facebook on 9 March, showing Miliband in Alex Salmond's (the former SNP leader's) pocket (Figure 21) and Nicola Sturgeon manipulating a Miliband puppet[116] (Figure 1 on page viii). These posters were, in turn,

---

[116] Rosa Prince, 'Election 2015: Nicola Sturgeon Is Ed Miliband's Puppet-Master in New Conservative Campaign Poster', *The Telegraph*, 18 April 2015, http://www.telegraph.co.uk/news/general-election-2015/11547853/Election-2015-Nicola-Sturgeon-is-Ed-Milibands-puppet-master-in-new-Conservative-campaign-poster.html, accessed 19 November 2015.

supported by a cartoon video[117] placed on YouTube on 22 March, showing Miliband dancing to Salmond piping a tune, drawing around a quarter of a million views by the middle of May[118].

Figure 21: Negative Conservative campaigning on the SNP issue

In addition, the theme "Don't let Labour wreck it" was incorporated into their final week party election broadcast, by depicting the economy as a clock in a bell jar, sledge-hammered by Labour were voters to choose them, was the implication. There was, however, a potential danger that such negative campaigning might actually entrench the SNP vote in Scotland[119]. UKIP responded with a spoof poster showing the EU

---

[117] *Alex Salmond: Ready to 'Call the Tune'*, 2015, https://www.youtube.com/watch?v=6JeYlBRvUeE, accessed 29 October 2015.
[118] Matt Walsh, 'There Now Follows a Party Election Broadcast', in Daniel Jackson and Einar Thorsen (eds.), *UK Election Analysis 2015: Media, Voters and the Campaign*, http://www.electionanalysis.uk/uk-election-analysis-2015/political-communication-and-image-management/there-now-follows-a-party-election-broadcast/, accessed 29 October 2015.
[119] John Mullin, 'The SNP Are Having the Last Laugh – Why Shouldn't They?', *The Independent*, 25 March 2015, http://www.independent.co.uk/voices/comment/the-snp-are-having-the-last-laugh-and-why-shouldn-t-they-10131106.html, accessed 29 October 2015.

Commission president, Jean-Claude Juncker, with a little David Cameron in his pocket. This new Tory approach then forced Ed Miliband onto the defensive and to respond in a speech in Scotland that there would be no formal deal with the SNP, although he stopped short of ruling out a confidence and supply arrangement[120].

Nevertheless, not all the Tories' messages were negative. In a party election broadcast "Securing a better future for your family", the message was aimed at persuading families that their future was better with the Conservatives. Celebrity endorsement came from Sol Campbell, Andrew Lloyd Webber and Simon Cowell.

Figure 22: Negative Labour campaigning on health

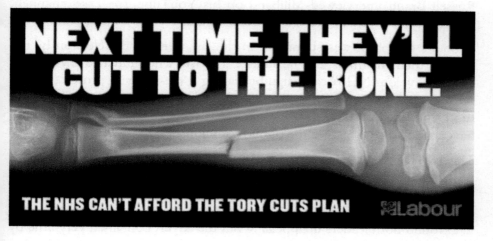

The Conservatives were not the only ones using negative adverts. Labour promised a clean campaign in January 2015 but then developed a poster attacking the Conservatives on the issue of funding the NHS in January[121], arguing they would return its funding "to levels of the 1930s when there was no NHS" and again in March[122], both highlighting the NHS issue on

---

[120] Hamish Macdonell, 'Miliband Goes on Attack over Salmond's "bluster"', *The Times*, 24 March 2015, 8.

[121] Tamara Cohen, 'Truth about Tory Poster', *Daily Mail*, 5 January 2015, 12.

[122] Rosa Prince, 'Labour Goes Negative with Poster Claiming Tories Would Cut NHS to Bone - Telegraph', *The Telegraph*, 20 March 2015, http://www.telegraph.co.uk/news/politics/labour

which they held a 23% lead over the Tories (see Figure 22). Labour also released an election pledge card in mid-March but many of Miliband's senior colleagues voiced privately concerns, arguing that his message was too negative and insufficiently aspirational[123].

One Labour poster released on 4 April claimed families were £1,100 worse off under a Tory Chancellor. Another, launched on 6 April, parodied the famous "Labour isn't working" poster with the message "The doctor can't see you now" and an almost identical picture of a queue except that many of those queueing were elderly, wearing bandages or in wheelchairs. But not all of their messaging was negative. Labour's PEBs tended to be more positive, aiming to inspire people to vote for a fairer society, and included plenty of celebrities, including comedians Jo Brand and Steve Coogan (and Russell Brand interviewed Miliband on his YouTube *The Trews* channel), actors Martin Freeman and David Tennant and TV cook Delia Smith.

Labour's campaign was supported in the last week of the election by the unions, their members and healthcare activists who launched the "Seven days to save our NHS" campaign by staging a 'die-in' (with protesters lying on the street wrapped in bandages and made up to look injured) outside the Department of Health on Whitehall[124]. This event however seems to have made little impact on the public consciousness.

The Lib Dems also got in on the negative campaigning act, unveiling a poster depicting images of flabby-mouthed versions of both Ed Balls and George Osborne, respectively the Shadow Chancellor and the Chancellor of the Exchequer (Figure 23). The poster was designed to appeal to voters who found both leaders unappealing but the advert contained very little by way of rationale for voting Liberal Democrat (a distinct weakness now that the Liberal Democrats were no longer seen as the obvious destination for protest voters). This was supported by a party election broadcast on the same theme, also released on YouTube, which mirrored their party election broadcasts, using the same theme.

/11485160/Labour-goes-negative-with-poster-claiming-Tories-would-cut-NHS-to-bone.html, accessed 29 October 2015.

[123] Tim Shipman and James Lyons, 'Miliband's "Miserable" Message Means He Can't Win, Say Third of His Cabinet', *Sunday Times*, 14 March 2015, 14–15.

[124] See the campaign website http://www.peoplesvotefornhs.org.uk/7_days_to_save_our_nhs, and Will Stone, 'Seven Days to Save the NHS', *Morning Star*, 30 April 2015, http://morningstaronline.co.uk/a-33d0-Seven-days-to-save-the-NHS/, accessed 29 October 2015.

The Liberal Democrats managed to secure John Cleese, as ever, to support them but only to help Nick Clegg rehearse for his debate performances[125]. But they also tried to deliver a more positive message aimed at rebuilding trust with voters in a poster launched during Easter on how they had delivered a tax cut, as they had previously promised. Their "it's decision time" party election broadcast was also more positive, arguing for a fairer society, a better NHS and "opportunity for everyone".

Figure 23: Negative Lib Dem campaigning poster

UKIP's messaging was completely different from what one might have expected. They released a poster on 7 April, showing a soldier holding his helmet outstretched like a begging bowl with the message "Don't make our heroes beg for more", perhaps in a bid to capture former BNP voters and the nationalist, patriot vote more generally. In late March, Nigel Farage unveiled a more negative poster, in Dover, showing escalators

---

[125] For a more detailed discussion of celebrity endorsement in the 2015 general election, see Mark Wheeler, 'Celebrity Endorsements and Activities in the 2015 UK General Election Campaign', in Daniel Jackson and Einar Thorsen (eds.), *UK Election Analysis 2015: Media, Voters and the Campaign*, http://www.electionanalysis.uk/uk-election-analysis-2015/section-7-popular-culture/celebrity-endorsements-and-activities-in-the-2015-uk-general-election-campaign/, accessed 29 October 2015.

rising up the white cliffs of Dover, with the message "Immigration is three times higher than the Tories promised"[126]. In their "Believe in Britain" party election broadcast, Farage stated that they stood "for the ordinary folks against the political class", a negative sideswipe against the Conservative, Labour and Liberal Democrat parties in general. The broadcast ended with a patriotic appeal, "If you believe in Britain, UKIP is the party for you", and in a strange bid to illustrate Farage's ordinariness, it ended with a post-production comment presumably to his producer, "I reckon that's all right".

Towards the end of the campaign, Tory strategists warned their candidates to be wary of Liberal Democrat "dirty tricks", suggesting they would make "false and exaggerated claims" and use "wicked" campaign tactics in a bid to save 35 of their key seats. All Lib Dem negative campaigning was to be reported to Conservative Central Office, the memo commanded. One Lib Dem suggested however that the Tory's suggestion that they were up to "dirty tricks" was in itself a dirty trick![127]

The SNP's initial poster on 4 January, early in the pre-campaign, showed an image of the leather seats of the House of Commons with a nationalist message: "The more seats we have here, the more powers we will have in Scotland". The SNP also lashed out at supposed 'dirty tricks', after a report that Nicola Sturgeon had commented to the French Ambassador that she preferred a Conservative-led government in the 2015 general election appeared in *The Telegraph*[128], something she flatly denied. Nevertheless, the SNP were not beyond conducting their own negative campaigning. Their whole *raison d'etre* was focused around 'keeping Cameron out of Downing Street' by projecting themselves as more anti-Tory than Labour. In her column for Glasgow's *Evening Times*, she articulated this position clearly, stating: "voting Labour in the past hasn't

---

[126] To see an online gallery of the various parties' posters, see 'General Election 2015: Political Poster Campaigns from All the Major Parties - Telegraph', *The Telegraph*, http://www.telegraph.co.uk/news/general-election-2015/11519856/General-Election-2015-Political-poster-campaigns-from-all-the-major-parties.html?frame=3258460.

[127] Ben Riley-Smith, 'Watch out for Liberal Democrat "Dirty Tricks" Campaign, Tories Warn Candidates', *The Telegraph*, 1 May 2015, -, http://www.telegraph.co.uk/news/general-election-2015/11578163/Watch-out-for-Liberal-Democrat-dirty-tricks-campaign-Tories-warn-candidates.html, accessed 30 October 2015.

[128] 'Election 2015: Nicola Sturgeon Hits out at "Dirty Tricks"', *BBC News*, 4 April 2015, http://www.bbc.co.uk/news/election-2015-32177315, accessed 30 October 2015.

protected Scotland against Tory governments"[129]. This same theme of Labour no longer 'standing up to the Tories' was also incorporated into their party election broadcasts, together with the theme of standing up to Westminster in general in order to ensure they stuck to the promises they made after the 2014 Independence Referendum. Celebrity endorsement came from the likes of actors Brian Cox and Martin Compston.

Plaid Cymru, in some ways, mirrored the patriotic positioning of the SNP. In a party election broadcast, they sought to position themselves as "the party of Wales" and "the only party standing up for Wales". It published over 80 posters in English and Welsh online[130].

The Greens also got in on the negative campaigning act, releasing their "Change the tune" party election broadcast (also aired on YouTube) which pulled in around 900,000 views. The broadcast featured a boyband (parodying leaders Clegg, Farage, Miliband and Cameron) singing "it's sweeter when we all agree, a party political harmony"[131] but their poster message was more inspirational, urging voters to "vote big, vote brave"[132].

But more generally, this was perceived to be an election in which PEBs were expected to make limited impact, largely because fewer people were watching TV[133] – but we shall see later that this was not the case – and the smaller parties secured airtime in a way that they had not in previous elections.

---

[129] Nicola Sturgeon, 'Nicola Sturgeon: We Need SNP MPs to Stop the Tories', *Evening Times*, 21 April 2015, http://www.eveningtimes.co.uk/opinion/13306348.Nicola_Sturgeon__We_need_SNP_MPs_to_stop_the_Tories/, accessed 30 October 2015.

[130] Vincent Campbell and Benjamin Lee, 'The Slow Shift to the Digital Campaign: Online Political Posters', in Daniel Jackson and Einar Thorsen (eds.), *UK Election Analysis 2015: Media, Voters and the Campaign*, http://www.electionanalysis.uk/uk-election-analysis-2015/political-communication-and-image-management/the-slow-shift-to-the-digital-campaign-online-political-posters/, accessed 29 October 2015.

[131] Aliya Ram, 'Greens Satirical Video Tops YouTube Polls', *Financial Times*, 9 April 2015, http://www.ft.com/cms/s/0/b5fc3c98-decc-11e4-852b-00144feab7de.html#axzz3oAXnpTm2, accessed 10 October 2015.

[132] 'Election 2015: Greens Launch "Vote Big" Poster Campaign', *BBC News*, 13 April 2015, http://www.bbc.co.uk/news/election-2015-32284353, accessed 30 October 2015.

[133] For more on the history of PEBs, see Leala Padmanabhan, 'The Story of the Party Election Broadcast', *BBC News*, 21 April 2015, http://www.bbc.co.uk/news/election-2015-31711345, accessed 30 October 2015. Also: Philip Cowley and Steven Fielding, 'Party Election Broadcasts', *BFI Screenonline*, http://www.screenonline.org.uk/tv/id/1389732/.

To a greater extent than previously, the 2015 election was much more about the ground wars fought in marginal constituencies. In a study of election leaflets in the British general election by Nottingham University, based on around 1,300 leaflets from nearly 300 constituencies, Labour turned out to be the most negative party based on the issues covered, the images used, and whether the party discussed its opponents in their local leaflet campaigning. 82% of Labour's leaflets attacked another party, compared to 81% for Lib Dems, 70% for the Conservatives, 40% for the Greens and only 35% for UKIP. It is perhaps easiest for the parties to be more negative using this medium, because leaflets are essentially direct mail and can be targeted to individuals, unlike posters or party election broadcasts which are visible to a mass audience[134].

Celebrity endorsements played a somewhat smaller role in the 2015 election than previously. Nevertheless, a letter published in *The Telegraph* from 103 business chiefs, some of whom had previously backed Labour, backing the Conservatives' policy on corporation tax cuts and other pro-business policies, made news early in the campaign period[135]. The letter came hot on the heels of the Labour party's launch of their business manifesto and after they had taken out a full-page advertisement in the *Financial Times*, which included pro-Labour endorsements from six business leaders, four of whom later distanced themselves from the advert[136]. Labour responded quickly crowd-sourcing its own letter in response from actors, writers, business leaders, nurses and 50 people on zero hours contracts using their party website[137].

Despite these stunts, however, the influence of celebrity endorsement over ordinary voters is debatable. As with commercial celebrity endorsement more generally, this influence is reduced considerably if the celebrity does

---

[134] Isabel Hardman, 'Revealed: The Party with the Most Negative Election Campaign', *Spectator Blogs*, 7 May 2015, http://blogs.new.spectator.co.uk/2015/05/revealed-the-party-with-the-most-negative-election-campaign/, accessed 30 October 2015.

[135] 'Election 2015: Bosses' Letter Backing Tories Fuels Business Battle', *BBC News*, 1 April 2015, http://www.bbc.co.uk/news/election-2015-32141412, accessed 30 October 2015.

[136] Peter Dominiczak, '100 Business Chiefs: Labour Threatens Britain's Recovery', *The Telegraph*, 1 April 2015, http://www.telegraph.co.uk/news/politics/labour/11507586/General-Election-2015-Labour-threatens-Britains-recovery-say-100-business-chiefs.html, accessed 30 October 2015.

[137] Patrick Wintour, 'Labour Offers Counterpunch to Daily Telegraph Business Letter', *The Guardian*, 1 April 2015, http://www.theguardian.com/politics/2015/apr/01/labour-offers-counterpunch-to-daily-telegraph-business-letter, accessed 30 October 2015.

something wrong which could affect the party image negatively (like avoiding paying some taxes as Gary Barlow – a 2010 Conservative endorser – was reported to have done[138]).

The public's response to negative campaigning

It is however something of a paradox that the public always say emphatically that they don't like negative campaigning and yet party strategists use it so ubiquitously. In 2015, 64% of the public said they thought "the election should be fought by the parties putting forward their own policies and personalities", and only 5% that "the election should be fought by the parties pointing out what was wrong with the policies and personalities in other parties" (Figure 24). But this wasn't what they felt they got (46% thought the latter description best fitted how it was actually being fought, and only 8% that it was being fought purely positively); and we certainly wouldn't deny that they were probably right.

Nevertheless, it is not all so black and white. More often, it is a matter of comparative arguments rather than a purely offensive one. It is one thing to decry a campaign that says "my opponent's policy is bad". But are we also to disapprove of the campaign that says "my policy is better than my opponent's"? If so, we may create a situation where the various campaigns are unable ever to make meaningful contact with each other, and where the debate between positions which the voters need to help them decide how to vote is effectively impossible. The wildest claims of the competing candidates would necessarily go unchallenged, and on those issues which essentially involve trading off one benefit against another (including almost any concerned with public expenditure) the public would be left in ignorance of the real meaning of any of the competing programmes.

There are signs that some of the voters accept this argument, and that they saw value in the comparative element to campaigning in the 2015 election. As many as one in five, 21%, thought that the election should be fought by parties combining both strategies, "putting forward their own policies

---

138 For details of his public apology, see Press Association, 'Gary Barlow Apologises over Tax Affairs', *The Guardian*, 2 September 2014, http://www.theguardian.com/culture/2014/sep/02/gary-barlow-apology-tax-affairs, accessed 30 October 2015.

and personalities" but also "pointing out what was wrong with the policies and personalities in other parties".

Figure 24: Public attitudes to negative campaigning

Q Which of the following comes closest to your views?

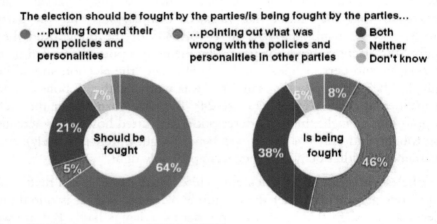

Base: 496 GB adults aged 18+, 26-29 April 2015
Source: Ipsos MORI Political Monitor

But negative campaigning may in any case be very much in the eye of the beholder. What seems an entirely negative and cynical attack to the supporters of the party which it attacks may appear entirely different to supporters of the party which disseminates it; a justified and indeed necessary warning on a relevant issue. It may be that, for many, this is not a case of negative campaigning being legitimate but, because the message seems so obviously germane to the decision that the voters must make, that it is not perceived as negative at all.[139]

---

[139] This is not the first time that this phenomenon has been observed. For example, in their empirical study of campaign advertising in the 1997 election, Dermody and Scullion found that when advertisements were considered informative and believable they were often not recognised as being negative – see Janine Dermody and Richard Scullion, 'Perceptions of Negative Political Advertising: Meaningful or Menacing? An Empirical Study of the 1997 British General Election Campaign', *International Journal of Advertising* 19 (2000): 201–223.

At any rate, it was very clear when we asked the public during the 2015 election which party had been running the most negative campaign (Table 33), very few of them reported it to be their own party. Conservatives named Labour, and to a lesser extent UKIP and the SNP, Labour supporters thought it was the Conservatives or UKIP, while Liberal Democrats and Scottish Nationalists picked both the major parties (though the Conservatives more often than Labour) and UKIP; meanwhile UKIP supporters detected most negativity in the Labour, Conservative and SNP campaigns in that order. Not a single one of our UKIP, Liberal Democrat or SNP supporters thought their own party was most negative. Overall, though, the Conservatives and Labour were perceived to be the most negative campaigners with the SNP, the Liberal Democrats and the Greens barely registering in this regard.

Table 33: Who was most negative?

Q Now talking about negative campaigning, for example making personal attacks on opponents or attacking opponents policies, which party and their leader, if any, do you think has the most negative election campaign so far?

		Voting intention				
	All	Conser-vative	Labour	Lib Dem	UKIP	SNP
	%	%	%	%	%	%
The Conservative party and their leader David Cameron	28	8	51	40	22	54
The Labour party and their leader Ed Miliband	23	42	7	21	34	24
The Liberal Democrat party and their leader Nick Clegg	3	2	3	0	3	2
The UK Independence Party and their leader Nigel Farage	18	18	23	22	0	13
The Scottish National Party and their leader Nicola Sturgeon	7	10	4	3	13	0
The Green Party and their leader Natalie Bennett	2	2	2	0	4	3
Other	1	0	0	2	2	0
None	5	7	4	5	4	4
Don't know	12	11	6	6	17	*

Base: 1,010 British adults 18+, 26-29 April 2015
Source: Ipsos MORI Political Monitor

Incidentally, most of the public also believed that they are not much influenced by negative campaigning, although others are. This 'third person effect' is common in advertising, in general[140]. Back in 2008 we found that 79% agreed that "I am more likely to trust/believe those politicians who concentrate more on explaining their own policies than those who concentrate more on attacking other politicians' policies". However the party campaign planners clearly believe that negative advertising works, and our research during the 2010 election[141] may show why that is the case, as it indicated that negative impressions of the leaders were more powerful than positive ones: distrusting or disliking David Cameron or Gordon Brown was much better as a predictor of voting against that leader's party than trusting or liking him was as a predictor of voting for them.

But negative campaigning can also serve a purpose of shoring up the troops and reinforcing their morale. In psychological terms it takes account of in- and out-group psychology, which is the idea that we like to psychologically identify with a particular group and in so doing denigrate non-similar groups (what psychologists call out-group derogation). Negative campaigning can therefore sometimes be seen as a 'core vote' strategy, but in fact it differs in important respects. A core vote strategy is typically aimed at reinforcing the party's appeal to voters who would support it anyway, to ensure they turn out or to cement their loyalties for the future in an election whose result is already decided. It emphasises those policies and appeals which distinguish the parties, and since activists and loyalists tend to be less moderate than supporters, it concentrates on the extreme voters more than on moderates. It has most effect in the party's safest seats, since that is where support is strongest, and may look remote from the task of winning an election which has to be fought in the marginals.

A strong turnout in safe seats which would be won anyway contributes nothing except to increase the apparent numerical bias of the electoral system against the party. But the safe-seat core voters have similarly-minded counterparts in the marginal seats, fewer in number but much more important to securing the outcome of the election. It may be that

---

[140] For more on this interesting phenomenon, readers are advised to see W. Phillips Davison, 'The Third-Person Effect in Communication', *Public Opinion Quarterly* 47 (1983): 1–15.

[141] Mortimore, Baines, Crawford, Worcester, and Zelin, 'Asymmetry in Leader Image Effects and the Implications for Leadership Positioning in the 2010 British General Election'.

campaigning in a way that appeals to this group, ensuring that they remember to vote, is a more efficient use of campaigning resources than trying to win over the floating voters in the centre; and the side-benefits of cheering the core members can also be important – higher morale among the campaigners, greater willingness to help the campaign on the ground and to spread the word-of-mouth and willingness to fund the party's campaigns.

Because of possible legal pitfalls and the potential for demands of corrective advertising, damages and injunctions, negative campaigns and 'knocking copy' are much rarer in commercial advertising – although not non-existent as Microsoft's anti-Google 'Scroogled' campaign (where Microsoft explains that Google's gmail invades users' privacy unlike their own Outlook service) demonstrates[142]. Indirect comparative advertising is more commonly used ('our powder washes whiter than the leading brand X', for example. But there is an important difference in the political situation, in that commercial marketing is not a 'zero-sum game' – everybody can lose. Suppose Coke and Pepsi put all their energies into knocking each others' products instead of promoting their own – the public might simply end up buying less cola, which wouldn't suit either of them. For the politicians, though, that possibility does not arise: somebody is going to win the election, however much the voters may be disillusioned with politics and the parties.

On the other hand, that is only the short-term view. In the long-term context, if the public lose faith in all existing parties, they might support new parties, or stop voting altogether, and turnouts will fall. The democratic legitimacy of governments elected by an ever-decreasing proportion of the population may be called into question, and there may even a breakdown in public order as opponents of the government or of the establishment lose faith in democratic processes as a channel for dissent and redress. This concern is the one most frequently cited as the greatest consequence of negative campaigning. The argument therefore goes that negative campaigning is 'bad for democracy'. But others have

---

[142] For a discussion of the effects of negative advertising in the commercial world, see Adrianne Jeffries, 'Fighting Dirty: Microsoft's Mean "Scroogled" Ads Are a Sign of What's to Come', *The Verge*, 13 February 2013, http://www.theverge.com/2013/2/13/3984700/microsoft-negative-scroogled-ads-sign-of-things-to-come, accessed 27 October 2015.

argued that it is good for democracy because it provides people with a greater understanding of the choices that they face[143].

---

[143] Dick Morris is perhaps the most prominent proponent of the pro-negative campaigners: see 'Dick Morris: Negative Campaigning Is Good for America', *US News & World Report*, 6 October 2008, http://www.usnews.com/opinion/articles/2008/10/06/dick-morris-negative-campaigning-is-good-for-america, accessed 27 October 2015. On the anti-negative campaign side, see Janine Dermody and Richard Scullion, 'Exploring the Consequences of Negative Advertising for Liberal Democracy', *Journal of Political Marketing* 2 (2003): 77–100.

The diverse elements of the campaign

A British election campaign is fought, of course, across a wide range of media and in a diverse selection of forums; the parties must choose not only the content of their messages but how to put them across in the most effective way to reach the most key voters.

Television has been by far the most influential single medium for informing the public about politics and influencing their decisions since the 1950s. But perhaps this has become so much a part of process of politics that it is taken for granted, and its importance is sometimes forgotten. Much of the talk before the 2015 election, as before the last few that preceded it, was about the importance and impact of new media, of online channels of communication, and especially of social media. Undoubtedly these are more important than they used to be, and it would be an unwise party or candidate that ignored them entirely; nevertheless, their impact pales into insignificance when judged against the more traditional, but much more pervasive, impact of TV coverage in all its various manifestations.

Before the campaign started, in February, we asked the public to consider a list of campaign elements and tell us which they thought would influence their vote.[144] Most significant by far from the list of eight possibilities was TV debates, which 37% thought would influence them, while 32% did not expect to be influenced by any of them. (This presumably reflected people's memories of the dramatic and well-received 2010 debates, as details of how the 2015 debates would be organised were still at this point being decided.) Next in line were newspapers, influential to 19%, and election broadcasts, 15%, so two of the top three items were televisual. Lower in the pecking order came leaflets (11%), social media (10%), opinion polls (7%), posters (4%) and telephone calls (2%).

These expectations accorded very closely with what people reported had actually influenced them at the end of the campaign. According to a

---

[144] The survey was conducted as part of the Wisdom of the Crowd project, a collaboration between Ipsos MORI, the Centre for Analysis of Social Media (CASM) at Demos and the University of Sussex (sponsored by Innovate UK, with funding contributions from the TSB, EPSRC and the ESRC): Ipsos MORI interviewed 1,142 GB adults aged 18+, face-to-face, on 6-16 February 2015. More about the project can be found at https://www.ipsos-mori.com/ourexpertise/ digitalresearch/sociallistening/wisdomofthecrowd.aspx, accessed 6 November 2015.

Panelbase survey conducted just a week before Election Day, voters were most influenced in forming their political opinions by television sources (62%) overall. Nearly two in five voters (38%) were influenced by the debates, nearly a quarter (23%) by TV news coverage, one in ten by party election broadcasts, one in four for newspapers (25%), just over one in six (17%) for websites, one in seven for radio (14%) and word of mouth from friends and family (14%). Only 11% reported that social media had been influential[145].

The real importance of social media, however, lies in the fact that its influence varies substantially across different groups, most obviously in that it is much more used by younger people – who are harder to reach than their older counterparts by other channels, tending to watch less television and reading fewer newspapers. Although only 10% of all adults expected in the February poll to be influenced by social media, 26% of 18-24 year olds thought they would.

Table 34: Interest in the campaign

Q How interested would you say you are in the following?

	Party election broadcasts	Politicians' speeches	TV leaders' debates
	%	%	%
Very interested	12	14	28
Fairly interested	33	44	34
Not very interested	28	26	17
Not at all interested	26	14	18
Don't know	1	1	2
Net interested/not interested	-9	+18	+27

Base: 1,010 British adults 18+, 26-29 April 2015
Source: Ipsos MORI Political Monitor

---

[145] Emma Thelwell, 'Election 2015: TV Debates "Most Influential" for Voters', *BBC News*, 9 May 2015, http://www.bbc.co.uk/news/election-2015-32673439, accessed 2 June 2015.

Research conducted on the Ipsos MORI political monitor indicated a negative net interest[146] by voters in party election broadcasts (-11%), a surprisingly positive net interest in politicians' speeches (+18%) and a large positive net interest (+27%) in the TV leaders' debates (see Table 34).

Voters' net interest in party election broadcasts appears to have become considerably less negative, but still negative, in the last election, compared to previous elections, perhaps indicating either that the format for these has shifted to one which is more entertaining (which is unlikely) or that many voters were less sure of who they wanted to vote for and were therefore more inclined to watch the PEBs in order to help them decide.

Table 35: Interest in party election broadcasts

Q How interested would you say you are in the following? Party election broadcasts

	1992*	1997	2001	2005	2015
	%	%	%	%	%
Very interested	8	5	5	8	12
Fairly interested	28	27	30	26	33
Not very interested	31	31	32	28	28
Not at all interested+	32	36	32	38	26
Don't know	1	1	1	1	1
Net interested/not interested	-27	-35	-29	-32	-9

Base: c. 1,000 British adults 18+ in each poll
Source: Ipsos MORI
asked as "party political broadcasts" in 1992; + "Not particularly interested" 1992-2005

A similar pattern of unusual voter interest, this time in politicians' speeches, can also be found. Whilst on average, a majority of voters have not previously found politicians' speeches interesting, in 2015 they said they did. This provides further evidence that voters were seeking to inform themselves of what politicians were saying in a bid to inform their vote.

---

[146] We calculate this by adding "very" and "fairly interested" and subtracting from it the score from "not very interested" and "not at all interested" to arrive at a net score. "Don't know" is disregarded.

Table 36: Interest in politicians' speeches

Q How interested would you say you are in the following? Politicians' speeches

	1992	1997	2001	2005	2015
	%	%	%	%	%
Very interested	9	7	7	10	14
Fairly interested	34	33	39	34	44
Not very interested+	28	30	29	26	26
Not at all interested	28	30	25	29	14
Don't know	1	*	*	*	1
Net interested/not interested	-13	-20	-8	-11	18

Base: c. 1,000-2,000 British adults 18+ in each poll
Source: Ipsos MORI
+ *"Not particularly interested" 1992-2005*

An analysis by PSONA Glasgow and Human Digital[147] indicated that early in the campaign (17 March–10 April), Labour enjoyed the most mentions on social media, followed by SNP, Conservatives and UKIP (see Figure 25).

Figure 25: UK political parties' share of chat

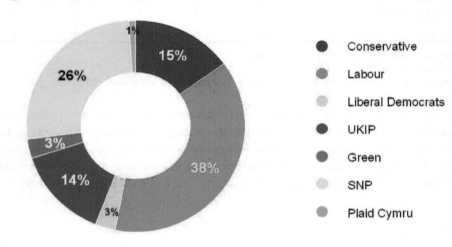

Source: Adapted from analysis by PSONA Glasgow/Human Digital (*Marketing*, May 2015)

---

[147] Analysis by PSONA Glasgow/Human Digital: see 'Will Conservatives' Investment in Social-Media Campaigning Make a Difference on Polling Day?', *Marketing*, May 2015, 18.

15% of the chat concerning the Conservative Party was on housing of which 45% was negative, 27% was positive and the rest neutral. In contrast, 85% of the commentary on the Labour Party and the economy was negative.

A slightly later analysis by Brandwatch and *The Guardian* of Twitter, Facebook and Instagram, mid-way through the campaign, indicated that the Labour Party was streets ahead of the other parties in terms of mentions, with 1.5 million, compared to 902,000 for UKIP and 855,000 for the Tories. The Lib Dems were barely present and almost eclipsed by the Greens online (see Figure 26).[148]

Labour's official Twitter account @uklabour had 388,109 tweets and retweets compared to @ukip's 212,418 and @conservatives' 158,158.

Figure 26: Party and leader mentions on social media by mid April

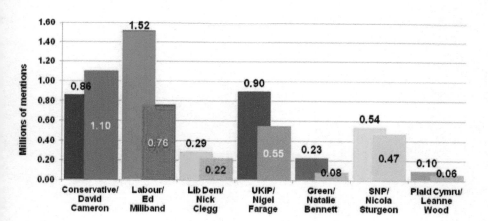

Source: Data from Brandwatch, reported in the *Guardian* (18 April 2015)

Nevertheless, whilst Labour were enjoying the most mentions in social media, and sending out more tweets (42,000 to the Tories' 27,000 by mid-March), the Tories were generating the most positive tweets in key election

---

[148] Esther Addley, 'The Electronic Election: Keyboard Warriors Go All out to Win Hearts and Minds', *The Guardian*, 18 April 2015, 11.

battlegrounds, according to research by the Centre for the Analysis of Social Media at Demos[149].

Nigel Farage, Ed Miliband and Leanne Wood were the leaders with the most popular individual Twitter accounts by the middle of the campaign; however, in terms of mentions across all social media, the general trend for leaders was the same as for party, with the exception of David Cameron, who obtained 33% of the total share of mentions, and significantly out-mentioned the other leaders – and, indeed, his own party. The difficulty with such analysis, however, is that contrary to the popular notion that 'any publicity is good publicity', much of the commentary would have been negative for all party leaders and therefore, the sentiment (positive and/or negative and the relative amounts of each) needs also to be analysed but was not reported here.

---

[149] Carl Miller, 'Tories Lead in Local Tweets', *Sunday Times*, 15 March 2015, 14.

The debates

At the 2010 general election, the televised debates between the leaders were by far the most prominent feature of the campaign. They dominated the media coverage, and they took up a huge proportion of the campaigning time of the leaders and their teams. And the voters liked them. The viewing figures were high (a peak audience of more than 10 million), and many said afterwards that the debates had affected their voting intentions.

Some observers assumed that because of their success the debates had already become so part of the fabric of a British election campaign that the exercise would automatically be repeated and that the leaders would take part without a second thought – or, at least, if they had second thoughts they would still feel they had no alternative. But the debates only happened in 2010 because all three leaders believed they could win and achieve a decisive advantage by taking part. Of course, at least two of them were wrong. In 2015, all the leaders would clearly make their calculations in the light of the experience of 2010.

Moreover, the situation was far less clear cut than in 2010 when the only question of scope about which there could be any conceivable doubt was whether the debates should include Nick Clegg, whose party could be expected to secure one vote in five but who had no realistic chance of becoming Prime Minister. The precedent having been set by Clegg's inclusion in 2010, serious consideration had to be given in 2015 to the inclusion of other competitors deemed by the broadcasters to be "major parties"; and that gave the leaders scope to make the inclusion or exclusion of other leaders a condition of their own participation, or at least a bargaining chip. In deciding whether to take part in the 2015 debates, and on what terms, David Cameron was naturally driven by whether he had more to gain (or lose) by taking part than by not doing so.

This is not new of course – it has taken Britain so long to have televised pre-election debates precisely because Prime Minister after Prime Minister has refused to take part in them, fearing that to do so would merely give the Leader of the Opposition credibility and exposure while offering no benefit to the incumbent party. Only James Callaghan, already facing defeat and calculating that he might have the advantage over his then-inexperienced opponent, Margaret Thatcher, was willing to take part and she, making similar calculations that the risks to her cause outweighed the benefits, declined. In 1997, John Major and Tony Blair both decided not to take part and each tried to blame the other. Gordon Brown was the first to agree knowing that his opponent would also do so, and the outcome for him was hardly an encouraging precedent for Mr Cameron.

On the face of it, Mr Cameron might have felt confident of outperforming Ed Miliband in a head-to-head confrontation. But that would not have been the only calculation. Mr Cameron was already the better-known, more popular and trusted of the two, and more popular than his party while Mr Miliband was less popular than his. He had a good deal to lose if a debate were to overturn that situation, probably much less to gain from a debate merely reinforcing it; and he will have remembered how he went into the 2010 debates confident of landing a decisive blow on Brown, only to see his calculations completely upset by Nick Clegg's show-stealing performance. The precautionary tactic was not to take the risk.

In the event, the head-to-head debate never happened, although Cameron did agree instead to what turned out to be a serial mauling by Jeremy Paxman, perhaps a little less unhelpful for him. What also happened was an unwieldy seven-leader debate.

When multi-leader debates have been discussed in the past, one of the biggest fears of Prime Ministers has been that the opposition leaders would naturally gang up on them, gaining a huge advantage in terms of the impression made on viewers. At first, the likeliest format seemed to be a four-way debate including Nick Clegg and Nigel Farage, a real danger for Mr Cameron, who might have ended up being attacked from right and left while Mr Miliband was given a relatively free ride. But with the inclusion of Green, SNP and Plaid Cymru speakers, all of whom could best serve their own cause by attacking Labour since it was the votes of ex-Labour supporters that they hoped to attract, the boot was on the other foot. When Ed Miliband also signed up for a second debate, without David Cameron or Nick Clegg but with the other four included, this was redoubled.

What did David Cameron have to lose by refusing? Mainly, of course, he risked that the voters would blame him for the debates not having taken place, or for his absence if they took place without him, and would resent it. He might have felt that he could shift the blame, onto the other leaders or the broadcasters. He might also have wished to argue that the debates were not a useful innovation in 2010, detracting from the rest of the campaign and encouraging even more concentration than usual on elements of the political 'game' and the horserace rather than real confrontation between the parties on issues of substance.

In one respect the risk for Mr Cameron was bigger than appears obvious at initial glance. It would be a big step for a voter to change her vote just because she is angry that there were no election debates (which of course is not what happened in the end), but there is a more subtle effect. Appearance at the debates was not an 'issue issue', it was an 'image issue': even people who do not feel strongly about the debates in themselves may have had their general impression of Mr Cameron changed, since it would have made him look afraid to face his opponents, even cynical or uncaring towards the voters or looking like he had something to hide.

Nevertheless, Cameron seems to have played his hand well. When a four-way debate, adding only UKIP, was proposed, Cameron refused to take part unless the Greens were included as well, attempting to ensure that Miliband would have to face attack from the left as he would face attack from the right. Some of the Conservative press attacked him for this, pointing out that if there was a case for including the Greens it was an even stronger case for including the SNP[150]. But the eventual outcome was the inclusion not only of both the Greens and the SNP, but of Plaid Cymru as well. Far from having painted himself into a corner, as seems to have been the supposition at the time, Cameron had thereby brought about a debate in which he could much more happily participate, with Miliband's position much more difficult than his own. Moreover – although the importance of this was not obvious as early as January – the national exposure which this gave to Nicola Sturgeon raised awareness of the SNP among voters outside Scotland, which was to become an important plank in the subsequent Conservative campaign.

The debates themselves proved less memorable than in 2010. The set-piece seven-leader debate was the only one in which the Prime Minister participated, and none of the seven was either outstanding or awful,

---

[150] Peter McKay, 'Why David Cameron Is Wrong to Dodge the TV Debate', *Mail Online*, 12 January 2015, http://www.dailymail.co.uk/debate/article-2905983/PETER-MCKAY-David-Cameron-wrong-dodge-TV-debate.html, accessed 3 November 2015.

although Miliband may have gained most simply because his competent performance exceeded public expectations. Sturgeon probably made the biggest impact, as a hitherto mostly-unknown leader who made the most of her chance to demonstrate that she was entitled to be considered on an equal plane with Cameron, Miliband and Clegg. But the format allowed none of the seven any real scope to take control and appear the dominant figure. Four different polls taken during the debate proclaimed four different 'winners'[151], but all agreed that viewers were completely split. Nobody can be meaningfully described as having 'won' a debate if only a quarter of the viewers thought they were better than the other competitors. But both Nigel Farage and Nicola Sturgeon were rated as best across the post-debate polls by far more people than they could reasonably have expected to vote for them (in YouGov's poll, Sturgeon was judged the winner by 28% and Farage by 20%), which was probably as much as they could have hoped to achieve.

Analysis of Twitter comment during the same debate by the Centre for the Analysis of Social Media[152] found, intriguingly, that all three female leaders elicited more positive than negative tweets (Nicola Sturgeon doing best, with an 83% to 17% balance), while for all four male leaders the negatives outweighed the positives, although only marginally so in the cases of Nick Clegg and Ed Miliband. For David Cameron, 32% of the mentions that leant one way or the other were rated as 'cheers' and 68% as 'boos'. (But, of course, the views of social media users do not necessarily reflect those of the wider voting public.)

The second debate proceeded without David Cameron or Nick Clegg, Cameron having declined to take part and Clegg having not been invited[153]. Their absence was noticed, of course, and Cameron's drew plenty of adverse comment on social media. It was reported that "Where is

---

[151] YouGov gave the verdict to Nicola Sturgeon and ICM to Ed Miliband, while Survation proclaimed a tie between David Cameron and Ed Miliband, and ComRes a three-way tie between those two and Nigel Farage. See 'So Who Won the ITV General Election Leaders' Debate?', 3 April 2015, http://www.telegraph.co.uk/news/general-election-2015/11513976/Who-won-the-ITV-general-election-leaders-debate.html, accessed 3 November 2015.
[152] As part of the Wisdom of the Crowd project (see note 144 above): http://ukelection.qlik.com/20150402/index.html, accessed 3 November 2015.
[153] "For clarity, I was not invited to #BBCDebate. I would have happily taken part and proudly defended our strong @LibDems record in government.", https://twitter.com/nick_clegg/status/588789689353695234?ref_src=twsrc^tfw, accessed 3 November 2015.

David Cameron?" was the second-most searched term on Google while the debate was in progress[154], and the Twitter analysis found that a higher proportion of tweets about Cameron were adverse than was the case for any of the leaders who took part. By the end of the debate, Nigel Farage had received by far the most attention – 18,000 tweets about him, mostly negative, with 10,000 on Miliband, mostly positive, and 7,000 about Cameron's 'empty chair'[155]. But there was no clear winner. The three women ganged up on Miliband (their 'group hug' at the end of the debate with Miliband forlornly looking on was perhaps its most memorable moment), while Farage lost his cool over the hostility of the studio audience.

In 2010 the first TV debate had provoked the biggest overnight movement in the campaign voting intention polls in British polling history; in 2015 there was no sign of any movement at all after either of the big debates. But if the exposure given to Nicola Sturgeon and the attacks she made on Ed Miliband gave force to Conservative arguments that their target voters should vote to prevent a Labour-SNP government, they may nevertheless not have been entirely irrelevant. As Toby Young argued in the *Telegraph*, "This is what a 'rainbow coalition' would look like – a weak Labour leader being pushed to the left by three anti-austerity party leaders'[156]; if that was the message Tory waverers took from the debates, David Cameron can be well satisfied with the outcome of his manoeuvrings over their composition.

---

[154] Rachel Babbage, "'Where Is David Cameron?" Hot Google Search Term during Election Debate', *Digital Spy*, 16 April 2015, http://www.digitalspy.co.uk/displayarticle.php?id=642346, accessed 3 November 2015.

[155] Carl Miller, 'How Twitter Judged the Challengers' Debate', Demos, 17 April 2015, http://www.demos.co.uk/blog/how-twitter-judged-the-challengers-debate/, accessed 3 November 2015.

[156] Toby Young, Untitled post in 'BBC Challengers' Election Debate: Live Analysis, Reaction and Fallout', *The Telegraph*, 16 April 2015, http://www.telegraph.co.uk/news/general-election-2015/11541093/bbc-challengers-general-election-debate-2015-live.html, accessed 3 November 2015.

The parties' segmentation strategies

Key basic segments of the electorate include young voters between 18-34 years of age (about 29% of the electorate, although because of low registration and low turnout they made up only 20% of voters in 2015), women (who represent about 51% of the electorate and 51% of voters) and older voters, aged 55 and over (about 36% of the electorate but 44% of voters). The Conservatives held a lead over Labour only in the second and third of these groups, but Labour was well ahead among young people. Labour's desire to increase the youth vote may have been behind Miliband's appearance on comedian Russell Brand's YouTube channel *The Trews*. But the Tories were also mindful of the need to target young voters, which may have explained why they were spending large sums on Facebook advertising and why they developed the YouTube cartoon video with Ed Miliband dancing to Alex Salmond's tune[157].

Women were also seen as an important segment, although thinking in terms of a single "women's vote" is probably a dangerous simplification. In the run-up to the election, women were more likely than men to say that they had not yet definitely decided how to vote: In January we found 54% of women compared to 48% of men who had a voting intention said they might still change their mind; in February it was 54% to 47% and in March 44% to 39%, and the press reported similar conclusions from other polls; however, by the first half of April, as the campaign got fully underway, that gap had disappeared.[158] Women were also less likely than men to be backing UKIP, suggesting that more of their wavering votes might be available to the two main parties, but this differential also narrowed as the campaign progressed.

Some of the parties had selected more women as candidates than in the past, perhaps partly with an eye to their attraction to female voters. Labour fielded 214, Conservatives 169, Lib Dem 166, UKIP 78, SNP 21 and Plaid Cymru 10, but it was the Greens with 216 who could boast the biggest

---

157 Helen Warrell, Chris Tighe, and Kiran Stacey, 'UK Parties Seek Elusive Youth Vote in Final Days of Campaigning', *Financial Times*, 1 May 2015, http://www.ft.com/cms/s/0/74e6f44e-f008-11e4-ab73-00144feab7de.html#axzz3pmtf0zeZ, accessed 29 October 2015.
158 Data from the Ipsos MORI Political Monitor: c. 800 GB adults 18+ with a voting intention were interviewed by telephone in each poll. See also Sam Coates, 'Wavering Women Will Decide the Fate of Mr Weird and Mr Smug', *The Times*, 25 March 2015, 14–15.

number.[159] Nor was the gender of candidates the only issue raised. The Greens came under pressure during the campaign when a UCL/Birkbeck study found that only 4% of their selected candidates were Black or Minority Ethnic, lower even than UKIP[160]. In the event, 41 minority MPs were elected, an increase on the 27 who succeeded in 2010: of these 23 were Labour MPs, 17 Conservative and 1 from the SNP.

The Conservatives, who were the principal force behind the introduction of the Marriage (Same-Sex Couples) Act in 2013, may also have been targeting the gay vote, and if they were, they might have been enjoying some success as (an albeit self-selected) poll for *PinkNews* showed that one in four readers (26%) intended to vote Conservative, putting the Tories level with Labour[161]. *PinkNews* urged its readers to vote for individual candidates supporting equality legislation rather than backing any party[162], and their poll found that 85% said they would vote against a candidate who did not support same-sex marriage[163]. Of the candidates in marginal seats that they singled out for support, two (Nick Clegg and Mike Freer) won and one (Lynne Featherstone) lost, while both of those they opposed (Matthew Offord and Bob Blackman) won with increased majorities against the general trend in London.

---

[159] Richard Keen, *Women in Parliament and Government*, House of Commons Library Standard Note (London: House of Commons Library, 19 June 2015), 19, www.parliament.uk/briefing-papers/SN01250.pdf, accessed 26 October 2015; Oliver Hawkins, Richard Keen, and Nambassa Nakatudde, *General Election 2015*, House of Commons Library Briefing Paper (London: House of Commons Library, 28 July 2015), 58–59, http://researchbriefings.parliament.uk/ResearchBriefing/Summary/CBP-7186, accessed 26 October 2015. The Greens could also, of course, claim the highest proportion of female MPs (1 out of 1, 100%), while the Lib Dems (0 out of 8), Democratic Unionists (0 out of 8), Sinn Fein (0 out of 4) and UKIP (0 out of 1) all scored 0%.

[160] Matt Dathan, 'Natalie Bennett Admits the Green Party Has a Problem Over Its Lack of Black and Ethnic Minority Candidates', *The Independent*, 22 April 2015, http://www.independent.co.uk/news/uk/politics/generalelection/general-election-2015-natalie-bennett-admits-the-green-party-has-a-problem-over-its-lack-of-black-10193937.html, accessed 4 November 2015.

[161] For more details, see 'The Gay Vote: Coming Out', *The Economist*, 11 April 2015, 28; André Rhoden-Paul, 'Tories Draw Level with Labour in Winning Gay Vote', *The Guardian*, 23 March 2015, http://www.theguardian.com/politics/2015/mar/23/tories-level-labour-gay-vote, accessed 4 November 2015.

[162] 'Here Is Who PinkNews Is Backing at the General Election', *PinkNews*, 6 May 2015, http://www.pinknews.co.uk/2015/05/06/editorial-reward-the-heroes-and-punish-the-villains-of-lgbt-rights-in-parliament/, accessed 4 November 2015.

[163] Nick Duffy, 'Exit Polls Project a Conservative Lead but Short of a Majority', *PinkNews*, 7 May 2015, http://www.pinknews.co.uk/2015/05/07/exit-polls-project-a-conservative-lead-but-short-of-a-majority/, accessed 4 November 2015.

The main move in the young people's vote was their desertion of the Liberal Democrats, with Labour, UKIP, the Greens and the SNP all making significant gains. Whereas the Liberal Democrat vote had stood at 29% among 18-34 year olds in 2010, only a fraction behind the Conservatives and Labour, this had plummeted to just 6% in 2015, leaving them behind the Greens and even the SNP. They were also punished by women voters where their vote was down 17 points to only 8% (see Table 8 on p. 38).

As in previous campaigns, political campaigners tend to use basic demographic groupings when developing their manifestos, but more granular segmentation techniques when developing their online, direct mail and canvassing campaigns. This would have been particularly important to the Labour Party, who had a target to complete four million doorstep conversations by the end of the campaign[164], where they believed the campaign would be won or lost, according to Douglas Alexander, their election co-ordinator[165].

The segmentation technique most often used in political marketing in the UK is geo-demographics, which involves classifying voters on the basis of the characteristics of their MOSAIC segmentation provides all sorts of lifestyle information by group, allowing the direction of campaigning resources to the most persuadable people in the most marginal seats, and therefore the best chance to appeal to floating voters making up their minds and to get out the vote for those who have already made up their minds how to vote. The Conservatives used this system, hiring Jim Messina in 2013, a US consultant specialising in digital political marketing and voter mobilisation[166]. Part of the Conservative segmentation also focused around a ruthless ground campaign in marginal Liberal Democrat seats, particularly in the Midlands and South-west of England[167]. They pursued a '40/40 strategy' targeting 80 seats to hold or win in order to

---

[164] Patrick Wintour, 'Miliband Campaign: Gains on the Ground Add up to Growing Optimism', *The Guardian*, 11 April 2015, 7.

[165] Lucy Tesseras, 'Election to Be Fought with Boots on the Ground', *Marketing Week*, 21 January 2015, https://www.marketingweek.com/2015/01/21/292942/, accessed 27 October 2015.

[166] 'Forget Mondeo Man: Tories Identify Eight Tribes to Win in 2015', *The Telegraph*, 5 November 2013, http://www.telegraph.co.uk/news/politics/conservative/10426747/Forget-Mondeo-Man-Tories-identify-eight-tribes-to-win-in-2015.html, accessed 27 October 2015.

[167] Kiran Stacey, 'How Cameron Killed His Coalition', *Financial Times*, 9 May 2015, 11.

secure a majority[168]. In addition, they made use of a million strong email address list. Labour apparently made use of the big six energy companies' customer lists and the 'bounty list' – a list of expectant mothers who sign up to receive free baby goods – in their targeting exercise[169].

Whilst certain groups like Scots and young voters were shifting their allegiances in 2015, the parties still tended to identify particularly faithful groups of voters based on their policies on particular issues. For Labour, this was the blue-collar worker (on unemployment), for Conservatives it was the young family (on the economy and health), for Liberal Democrats it was the centrist voter (on the environment and health), UKIP were targeting pensioners (on immigration and the cost of living), the Greens were targeting students (on housing, austerity and the environment) and the SNP were targeting the 'Yes' Scottish Independence voters (on austerity as well as independence)[170].

Table 37 outlines what specific manifesto commitments each of the main GB-wide parties were making which might impact on younger, female and older voters, which party was seen by members of those groups as having the best policies on the issues that might be of particular interest to them, and how these groups finally voted.

---

[168] Andy Beckett, 'Everyone Knows That Lynton's In Charge', *The Guardian*, 17 March 2015, sec. G2, 6–11.

[169] Tim Shipman and James Lyons, 'It's Cyberwar!', *Sunday Times*, 5 April 2015, http://www.thesundaytimes.co.uk/sto/news/focus/article1540007.ece, accessed 27 October 2015.

[170] Philip Webster, Danielle Sheridan, Callum Jones, and Katie Gibbons, 'You Could Be the Mondeo Man of This Election', *The Times*, 27 April 2015, sec. Red Box Supplement 3 Britain Decides, 2–3.

Table 37: Key demographic voter segments in 2015

Group	Young voters (aged 18-34) / 20% of voters*	Women /51% of voters*	Older voters (aged 55+) / 44% of voters*
Key Manifesto Focus/ Commit-ments**	**Labour:** Cut university fees to £6,000 per year, and guarantee paid work for all young people out of a job for a year, and increase minimum wage to £8 per hour by 2019. **Conservative:** No tax for those working 30 hours on minimum wage, tuition fees to stay at £9,000. **Lib Dem:** Give 16 year olds the vote, introduce specialist drugs courts, end continuous nuclear weapons patrols, ban some arms exports and minimum unit pricing for alcohol. **UKIP:** No specific youth-oriented policies. **Green:** Remove restrictions on foreign students, minimum price on alcohol of 50p per unit, decriminalise cannabis, raise age of criminal responsibility from 10 to 14, increase minimum wage to £10 per hour.	**Labour:** 25 hours of free childcare for working parents of 3 and 4 year olds, wrap around care for primary school kids from 8am to 6pm, GP appointments within 48 hours, extra £2.5bn for NHS, spend £800m to protect police numbers and bring in Britain's first victims' law. **Conservative:** 30 hours of free childcare to working parents of 3 and 4 year olds, more free schools and failing schools turned into academies, increase NHS spending in England by at least £8bn, tougher sentencing and give police more power to monitor online communications. **Lib Dem:** Extra £2.5bn for England's education budget, 20 hours per week of free childcare for all 2-4 year olds, free school meals for all primary school pupils, £8bn more for NHS by 2020 and extra cash for mental health. **UKIP:** More grammar schools, scrap sex and relationship education for children under 11, wrap-around childcare with breakfast and after-school clubs, extra £3bn a year for NHS by 2020, scrap hospital car parking charges and limit child benefit to two children for new claimants. **Green:** Abolish grammar schools, cut class sizes to 20, end tuition fees, increase NHS budget by £12bn.	**Labour:** GP appointments within 48 hours, pensioners on 40p tax rate lose fuel payments, freeze energy bills until 2017, freeze rail fares in 2016. **Conservative:** Increase inheritance tax threshold to £1m, state pension to rise by minimum 2.5%, cuts in tax relief on pension contributions for people earning above £150,000, 7-day access to GPs, same-day appointments for over-75s, keep bus passes, free TV license and OAP's winter fuel allowance. **Lib Dem:** Increase the income tax allowance to £12,500 by 2020, state pension to rise by minimum 2.5%, single rate of tax relief for pensions, extra cash for mental health, cut winter fuel payments and free TV licenses for richer OAPs, **UKIP:** Raise the personal allowance to £13,000, scrap inheritance tax, and scrap hospital car parking charges, Flexibility to take slightly lower state pension at 65 as pension age rises. **Green:** New citizen's pension set at £180 per week for single pensioner and £310 per week for couple, free prescriptions, abolition of the TV license and free £5,000 of home insulation.
Best Party on… (among segment members, 12-15 April 2015) *	**Education** = Lab 33% Con 19% None/DK 29% **Unemployment** = Lab 29% Con 26% None/DK 30% **Environment** = Other (Green?) 41% LD 10% Lab 9% Con 8% None/DK 30%	**Healthcare** = Lab 33% Con 23% None/DK 26% **Crime/anti-social behaviour** = Con 28% Lab 20% None/DK 41% **Education** = Lab 30% Con 22% None/DK 28% **Unemployment** = Con 31% Lab 30% None/DK 28% **Looking after interests of women** = Lab 23% Con 14% None./DK 39%	**Healthcare** = Lab 33% Con 30% None/DK 20% **Pensions** = Con 37% Lab 23% None/DK 30% **Taxation** = Con 36% Lab 26% None/DK 19%
Vote*	Lab 38%, Con 31%, UKIP 10%, Green 7%, LD 6%, Other 8%	Con 37%, Lab 33%, UKIP 12%, LD 8%, Green 4%, Other 6%	Con 43%, Lab 26%, UKIP 15%, LD 8%, Green 2%, Other 6%

Sources: *Ipsos MORI ** *Daily Star*, 23 April 2015, 24-25; *The Guardian*, 1 April 2015, 43.

The party finances

To finance their electoral strategies, British political parties began soliciting donations in earnest in the year prior to the election, as few voters are prepared to donate for an election campaign inside the parliamentary cycle. In 2014, according to figures from the Electoral Commission, a total of £65.7m was donated to political parties in the UK, £20.3m of which was received in the last quarter of 2014. By the end of 2014, Labour owed around £10.75m, the Conservatives £1.1m with credit facilities for a further £5.5m, and the Liberal Democrats owed £414,000 with credit facilities for a further £572,500[171].

Table 38: Party donations

Party	Value of large party donations in 2014	Large donations and loans made and reported during campaign period (30 March – 7 May 2015)	
		Number	Value
Conservative	£28.93m	163	£6,120,129
Labour	£18.75m	45	£6,509,673
Liberal Democrats	£8.75m	19	£601,000
UKIP	£3.85m	12	£1,684,728
Scottish National Party	£3.77m	1	£10,000
Green Party (including Scottish Greens)	£0.66m	3	£27,594
Plaid Cymru	£0.18m	n/a	

Sources: *The Independent*, 17 April 2015, Electoral Commission

By far, the party with the biggest campaign war chest was the Conservatives (see Table 38). During the campaign period, the parties were required to report all large donations and loans (over £7,500) at weekly intervals. The Conservatives received the highest number of donations but the average size of those to the Labour Party was bigger, so that both by the end of the campaign had added more than £6m to their available resources, and UKIP received a surprisingly high £1.7m. All parties received their funding from a mix of individuals, associations and

---

[171] 'General Election 2015 Explained: Who Finances Political Parties, Who Gets the Most - and How Much Does the Election Cost?', *The Independent*, 17 April 2015, General Election 2015 explained, http://www.independent.co.uk/news/uk/politics/generalelection/general-election-2015-explained-who-finances-the-parties-who-gets-the-most-and-how-much-does-the-10186008.html, accessed 27 October 2015.

companies although the biggest donations to the Conservatives were from individuals while the biggest to Labour were from Trade Unions[172]. More surprisingly, given the large amount of money it had received in the previous year, Liberal Democrat financing dropped off markedly, perhaps as its supporters realised that their campaign was a busted flush.

---

[172]   http://www.electoralcommission.org.uk/find-information-by-subject/political-parties-campaigning-and-donations/donations-and-loans-to-political-parties/weekly-pre-poll-donations-and-loans, accessed 4 November 2015.

The election and the polls

What the polls said in 2015

There were more, many more, opinion polls published during the 2015 general election than at any previous election. They gave a broadly consistent message, of a contest that was absolutely neck and neck in terms of vote share at the time the interviewing took place, and with no impression that any systematic movement of opinion was underway during the campaign up to the eve of election day. When the final pre-election polls were published, they were right in line with what had gone before, portraying an election that in terms of votes was too close to call. But as voting ended at 10 p.m. the broadcasters revealed the results of the Exit Poll, and that said that the Conservatives would be the clear winners with the largest share of seats. When the votes had been counted, it proved to be the Exit Poll that was 'right' and the other polls that were 'wrong', according to the commentators. Since the evidence about public opinion on which we rely in this book is taken from the pre-election polls and others throughout the last parliament, we need to explain what happened and what, if anything, it tells us about their reliability as an indicator of what the public thought about politics.

The pre-election polls

The final polls in the 2015 election all predicted a very close result between the Conservatives and Labour (Table 39) and the 'poll of polls' (i.e. all the final election polls averaged for each party's vote share) suggested a dead heat. In fact, the Conservatives won easily on this measure. Still, if there was consistency of the finding by eleven different polling agencies, using different (in most cases) field interviewers, different sampling methodologies, different question placement of the turnout question and different weighting, get the same result, it seems clear that they are measuring something important.

But just how inaccurate were the polls? Polls measure shares of the vote, not gaps between parties. When the press or the pundits mention, as they sometimes do, that the polls have a 'margin of error' of three per cent, what they should be saying is that each party's share of the vote in the poll should be within three percentage points of the real figure 95 times in 100. This gives some perspective to the somewhat hysterical post-election reaction, which often implied that the 2015 polls had been many more times inaccurate than the margin of error should allow. They weren't.

On average the final polls were 4.1 points adrift of the Conservative share on election day, and 2.3 away from Labour's. Some were higher than average for both main parties, some lower, but all but one had the parties level or one party a single point ahead of the other. So the average "error" for the two parties was 3.2 points, against a frequently-quoted 3.0 margin, **or 6.4 points on the lead against the equivalent 6.0 margin**. A bigger difference than it ideally should be, and certainly a big enough difference to have dramatic political implications in terms of the governmental outcome of the election, but not as ludicrously far from the truth as many of the media pundits seemed to suppose. The error was bigger than has been the case in recent general elections, however, although not as big as in 1992, the previous election with which some commentators made comparisons. (The gap between the final polls and the election result in 2015 was about two-thirds of the size of the gap in 1992.)

Table 39: Final pre-election polls in 2015

Polling Organisation	Con %	Lab %	LD %	UKIP %	Green %	Other %
ComRes	35	34	9	12	4	6
ICM	34	35	9	11	4	7
Ipsos MORI	36	35	8	11	5	5
Lord Ashcroft	33	33	10	11	6	8
Telephone poll average	**34.5**	**34.3**	**9.0**	**11.3**	**4.8**	**6.3**
BMG	34	34	10	12	4	6
Opinium	35	34	8	12	6	5
Panelbase	31	33	8	16	5	7
Populus	33	33	10	14	5	6
Survation	31	31	10	16	5	7
TNS	33	32	8	14	6	7
YouGov	34	34	10	12	4	6
Online average	**33.1**	**33.1**	**9.1**	**13.7**	**5.0**	**6.2**
Telephone v Online difference	**−1.4**	**−1.2**	**+0.1**	**+2.4**	**+0.2**	**−0.1**
Overall average	**33.6**	**33.5**	**9.1**	**12.8**	**4.9**	**6.2**
Actual result	**37.7**	**31.2**	**8.1**	**12.9**	**3.8**	**6.3**
Overall difference	**−4.1**	**−2.3**	**−1.0**	**−0.1**	**+1.1**	**−0.1**

Source: Data from www.britishpollingcouncil.org and www.politicalbetting.com

The point must be made, also, that the polls' measurement of all the parties' votes apart from those of the Conservatives and Labour was accurate (and well within the margin of error). It may not be much consolation, since it is the relative fortunes of the two biggest parties in which people are most interested and which dictate who wins the election, but the polls were right about the Liberal Democrats, right about UKIP, right about the SNP. This achievement should not be trivialised. In many ways, this should have been far harder than sorting out vote shares for Labour and the Conservatives, because it involved far more dramatic movements of votes and changes in some of the assumptions about the political ground rules which underlie decisions about polling methodology. Since the election, this success has been rather taken for granted, perhaps because the correct final polling was fully in line with what had gone before, so that the results were no longer a surprise. If poll after poll for months before the election had not continually hammered home the fall of the Lib Dems and the rise of UKIP and the SNP, so that it was not a surprise when it happened, might the final election polls be given more, deserved, credit for predicting some quite improbable things and being right?

Nevertheless, the overall accuracy of the final polls was certainly a disappointment to the pollsters. As Table 39 shows, there's little to choose between the various polls, and in particular not much difference between the telephone and online polls. (The online polls tended to put both Conservatives and Labour slightly lower and UKIP higher, but with little impact on overall accuracy.) Nor was there much difference between the final polls and those published during the campaign. Some might argue that the polls were 'wrong' all along, but it would be equally possible that they were right all along and the problem was that people were changing their minds as to whether to vote or whether not to bother in the final hours after the polls finished interviewing.

One mustn't forget that people can change their mind not just on for which party they are intending to vote for, shifting away from their original intention and to another, but also on whether they vote at all. If a person is a staunch supporter of Labour, and so will not vote for their 'usual' party, Labour, but won't vote for them at this election as they do not want the Labour Leader to become Prime Minister, they may well abstain.

The Exit Poll

Our poll published on election morning in the *Evening Standard* (or sometimes in the past in *The Times*) used to be our final word on an election, but for the past five elections we have also been engaged in conducting an Exit Poll, interviewing the voters on election day as they emerge from the polling stations and leading to a prediction of the outcome, broadcast at 10 p.m. that evening, after the last vote has been cast but before any of the votes have been counted. In 1997 and 2001, MORI provided ITV's Exit Poll. Since 2005 we have joined forces with our friends at GfK NOP to conduct the single Exit Poll that is commissioned and used by both ITV and the BBC (and latterly also by Sky News), providing the data for the academic team of political scientists led by John Curtice. This team conducts the statistical analysis which translates the findings into a prediction of the number of seats each party will win.

Table 40: The record of the British exit polls, 1997-2015

Projections of seat numbers for biggest party (Labour to 2005, Conservative 2010-15)

	MORI for ITV	NOP for BBC	MORI/NOP average	MORI/NOP for BBC & ITV	Election Result
1997	410	429*	419.5		**419**
2001	417	408	412.5		**413**
2005				356	**356**
2010				305	**307**
2015				316	**331**

*In 1997 the precise NOP projection was not broadcast, but was reported as indicating an overall majority of "about 200".

We are pleased to be able to say once again that the record of the Exit Polls over the years in which we have been involved is phenomenal. In 2010, the Exit Poll predicted that Labour would win 305 seats; Labour won 307. In 2005, it predicted Labour to win 356 seats, and Labour won 356. In 2001, there were two Exit Polls: MORI's predicted Labour would win 417 seats[173], NOP's that they would win 408; they won 413. In 1997,

---

[173] 'ITV Election 2001 (opening)', *ITV Election 2001* (ITV, 7 June 2001), https://www.youtube.com/watch?v=E3oNO-_cg7M, accessed 21 May 2015 (at 5:24).

MORI predicted 410, NOP "an overall majority of about 200"[174], which was equivalent to 429 seats; splitting the difference between the two gives a figure of 419.5, and Labour won 419.

Predictions as accurate as this are partly a matter of luck: sound methodology can get the result within a few seats, but the Exit Poll is still a statistical exercise based on sampling, and has a margin of error – you can expect to be near to the centre of the target but you can't guarantee to hit the bullseye every time. The 2015 Exit Poll, predicting 316 Conservative seats against an actual outcome of 331 was not as close as the previous two but still as accurate as can reasonably be expected (the 15-seat gap equates to about a 1% error in vote share in the decisive seats).

You would think that by now politicians would have got the message that rubbishing the Exit Poll predictions on live TV tends to be a quick route to embarrassment, as has happened to both party spokesmen and pundits in each of the last few elections. (Iain Dale, publisher of some of the earlier books in this series, could tell them about that.) But still they do it. Harriet Harman, for one: "I have been on television where I have been commenting on Exit Polls in the past where the Exit Polls were wrong."[175] When was that? Not recently, that's for sure.

Paddy Ashdown was on the same track – "We have seen a lot of water flow under the bridge, including a lot of very inaccurate Exit Polls"[176] – but unwisely allowed Andrew Neil to lure him into going further:

> Ashdown: "If this Exit Poll is right, Andrew, I will publicly eat my hat on your programme."
>
> Neil: "Have you got a hat?"
>
> Ashdown: "No, but I'll get one specially for the occasion."
>
> Neil: "Can I get the hat?"

---

[174] In fact the precise NOP estimate was 434 seats, but this was not broadcast on the night and the figures were only revealed later. See P. J. Brown, D. Firth & C. D. Payne, "Forecasting on British Election Night 1997", *Journal of the Royal Statistical Society, Series A,* Volume 171, 211-26 (1999).
[175] 'BBC General Election 2015 - 1st Hour' (BBC, 7 May 2015), https://www.youtube.com/watch?v=7wixn14r9y0, accessed 21 May 2015 (at 25:38).
[176] Ibid. (at 23:19).

> Ashdown: "You can get the hat, providing it's made of marzipan... I'll bet you my hat, eaten on your programme, that that's wrong." [177]

Being a man of his word, Ashdown duly appeared on television a couple of days later to eat a marzipan hat. Of course, party spokesmen are at liberty to doubt the accuracy of poll predictions. If they do so after all the votes are cast, with the certainty that it is already decided whether they are right or wrong and that the outcome will be revealed in a few short hours while their pronouncements are still fresh in the nation's memory, perhaps they deserve to get egg on their faces as often as they do. But the charade, election after election, of those who dislike the predictions lining up to parrot in unison that "Exit Polls are usually wrong" is a particularly unedifying one. It just isn't so – and they must know it. In which case, why pay any attention to anything else they say?

A reasonable question, which we have been asked a number of times since the election, is why the Exit Poll seems less prone to errors in its prediction than the pre-election telephone and online polls. It is not to do with the much bigger sample size, although the average telephone survey will often include less than 1,000 voters and the Exit Poll conducts in the region of 20,000 interviews. The Exit Poll by its nature avoids some of the main problems that the pre-election polls have to solve. Accurate pre-election polls depend on meeting three challenges:

1. Not everybody will take part in polls, so the pollsters can only make their samples representative if they can work out how to allow for the difference between those people who agree to participate and those who don't.

2. Not everybody votes, so the pollsters must avoid being misled by the opinions of those who don't get to the polling station, but are happy to take part in opinion polls.

3. The polls have to rely on there being a close link between what people say they will do and what they actually do a day or more later, or find a way of detecting when this is not true and correcting it.

---

[177] Ibid. (at 21:46).

None of these apply fully to an exit poll. There is no turnout calculation to make – interviews are conducted as voters come out of the polling stations, so every person interviewed is known to have voted. Non-response is still a potential problem, but a much less acute one: the Exit Poll gets a response rate in the region of 80%, much better than most opinion polls (or for that matter virtually any other survey). And if people change their minds at the last minute before they vote, that will be after they answer the final pre-election polls but it will have happened by the time they answer the Exit Poll. Of course, if a lot of people were lying to pollsters that might affect the Exit Poll as much as the other polls, but the fact that the exit polls are usually right is one of many reasons why we don't believe that happens.

That doesn't mean that exit polls are simple to conduct: they face a whole separate set of challenges of their own; but that is another story[178]. But the accuracy of the Exit Poll does not directly tell us much about why the pre-election polls under-estimated the Conservative lead.

---

[178] The most complete account of how the exit poll works can be found in John Curtice and David Firth, 'Exit Polling in a Cold Climate: The BBC–ITV Experience in Britain in 2005', *Journal of the Royal Statistical Society: Series A (Statistics in Society)* 171 (2008): 509–539. This describes the 2005 exit poll, but the methodology was essentially the same in 2015 except that the modelling had to be expanded to predict SNP and UKIP votes separately, which was not necessary for the 2005 prediction. In 2015 the poll was conducted at 141 polling stations.

Ipsos MORI's final poll in 2015

Why did the polls not see it coming in 2015, having got it pretty well right in 2010 using the same methods? We can only answer that with any degree of authority for Ipsos MORI's polls, not having seen the detailed data from any of our competitors. The British Polling Council has set up an independent investigation, led by the academic methodologist Patrick Sturgis, which will look at the evidence from all the various polls and report some time in 2016. We await its conclusions with interest, not least because it is possible that the evidence from some of the other companies' polls may help us understand our own: if they measured things that we didn't, it may tell us things about the state of public opinion that we didn't know, and even though some of our methods differ we were all trying to measure the opinions of the same public at the same time, and may have been confounded by the same unforeseen problems.

It is not in any sense impossible that different problems may have affected different pollsters, or at least that the same problem manifested itself in different ways, because there are many significant differences in the methods that we use to conduct voting intention polls. The essential point to understand is that every poll aims theoretically to assemble a perfectly representative sample of British voters, but in practical terms that is an impossibility: all we can do is to assemble an imperfect sample and then attempt to correct for its imperfections.

Different companies have different ideas about the best way to do this, and so the imperfections with which they must deal in their raw samples are very different. For example, a telephone sample is very different from an internet panel sample. (In theory a telephone sample is able to choose from among almost the whole of the adult population at random, but is limited to those available to answer their phones at the periods when the poll is being conducted. An internet panel sample is chosen only from panel members, people who have previously volunteered to take part in such surveys: This excludes anybody who is not online, but allows participants to answer at any time that suits them within a quite wide window of time). They may also answer questions differently, since one is responding as they are read out by a human interviewer, the other reading the questions for himself or herself and filling out a computer form. Clearly, the data from these two polls might need to be corrected in different ways to reach the same right answer, and so a problem that disrupted the accuracy of one might not necessarily affect the other in the same way.

Nevertheless, with all the polls displaying similar errors in their final predictions of the election outcome, the likeliest explanation is that the same problem was affecting all of them. Different problems leading to the same result would be possible, but quite a coincidence. In fact it seems clear from what they have said at various post-election discussions that some, although by no means all, of the other pollsters have come to the same conclusions as us.

So what is that conclusion? In the simplest terms, we think that the turnout of Labour supporters was not as high as we expected. The most fundamental point to understand is that, contrary to the general supposition, **our polls did not under-estimate the number of Conservative voters: they over-estimated the number of Labour voters and under-estimated the number who would not vote at all.** Because these figures were then converted into share of the vote, this still meant that our prediction of the Conservative percentage share was too low, but not because we didn't have enough Conservatives in our sample.

To expand that explanation slightly: in recent past elections, a higher proportion of Conservatives than of Labour supporters have voted, but we have detected that by asking people how likely they are to vote, and have corrected for it. In 2015, however, Labour supporters told us that they were just as likely to vote as Conservatives, and we took them at their word; if they had done as we expected and as they had told us they would, people who had not voted in the recent past would have voted and so turnout would have been up. But they did not and turnout was not up, and the result was that we over-estimated the size of the Labour vote. This meant that, **even though we had predicted the size of the Conservative vote correctly**, the vote percentages and the scale of the Conservative lead in our prediction was wrong.

This should become clearer when we compare our final poll prediction with the election result in two different ways. The conventional – but highly misleading – way to judge the poll is simply to compare the voting intention proportions for the various parties with the shares of the vote obtained by those parties, as in Table 41, with the don't knows and non-voters ignored. Here we can see, it is true, that our final poll missed the mark, but it gives a very misleading impression of the reason, seeming to imply that Labour is over-represented at the expense of the Conservatives and other parties.

Table 41: The final poll and the election result

| | Election result | | Ipsos MORI final poll | |
	Millions	%	numbers	%
			1,186	
Conservative	11.3	37.7%	293	36%
Labour	9.3	31.2%	286	35%
Other parties	9.3	31.2%	245	30%
Not voting			362	

We can see much more clearly what the problem is in Table 42, which includes the non-voters. This, remember, is the basis on which the poll is conducted. There is no way of directly drawing a sample of voters – all we can do is to draw a sample of all adult members of the public, and then hope to exclude the non-voters from them before we make our voting 'prediction'.[179]

Table 42: The final poll and the election result (including abstentions)

| | Election result | | Ipsos MORI final poll | | |
	millions	%	numbers	%	millions (projected)
Total	50.5		1186		
Conservative	11.3	22.4%	293	24.7%	12.5
Labour	9.3	18.5%	286	24.1%	12.2
Other parties	9.3	18.5%	245	20.7%	10.4
Will not/did not vote	20.5	40.6%	362	30.5%	15.4

---

[179] Note that in this table the turnout shown, 59.4%, is considerably lower than the official turnout of 66%. This is because the official turnout is calculated based on the number of names on the electoral register: the proportion of the resident adult population who vote is considerably lower, since many are either ineligible to vote or, despite being eligible, are not registered. Since our poll starts from a sample representing the whole resident adult population, including the ineligible and unregistered, it is with this lower turnout figure that our poll needs to be compared.

From this table it can be clearly seen that the poll under-represented non-voters and over-represented voters for all the parties; but Labour voters were over-represented most, and that produced the error in the final poll. The overall exaggeration of turnout was not in any sense unexpected; we invariably find that a much higher proportion of poll respondents claim they are "absolutely certain" to vote than the proportion of electors who actually do so. But in recent past elections we have, nevertheless, managed to correct for the differences in exaggeration by supporters of different parties so as to reach roughly the right vote proportions. In 2015 we didn't.

To understand why we think this was where the problem was, it is necessary first to explain how the polls are conducted and see in detail how the voting 'prediction' is calculated from the data that we collect. Crucially, the methodology was in all its essentials identical in 2015 to what we did in 2010[180]. Ipsos MORI's political polls are conducted by telephone, and for each poll we interview a fresh sample of between 1,000 and 2,000 respondents. The process consists, in essence, of three separate stages:

1. We contact a roughly representative sample of British adults[181] and ask them a series of questions.

2. We adjust the data by weighting to make that sample more fully representative.

3. Using the answers they have given to our questions, we attempt to predict whether each respondent will vote and if so for which

---

[180] As a matter of principle we make a point of full transparency in our methods, and the details of every poll we publish (question wording, sample size, fieldwork dates, the weighting applied to the data, etc) are always posted on our website (www.ipsos-mori.com). Most other polling companies do the same, and this is now a requirement of the British Polling Council (BPC), of which Ipsos MORI was a founder member. In fact we go much further than our membership of the BPC requires: it is always possible, for example, to see from our computer tables the exact steps in calculating the voting projection and the impact that each step has (so that it can be seen what the result would be if the calculation were done in different ways); and we are often able and willing to provide much greater detail on request, to conduct extra analysis or even to hand over the raw data for other researchers to analyse for themselves.

[181] Covering Great Britain but not Northern Ireland: people in Northern Ireland are sometimes included in other Ipsos MORI surveys, but the universal convention is to exclude them from voting intention surveys since the main parties do not contest seats in Northern Ireland.

party, discarding those we identify as non-voters and counting up the rest to produce a percentage prediction.

We select telephone numbers using 'random digit dialling' (which ensures that we don't leave out people who are not listed in the phone book). This now includes a fixed proportion of mobile phone numbers as well as landline numbers.[182] When somebody answers the phone, if there is more than one person in the household we choose one of them to take part in the survey with the help of quotas. These are calculated to ensure that the sample broadly matches the adult population in the distribution of the sexes, of age, of social class and of working status (that is whether the respondent works full-time, part time or not at all), as well as geographical spread.

Once our chosen person has agreed to take part (we may arrange to phone them back at a more convenient time if they are willing but unable to participate immediately), we now ask them each of the questions in the poll, including a series of demographic questions which we use to ensure that the sample is truly representative. The interview begins with a few basic demographic details, to ensure that the person we are talking to fits the quotas, and then proceeds with the political questions: these always begin with the questions about voting – whether they are registered to vote, whether they have already voted by post and if not, how likely they are to vote, and which party they intend to support (or have already voted for), in that order. These are followed by another dozen or so questions about aspects of the election, and further questions about themselves – detailed demographics, newspaper readership and so on. We also ask their postcodes, so we can work out which constituency and what sort of neighbourhood they live in. The interviewers use CATI (computer-assisted telephone interviewing) technology, which brings up the questions on a

---

[182] This is one minor difference between our methodologies in 2010 and 2015. The proportion of the population who can only be contacted by mobile phone is steadily increasing, and so we decided that adding mobile numbers to our sample was a necessary precaution in case the views of mobile and landline users got out of step, and to ensure that as many eligible voters as possible would have the chance of being asked to take part in our polls. But in fact at the moment, as we have found to be the case for a number of years, there is no significant difference between the political views of mobile users and landline users once demographic differences are taken into account. It would have made no difference at all to our prediction of the Conservative and Labour vote shares if the mobile users had been excluded from the final poll.

screen in front of them and allows them to key in the response directly. These responses form our unweighted or raw data, which in 2015 consisted of 1,186 interviews, carried out on Tuesday 5 May and Wednesday 6 May, the last two days before the election.

The next stage is to weight the data to make it fully representative. This sounds complicated to anybody who is not familiar with it, and the mathematics behind it is fairly complex, but the idea is a very simple one. For example, it turned out in our raw sample of 1,186 that 621 (52%) of the people we talked to were men and only 565 (48%) were women. This meant that men were slightly over-represented, because in the British public as a whole, around 49% of adults are men and 51% are women. If the views of men and women are different this would mean we would get an inaccurate reading of public opinion. But we can correct for this by counting each woman as slightly more than 1 and each man as slightly less than 1, so that the final total works out right. In this case we would count each man as 0.93 (roughly, 49 divided by 52), and each woman as 1.08 (51 divided by 48): that would mean the men in total added up to 577 and the women to 609, the right proportions. With this straightforward example, correcting for only a single factor, the mathematics is simple enough to do with a calculator. However, to combine several factors at once we use a more complicated procedure called rim weighting, and we have to leave it to the computer to calculate the corrections[183]; but the basic principle is the same. In fact the effect of demographic weighting is normally small, since the combination of quotas and randomly selected telephone numbers generally prevents the raw sample diverging very much from the ideal; it is really only a fine-tuning process.

Having assembled (what we hope is) a representative sample, the final stage is to calculate a voting intention projection from their answers to our questions. That is not as simple as counting up each party's supporters, because not everybody will vote and some of those who will vote won't tell us which party they support. And, of course, there is the possibility

---

[183] We weight by region, sex, age, social class (occupation), housing tenure, ethnic group, number of cars in the household and working status (including whether respondents work in the public or private sector). Data for both weights and quotas are derived from the Census, from the ONS midyear population estimates (the official annual updates of the census figures), the Labour Force Survey and the National Readership Survey, as well as from other Ipsos MORI surveys where appropriate.

that some people will change their minds after they talk to us and vote for a different party – although in fact the evidence suggests that these last-minute swings rarely make a big difference. (The last time it affected the accuracy of the polls may have been 1970, when the polls stopped interviewing a lot longer before the election than they do today.) Last-minute changes of mind about whether to vote at all, however, may be a different matter.

Our estimate of each participant's voting behaviour effectively has two components: whether we think they will vote, and which party we think they will vote for if they vote at all. The turnout calculation is based mainly on the question "And how likely will you be to vote in an immediate General Election, on a scale of 1 to 10, where 10 means you would be absolutely certain to vote and 1 that you would be absolutely certain *not* to vote?": we take everybody who says they are "absolutely certain to vote" (10 on the 1-to-10 scale) as likely voters, and everybody else as non-voters; we also exclude those who have told us they are not registered to vote, of course. Anybody who has told us they have already voted by post is also, naturally, included with the voters. In 2015, of our original sample of 1,186, 82 had told us they were not registered to vote, 265 that they had already voted by post, and of the remaining 839, 649 told us that they were absolutely certain to vote[184]. This means that, taking the weighting into account, 74% of the total and 82% of those who claimed to be on the electoral register were being regarded as probable voters, much higher than the turnout was likely to be. But there was nothing unusual in this, we have always found that the 'predicted' turnout from the polls is higher than the real turnout.

There are probably two reasons for this. It is very clear that the public exaggerate their likelihood of voting – a good many of those who say they are "absolutely certain" will not, in fact, vote after all.[185] This error arises from 'social desirability bias', where some people indicate that they are likely to vote because this is what they think the interviewer expects to hear. Probably, also, people who are least interested in politics are also

---

[184] These are the unweighted figures, counting the actual number of people giving these answers; the proportions after weighting were slightly different, as Table 43 shows.
[185] After the election, some of them will tell us they have voted even if they have not, as can be confirmed by checking the marked electoral register which records who voted.

least likely to take part in opinion polls, so our samples may over-represent those who vote, even though we try to correct for this. Nevertheless, we have always taken the view that asking people whether or not they are going to vote is the most reliable basis for estimating whether they will or not.

Table 43: Calculating the voting 'prediction' in Ipsos MORI's final poll

	Unweighted	Weighted	Exclude undecided/ will not vote	Already voted/ 'Certain to vote'	With refusers
Number					
Conservative	323	322	322	270	293
Labour	301	309	309	265	286
Other party*	310	280	280	229	245
Undecided	66	70			
Will not vote	27	.24			
Refused to say	77	74	(74)	(60)	
Unregistered	82	107			
Total	1,186	1,186			
Percentage					
Conservative	27%	27%	35%	35%	36%
Labour	25%	26%	34%	35%	35%
Other party*	26%	24%	31%	30%	30%
Undecided	6%	6%			
Will not vote	2%	2%			
Refused to say	6%	6%			
Unregistered	7%	9%			
Total	100%	100%			

Source: Ipsos MORI. Figures may not sum exactly to totals because of rounding error.
*Other parties are measured separately in the poll, but combined here for clarity.

Each person has also been asked which party they intend to vote for (or have already voted for, in the case of postal voters). This uses a two-part question: if they say they are undecided or prefer not to say which party they intend to vote for, we ask a follow-up 'squeeze' question, "Which party are you most inclined to support?". Only if they still tell us they are undecided or are still unwilling to say, or if in answer to either question they tell us directly that they will not vote, do we dismiss them as "don't knows". Typically in one of our normal monthly polls, about two-thirds will give us a voting intention at the first prompt, but a third of the rest respond positively to the 'squeeze', so that we can class four in every five adults as supporters of one of the parties. Of the remainder, fewer than one in ten (under 2% of the total sample) are refusers who might vote but won't say how; the rest are genuine "don't knows" and given the turnout, we judge unlikely to vote. In the final election poll, however, we found – as we usually find – that the numbers refusing to tell us which party they have voted or are about to vote for increases substantially (6% in this case). Table 43 shows the detailed figures.

To calculate our final voting prediction, we count up the voting intentions of those who are certain to vote or who have already voted. But with so many refusing to reveal their party (about 7% of all those we think will vote), they cannot safely be ignored in case they come disproportionately from one party or another. However, we can estimate how this group will vote on the basis of the newspapers they choose to read. (Of the things we measure, newspaper readership is one of the most strongly correlated with voting, and even people who don't want to tell us how they will vote don't mind telling us which papers they read.) As the table shows, we can then add the refusers into the final totals, which however made only a small difference to the party shares of the vote.

It should be understood that we have never been suggesting that the '10 out of 10 certain to vote' criterion necessarily identifies exactly those respondents who will vote. Of course, some '10s' will fail to vote (we estimate that one in ten of these will in fact not cast their ballot) and many '8s' and '9s' will get to the polls (about half do, although our past analysis shows that not many '7' or below vote at all). Therefore, we've come to the conclusion from our experience in previous elections that it gave us the best approximation of the political profile of those who do vote, that the relative proportion of each party's supporters who were "absolutely certain to vote" is the best available indicator of differential turnout, and therefore produces the best indications from a representative sample of how the country will or would vote.

In other words, we do not really expect that we can draw an exactly-representative poll sample and literally predict the voting behaviour of every respondent in it so as to be a perfect microcosm of the entire adult population. It would be much simpler if that were possible, of course, but – as already mentioned – in practice accurate polling is always a matter of recognising the imperfections in the data and correcting for them. We expect our final poll to deliver us two measurements: the relative proportions of the public supporting each of the parties, and the relative differences in turnout between those parties. So each poll prediction can be presented as a 'raw' party share before the turnout correction and a turnout percentage applied to each party which applies that correction. Viewing Ipsos MORI's final polls at the 2010 and 2015 elections in this way enables us to compare them and see exactly why one gave a sufficiently accurate prediction of the voting and the other did not.

In fact this is very easy to see in hindsight. The 'raw' voting intention lead for the Conservatives over Labour, demographically weighted but with no account taken of turnout, was very similar in our final poll in 2015 to what we had in 2010; **what was different was how likely people said they were to vote.**

Figure 27: Turnout in general elections in Great Britain, 1945-2015

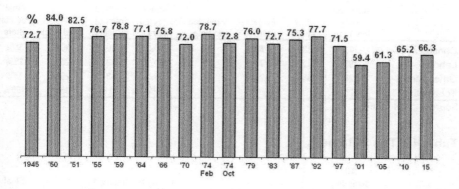

Note: Figures given are for turnout in Great Britain only, excluding Northern Ireland

In 2010, 76% of people in our poll said they were *"absolutely certain to vote"* (or had already done so); in 2015, 82% said so, which should have indicated a six-point rise in turnout, yet in fact the turnout was barely up at all. (Figure 27.) And **that increased certainty to vote was almost entirely concentrated among Labour supporters:** 85% of Conservatives said they were certain to vote in 2010, 84% in 2015, only one point different, while **74% of Labour supporters said they were certain to vote in 2010 but 86% that they were certain to vote in 2015,** a 12 point difference, and other parties 79% and 86% respectively. This is the rationale on which our "It wasn't shy Tories, it was reluctant Labour who gave Cameron his comeback" is based.

Table 44 and Table 45 give the figures from Ipsos MORI's final polls in 2010 and 2015, respectively, showing the effect of these turnout corrections on the raw figures.

Our poll was telling us that in terms of overall support, the Conservative lead over Labour had not significantly changed, although both parties had gained from other parties. However, it also told us that turnout would be up substantially, and that the increase would come entirely from supporters of Labour and the smaller parties (which meant that the same number of Conservatives would amount to a smaller percentage of the overall vote). We now know that turnout was not up substantially.

Table 44: The 2010 poll

	All declaring voting intention	"Raw" share	Projected turnout	Expected to vote	Turnout corrected share	Imputed votes of refusers	Final total	Final predicted share
Conservative	308	33%	*85%*	263	35%	40	303	**36%**
Labour	293	32%	*74%*	218	29%	33	251	**29%**
Other parties	328	35%	*79%*	260	35%	38	298	**35%**
Total voting	929			741	100%	111	852	**100%**

Source: Ipsos MORI

Table 45: The 2015 poll

	All declaring voting intention	"Raw" share	Projected turnout	Expected to vote	Turnout corrected share	Imputed votes of refusers	Final total	Final predicted share
Conservative	322	36%	*84%*	270	36%	23	293	**36%**
Labour	309	34%	*86%*	265	36%	21	286	**35%**
Other parties	267	30%	*86%*	229	31%	16	245	**30%**
Total voting	898			764	103%	60	824	**100%**

Source: Ipsos MORI

If we had disbelieved the likelihood of voting answers and had instead applied the 2010 turnout correction to the 2015 poll, we would have had Conservative 38%, Labour 32%, pretty close to perfect (see Table 46). But of course we had no way of knowing that at the time.

Table 46: The 2015 poll using the 2010 turnout percentages

	All declaring voting intention	"Raw" share	Projected turnout	Expected to vote	Turnout corrected share	Imputed votes of refusers	Final total	Final predicted share
Conservative	322	36%	85%	275	38%	23	298	38%
Labour	309	34%	74%	230	32%	21	251	32%
Other parties	267	30%	79%	212	30%	16	228	29%
Total voting	898			717	100%	60	777	100%

Source: Ipsos MORI

So the 2010 poll was consistent with the outcome. If intending voters in 2015 had given us the same answers about how likely they were to vote in 2010, the 2015 poll would also have been right; and the answers they gave us instead, promising an increased likelihood of voting, did not fit the reality of an almost unimproved turnout.

Taking these points together, there are two possible conclusions. One is that the problem is caused by people telling us they were sure to vote and then not doing so: **voters were more inclined to exaggerate their likelihood of voting in 2015 than in 2010, and that this extra exaggeration was disproportionately among Labour supporters rather than Tories.**

The other possibility is that the people we spoke to predicted their own likelihood of voting accurately, but we didn't succeed in talking to enough non-voters, and this problem was bigger among Labour-supporting than among Tory-supporting groups of the public. This would also cause us to over-predict turnout for both parties, but to over predict Labour turnout by more. The second possible explanation is therefore **that the difference in willingness to be polled between Labour voters and Labour non-voters was bigger in 2015 than in 2010**, so we ended up with a higher proportion of voting Labour supporters and a lower proportion of otherwise-similar non-voters than we should have done.

Either of these situations, or a combination of the two, would have had exactly the same effect on our polls, that our estimate of Labour turnout was increased even though there was no real increase in Labour turnout.

Although we will not know in full what conclusions can be drawn from the other companies' polls until the BPC investigatory team reports in 2016, some of the evidence which has already been published would seem

223

to tend towards the same conclusion that we have drawn on different grounds. The British Election Study internet survey (which is run on YouGov's panel but directed by an academic team) found substantial evidence to suggest that many of their participants claim to have voted when this is not the case:

> "20% of respondents in areas without local elections claim to have voted in them in 2015; 3-6% of respondents in the campaign wave claim to have voted by post before the postal ballots were actually issued and 46% of respondents who we could not verify as registered to vote in June 2014 claim to have voted in the 2014 European Elections."

And, significantly, they add that "In all of these cases, the fibbers lean significantly more Labour than other respondents."[186]

We might have been more suspicious of the increase in declared likelihood of voting by Labour supporters in our polls if had been a one-off change, out of line with the previous polling. But it wasn't. In fact we had been consistently finding that in our monthly polls throughout the parliament, that more Labour supporters were saying they were certain to vote than had been the case in the past.

The switch took place almost immediately after the 2010 election (Figure 28), and on the face of it there was nothing very implausible about it. The sudden shock of a Conservative-led government after 13 years when their own party had been in power might easily have sufficiently galvanised Labour's supporters into a greater determination to do their bit to throw the Tories out again at the next opportunity. But it seems not to have materialised in practice.

---

[186] Jon Mellon and Chris Prosser, 'Why Did the Polls Go Wrong?', *British Election Study*, 15 July 2015, http://www.britishelectionstudy.com/bes-resources/why-did-the-polls-go-wrong-by-jon-mellon-and-chris-prosser/#.Vadz0LXz-tL, accessed 14 October 2015.

Figure 28: "Certain to vote" by party in Ipsos MORI's polls 2008-15

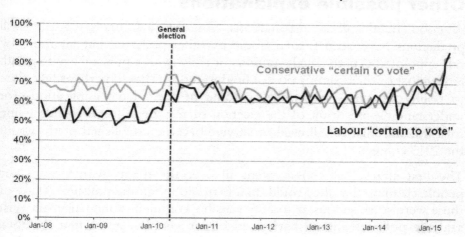

Source: Ipsos MORI Political Monitor

This leaves us with a conundrum. Although we are now fairly sure that the direct cause of our previously-successful methodology breaking down was that Labour supporters began exaggerating their likelihood of voting more than in the past or the sample imbalance between Labour voters and Labour non-voters was bigger than in the past, we don't know why this happened. It is possible to speculate, but as far as we know there is no convincing evidence. (One suggestion that has been floated is that the people who said they would vote Labour and failed to do so in 2015 were the same people who said they would vote Liberal Democrat in 2010 and failed to do so, causing all the polls to overestimate Liberal Democrat strength then. But that is purely a guess, and not everybody accepts that that was the reason why the Liberal Democrat vote was over-stated in any case.) That makes correcting our methods to prevent the same difficulties arising in future a tricky task. We are working on it, you may be sure, but have not yet reached a firm conclusion how our methodology should change for 2020.

Other possible explanations

A good many other 'explanations' for the inaccuracy of the poll predictions have been floated, some by other pollsters, but far more by self-appointed experts, media pundits or those with a political axe to grind. Since most of them simply do not hold water, we should perhaps take time to point out why – especially as some of them have implications for understanding the result of the election or for the political agenda going forward, and might if allowed to survive become established myths about the 2015 contest.

The first attacks, of course, were all over the media within hours, by people claiming that they could do a better job than the pollsters. Many of these were so ridiculous as to defy sensible comment. One party strategist said the pollsters should have used bigger samples: given that the total number of interviews during the campaign, all contributing to polls finding basically the same results, was well into six figures, one wonders how big a sample he would like! But since every one of the polls displayed an error in the same direction, the cause patently had nothing to do with sampling error, and so the sample size was entirely irrelevant. This is not a criticism that reveals much understanding of survey research.

We have also heard various people claiming that the parties knew from their private polls that the published polls were wrong. That is almost certainly nonsense. At any rate, Danny Finkelstein told ITV soon after the Exit Poll forecast was broadcast that "The Conservative figure [in the Exit Poll] looks very high. Internal forecasts in the Conservative Party – the most punchy – were saying 302"[187], and Labour's pollster James Morris tweeted after the results were known that "At 9.59 Thurs I expected a Lab government. Our final poll had it borderline but public polls showed us likely winners and votes moving to us.".[188]

One journalist suggested the polls got it wrong "because they lied"[189]. We didn't, of course. Nor do we manipulate our results to suit the preferences

[187] 'ITV News: Election 2015 - Opening', *YouTube* (ITV News, 7 May 2015), https://www.youtube.com/watch?v=6KIPdDAHdwM, accessed 14 May 2015 (at 8:01).
[188] https://twitter.com/JamesDMorris/status/598124531061018625, accessed 14 October 2015.
[189] Dan Hodges, 'Why Did the Polls Get It Wrong at the General Election? Because They Lied', *The Telegraph*, 24 June 2015, http://www.telegraph.co.uk/news/general-election-2015/politics-

of our clients. Every pollster in the BPC is required to be entirely transparent about its methods, and as far as we know they have all provided their raw data to the independent enquiry team for the academics to pore over and dissect: if there was any manipulation or misreporting of the data it would certainly be found. The main point of his argument seems to be that the close agreement of all the final polls can only be explained by 'herding', deliberate manipulation of some of the polls' results to fall into line with the others. This relies entirely on statistical ignorance. As the independent analyst Matt Singh demonstrated the following day, there is no evidence whatever of 'herding' in the polls: in fact the spread of predictions is slightly wider, not narrower, than would be expected by sheer random chance[190].

Another suggestion, widely believed to be true, is that "people lie to pollsters". We don't think that is generally the case, either.

But there are some 'explanations' which have been widely canvassed that are worth addressing. These include the late swing hypothesis, 'shy Tories' and the swinging don't knows. We consider each of these, next.

Late swing

We should start with the most obvious possibility, a late swing by voters after they were interviewed in the final polls, which would be a convenient explanation for us were it true, because to some extent it would absolve the polls from any error. Try as we might to predict the future we make no claims to clairvoyance, and if the polls are right at the moment they are conducted, with the respondents themselves unaware that they will change their minds, that is, after all, what election campaigns are about.

However, **there seems to be no evidence to support the idea that there was a late swing in the voting intention**. It is a possibility that we are always wary of before an election, but our figures gave us no reason to expect one.

---

blog/11695816/Why-did-the-polls-get-it-wrong-at-the-general-election-Because-they-lied.html, accessed 13 November 2015.

[190] Matt Singh, 'Is There Evidence of Pollsters Herding?', *Number Cruncher Politics*, http://www.ncpolitics.uk/2015/06/is-there-evidence-of-pollsters-herding.html/.

In our final poll, with interviewing the two days before the election, we found that 21% of those of our respondents who had a voting intention told us that they might still change their minds -- a high figure. But while it is true that this is much higher than it once was (only 10% in 1983 and 11% in 1987), it was not as high as at the last two elections: in fact 30% were still undecided on election eve in 2010, and 27% in 2005; this year's 21% was the same as in 1997 and 2001.

Table 47: Last minute decisions?

Q. (All with a voting intention) Have you definitely decided to vote for (party) or is there a chance you may change your mind before you vote?

		Conser-		Current voting intention			
	All	vative	Labour	Lib Dem	UKIP	Green	SNP
	%	%	%	%	%	%	%
Definitely decided	78	74	75	70	59	54	89
May change mind	21	24	25	30	41	46	11
Don't know	1	2	*	0	0	0	0

Base: 923 British adults 18+ declaring a voting intention, 5-6 May 2015
Source: Ipsos MORI Political Monitor

Q. (Those certain to vote) Have you definitely decided to vote for (party) or is there a chance you may change your mind before you vote?

		Conser-		Current voting intention			
	All	vative	Labour	Lib Dem	UKIP	Green	SNP
	%	%	%	%	%	%	%
Definitely decided	75	76	78	71	61	61	91
May change mind	24	22	21	29	39	39	9
Don't know	1	2	1	0	0	0	0

Base: 923 British adults 18+ declaring a voting intention, 5-6 May 2015
Source: Ipsos MORI Political Monitor

Of course, even if there were no more people considering changing their mind than in the past, that is no guarantee that more of them may not actually have done so when it came to the point. But, again, there is nothing in the figures to suggest the likelihood of a late swing by Labour supporters to the Tories that might explain the error in the polls. Quite to the contrary. To begin with, Labour's intending voters were no more likely than average to say that they had not yet definitely decided – in fact, with the exception of the Scottish nationalists they claimed to be the most determined of all the parties (see Table 47).

The most waverers were to be found among Greens and UKIP supporters, reasonably enough as both had far more reason to consider voting tactically than those who preferred the other four big parties[191].

The analysis can be taken further. Every participant in the final poll who said that he or she had not definitely decided was asked which other party they might vote for instead, if they were to change their mind. Only 15% of those who were wavering about voting Labour thought they might vote Conservative instead – they were as likely to be considering a vote for UKIP, and more likely to be thinking of voting Green or Liberal Democrat. Even if every one of them had been counted in our poll as a Conservative voter instead of a Labour voter, the projected Conservative lead would only have been increased from one percentage point to two points. And, in fact, we found more of our Conservative supporters saying that they were still contemplating voting Labour than the number who were considering moving in the other direction.

What is more, as part of our final poll we also carry out a separate exercise in the hope of detecting any late swing, interviewing a sample of the public on the Tuesday and then calling back some of them on the Wednesday to see if their intentions have changed. Had we found any swing, we would have adjusted our prediction accordingly, as we have sometimes done in the past. This time, however, we found no evidence of any swing in progress, so no adjustment was made.

Some of the other pollsters have further evidence towards the same conclusion. On election day, YouGov re-contacted 6,000 of the people it had polled earlier in the week, and found that although 5% had changed their minds, all the switching cancelled out, and there had been no net swing in progress.[192] And the British Election Study internet panel survey conducted a post-election re-contact survey, which also found no evidence of any swing by those it had talked to before the election.[193]

---

[191] Of course, tactical voting for the Tories by supporters of the smaller parties, even if it took place at the last minute, would not explain the over-estimation of the Labour vote.
[192] Peter Kellner, 'We Got It Wrong. Why?', *YouGov*, 11 May 2015,
https://yougov.co.uk/news/2015/05/11/we-got-it-wrong-why/, accessed 14 October 2015.
[193] Mellon and Prosser, 'Why Did the Polls Go Wrong?'

'Shy Tories'

Another frequently expressed idea was that it was all because of 'shy Tories', people who knew they were going to vote Conservative but were reluctant to admit it to a pollster, and since this is generally accepted as one of the factors that contributed to the under-estimate of the Conservative lead by the polls in 1992, perhaps it is not surprising that people should be looking for it again in 2015.

But note that this would not help at all to explain the fault in our figures. We were not short of Conservatives. We had enough people in our sample who said they were going to vote Tory and were certain to vote to account for all the Tory votes in the election. (And, as a check, we also had enough people in our sample who said they had voted Tory in 2010 to match the previous election result.)

In any case, regardless of the prediction polls, there are no signs of any 'shy Tory' problem at the moment – and you may be sure that since 1992 it is one of the things that we look for. The 'shy Tory' phenomenon is one example of the 'social desirability bias' effect. This is a well-known problem which affects all types of survey research and indeed other forms of communication: the doctor who finds that his patients under-report their drinking or smoking is facing social desirability bias. Studies of sexual behaviour find that men tend to exaggerate in their reports the number of sexual partners that they have had, women to do the opposite. People feel under pressure to conform to social norms, are reluctant to give answers they fear might demean them in the eyes of the person to whom they are speaking, and this can create significant bias in survey responses. If people believe that voting Conservative is unfashionable, or may cause other people to think less well of them, then the result will probably be that Conservative support is undercounted in the polls unless the pollsters are alert enough to detect and correct for it.

The 1992 election has also frequently been cited, perhaps less convincingly, as an example of a related but wider phenomenon in public opinion, a "spiral of silence".[194] In a classic spiral of silence, apparently unpopular opinions are suppressed not only in opinion poll responses but in a wider social setting, and this has the potential to affect public opinion

---

[194] See Elisabeth Noelle-Neumann, *The Spiral of Silence* (Chicago: University of Chicago Press, 1984).

itself: the impression that the opinion in question is unpopular becomes deepened by the unwillingness of those that hold it to express it, and this may eventually cause those holding it to question their own views and public opinion as a whole to move genuinely towards the more-widely expressed point of view.

But it does not seem to be true that voting Conservative is perceived as having the same stigma as it did in the 1990s. One way we measure this is with our 'word-of-mouth test' – adapted from the polling that we use to test companies' corporate image – which asks people whether they would encourage or discourage people from voting for a party, and whether they would wait to be asked or feel so strongly they would give such advice without being asked. Back in 1997 we found that less than half of the Conservative Party's supporters would advise somebody else to vote the same way even if asked: 46% in total would advise somebody else to vote Conservative (including the 10% who would do so without being asked), but another 46% would be neutral if asked for an opinion. In 2015, 60% of Tories said they would encourage others to vote the same way, and only 35% were so weak in their support or so reluctant to admit it that they would be neutral. These figures are only a little weaker than those for Labour supporters (65% would encourage somebody else to vote Labour, 30% would be neutral about it), which are almost identical to Labour's ratings in 1997.

Nor do we see the symptoms we would expect in the political polling if there was significant reluctance to admit Conservative support. As already mentioned, we monitor the number of people in our polls saying that they voted for each of the parties at the previous general election[195]: throughout the parliament, we have been finding too many, rather than not enough, of our respondents telling us they voted Conservative, which suggests 'shy Tories' are not a problem at the moment.

---

[195] Many other companies weight their samples by this reported past vote. We prefer not to do so, as we believe that it potentially distorts the data and is quite unnecessary provided the sampling procedures are adequate. (Weighting our poll by reported past vote in 2015 would not have prevented the under-estimation of the Conservative lead.) Nevertheless, we do regard it as offering a useful warning sign of the possibility of an unrepresentative sample, and so pay close attention to it.

Moreover, if social desirability bias were a big distorting factor in the 2015 polls, we would probably expect to find a difference between the online polls and those that use live interviewers. Advocates of online opinion polling have argued, reasonably enough, that one of its advantages is that it uses a self-completion questionnaire, which reduces the likelihood of social desirability bias. Certainly, the evidence seems to suggest that an important factor in social desirability bias is the interaction between the survey respondent and the interviewer (whether face-to-face or by telephone), with the respondent's reluctance to admit an opinion or behaviour of which he or she fears the interviewer may disapprove being the driving psychological factor. There is, therefore, some reason to suppose that self-completion survey methods, in which the respondent's views do not become known to an interviewer, may produce more honest answers in cases where there is a risk of a social desirability bias[196]. But if this is true, then the lack of any systematic difference between the telephone and online polls in their measurement of Conservative and Labour vote share would argue that the problem was not, after all, connected with social desirability bias.

The swinging don't knows

Another suggestion which was voiced in several quarters after this election as in every other since polling began was that the pollsters are too negligent of the don't knows, assuming that they would split proportionately between the parties when in fact in 2015 they split very substantially in the Conservatives' favour.

This is another apparently convincing idea which, however, simply doesn't fit the data. As already noted, any explanation which assumes that, for whatever reason, we talked to people who eventually voted Conservative but had told us that they were going to do something else, does not account for the discrepancy in our figures – it finds us extra Tories, and we had enough Tories already. What we were short of was non-voters. If our samples were more Conservative than we realised, that simply creates a

---

[196] For experimental evidence see Frauke Kreuter, Stanley Presser, and Roger Tourangeau, 'Social Desirability Bias in CATI, IVR, and Web Surveys: The Effects of Mode and Question Sensitivity', *Public Opinion Quarterly* 72 (2009): 847–865.

second discrepancy and leaves even more to be explained by some further unspecified problem.

Besides, the suggestion of differential voting by don't knows does not work, because there are simply not enough don't knows, at least in our polls[197]. We base our final voting prediction on those who say they are registered to vote and absolutely certain to vote. Only 5% of these in our poll said they were undecided which way they would vote. Our method of dealing with the undecideds is simply to leave them out altogether, and re-percentage the remaining figures – we think most of them will not vote at all and that those who do are unlikely to split hugely more to one party than another. However, if we had instead added them into the figures and assumed they would massively favour the Conservatives, it still would not solve the error: we already have too many saying they would vote Labour even without the don't knows. We had 293 respondents projected as voting Conservative, 286 Labour and 245 for other parties. There were only 43 don't knows. [198] Even if we had added every single don't know as a Conservative voter, that would still only push Labour down to 33%.

---

[197] Some of the other polling companies do not use a 'squeeze' question in measuring voting intention and consequently have to deal with many more respondents who have not given a voting intention than we do. But since our forecasts in 2015 were all fairly similar, this difference in methodology was plainly not a major contributory factor to the error.
[198] These numbers are weighted.

So were the polls wrong all along, or not?

If we are right about the main cause of the error in the polls being a lower turnout among Labour supporters than we expected, what does this tell us about the reliability of the polls during the election campaign and since the 2010 election? In one sense, it looks as if it could be argued that they were "wrong all along" – the rise in predicted turnout by Labour supporters began almost immediately after the 2010 election, and almost certainly throughout the parliament we were counting as Labour voters people who were still Labour supporters at the time of the election but didn't vote.

But should these polls be regarded as wrong? At what point does a potential voter become a non-voter? Suppose we were able to predict with absolute accuracy whether somebody was going to vote at the next general election, some years away, would we be justified in refusing to take any notice of their voting intentions in our polls? That is not necessarily an easy question to answer. Some of the 'likely voter' calculations used by U.S. pollsters in effect try to do exactly that. But on balance we do not believe that we should. What we are talking about is a bloc of real people, who really did support the Labour Party, and who really had the possibility of voting Labour right up to the moment on election day when it was too late to get to the polling station. Very probably they did not know themselves whether they would vote or not.

Of course, our final polls should ideally include them only if they are going to vote. One academic observer takes the view that we should only interview people who we knew would vote, but didn't have the answer to the question of how do we know if they were asked, and answered honestly, that they were going to vote, and were committed to voting for a party certain, and were not in the 'may-change-mind' camp. On this occasion we included them and they didn't vote, and so the polls were more inaccurate than they should have been; on some other occasion, perhaps, they would have voted and the polls would have been right if they were included and wrong if they were left out. We accept that we will get complaints if we fail, but nobody should assume that it is an easy job – perhaps it is not even a possible one. The difference between somebody voting and not voting is a far smaller psychological step than changing from one party to another, and for that reason probably much harder for the respondent himself or herself, let alone the pollster, to predict.

But what about the polls before the final poll? How predestined is a potential voter's decision to vote or not to vote at that point? If we are right about why the final prediction was wrong, then the campaign polls before the final polls, eleven of them, were completely justified in saying that Labour and the Conservatives were neck and neck in their number of supporters across the country – it was simply that when it came to the point days or weeks later, fewer of Labour's intending voters turned out. They may have been misleading as predictions, but as far as our poll two days before the election, it was not intended to predict; it is a snapshots of the state of play at the moment the respondent was interviewed and we believe that it was accurate at that moment. That is our view of our survey taken two days before the voting; other pollsters will have to defend their own election eve polls, some claim they are predictions, we don't. Finding real Labour supporters who really could have voted Labour and still at that point really intended to do so ; if the polls had succeeded in only counting those who would eventually vote, and so reported a substantial Conservative lead throughout the campaign, is there not an important sense in which that would have been just as misleading and inaccurate?

Implications

There are two implications that follow. The first is that there is no reason to be suspicious about the reliability of other findings of the opinion polls in the five years up to the 2015 election: the samples were adequate, the participants do not seem to have been dissembling on their opinions except, perhaps, over their enthusiasm and determination to vote, and they should be able to provide robust evidence to understand public opinion over that period and the outcome of the election, provided that allowance is made whenever voting intentions are considered for Labour's supporters to exaggerate their likelihood of voting more strongly than those of other parties.

But the more important consideration, perhaps, relates to the public role of polls in allowing the media to report the 'horserace' during the election and, perhaps, influencing some voters by doing so. Much of the comment on the polls immediately after the election centred on the possibility that they had painted a misleading picture during the campaign, showing a tight race in which a thoroughly-hung parliament was a probable outcome rather a Conservative lead sufficient to ensure that Labour had little chance of government: this, it was suggested, lent weight to the Conservative campaign about the dangers of SNP influence on a Labour administration, and may have swayed the votes of floating voters.

The more hysterical of these arguments are self-defeating. If it was only fear of the SNP that led to the Conservative victory, and fear of the SNP was caused by what the polls were saying about the state of the parties, then surely the polls must have been right before the voters reacted to what they were saying and swung to the Conservatives? But in fact there is little sign of movements in support at any stage of the campaign. No doubt the state of the polls provided moral support for the argument that the Conservatives were deploying; but if it affected voters it would seem to have been mainly in terms of morale, perhaps boosting Conservative turnout and/or depressing Labour turnout. But, once again, the argument descends into a vicious circle: the bigger the effect of the polls on the voters is supposed to be, the more accurate the polls must have been before that effect kicked in.

But there is another point to be made on the SNP. The polls may have had a misleading effect in the conclusions that were drawn about the likelihood of a Labour government; but they were entirely accurate, despite pointing to an outcome that was very surprising indeed, in measuring the SNP's rise and Labour's collapse in Scotland. What if there had been no polls, or if nobody had believed them? Then the public would inevitably have been totally unaware of the likely number of MPs that the SNP would have after the election. In 2010, they had had 6; had they claimed, purely on the basis of their canvassing, that they expected to increase this to 16, it would probably have been dismissed as optimistic exaggeration. (Indeed, they might even have felt it in their interests to play their expectations down.) In that event, their arrival at Westminster the day after the election with 56 MPs would have come completely out of the blue to voters in England and Wales. Was this not information to which they were entitled when considering how to cast their own votes?

These are questions that need to be considered when the idea is raised, as it was after the 2015 election, of banning polls altogether during election campaigns. In the eighty years over which opinion polls have existed, many have been the theories about their effects on voters. Some claimed that would inevitably cause 'bandwagon effects', with voters flocking to support the party they were told was already ahead; others expected the opposite, an 'underdog effect', with fear of the expected outcome or a preference for restricting the scale of the victory lending support to whichever party was trailing. But neither effect has ever been convincingly demonstrated even in a single case, either in Britain or anywhere else, and certainly neither has proved an inevitable consequence of poll coverage.

But few pollsters would deny that some voters' opinions may be affected by their reading of the polls. Is this necessarily a bad thing? If some people want to know what other people think, and to take that into account in their own voting, that would seem to be their business – in a democracy it is every voter's right to make up their mind how to vote in their own way, and nobody may dictate what considerations they can allow to influence them. Naturally, if the opinion polls are one of those influences then it is disturbing if the polls are inaccurate, but ideally the solution is that voters should understand and take into account that polls cannot be infallible, not to suggest that polls should be banned in case they are wrong. (If we are worried about voters being misled by inaccurate predictions during election campaigns, perhaps we ought to start by banning manifestos?)

We would be the first to say that blind reliance on the gospel truth of every poll finding to the umpteenth decimal place is misguided and even dangerous. We discuss this further below (pp. 241–245). But if people want information about what other people think, or what other people (say they) are going to do, the polls – with all their imperfections – are still the best source.

Table 48: Interest in opinion polls during elections

Q How interested would you say you are in the following? What opinion polls say about the election

	1992	1997	2001	2005	2015
	%	%	%	%	%
Very interested	8	7	5	8	18
Fairly interested	32	26	30	31	44
Not very interested*	33	38	34	29	21
Not at all interested	25	28	30	30	14
Don't know	2	1	1	2	2
Very/fairly	40	33	35	39	62
Not very/Not at all	58	64	64	59	35
Net Interested	-28	-31	-29	-20	+27

Base: c. 1,000-2,000 British adults 18+ in each poll

Source: Ipsos MORI

* "Not particularly interested" 1992-2005

Because, make no mistake about it, there is an insatiable demand for this sort of information (Table 48). Not everybody is interested, of course, but many are, and if they cannot get it from polls they will look for it somewhere else.

Of course, there is no shortage of other sources offering to interpret public opinion. The politicians generally feel that understanding the way voters think is one of their professional skills, and they are rarely reluctant to explain the state of public opinion – which, curiously, always seems to back their own position! They like to decry the polls if they point in a different direction, but how do they judge opinion themselves? Perhaps, as Stanley Baldwin speculated of a previous generation of MPs who claimed to be in touch with opinion in their constituencies, they simply ask the stationmaster. Journalists and editors too are sometimes confident of their ability to read public opinion, but when they are not relying on polls to help them do so it is remarkable how often what they find seems to fit the narrative of the tale they are already telling. (Indeed, one of our professional skills as pollsters sometimes has to be making sure that the polls that journalists commission from us are not inadvertently designed to fit into that same narrative, rather than coming to the question afresh.) Objective measurements with no axe to grind, no point to prove, no story to substantiate, only a curiosity to satisfy about how the public mind works, that is the purpose of the professional polls and almost their exclusive preserve.

We should make the point that almost all opinion polling in Britain is conducted as one specialised part of the business of bigger research companies. Polling is not a particularly profitable part of our business, and the same is true as far as we know for the other companies that publish polls: for most of us it represents only a tiny part of our turnover. But it is our shop window, the most visible part of our business, our opportunity to demonstrate our competence to our customers and potential customers, and no pollster has any incentive whatever to do anything except be as accurate as possible. We are in one of the very few businesses where the only thing we are paid for is to speak the truth.

Suppose there were no polls, as there were not in this country before the 1930s. Who could the public rely upon then to tell them what other people were thinking? Would people trust the politicians to interpret public opinion? Probably not, because most people seem to take the view eloquently expressed by a participant in one of our online focus groups during this election, that "honest politicians are like the Loch Ness monster – a few people claim to have seen one, but nobody can prove it". And even the honest politicians (who, to be fair, are much more common than the public's cynical view would admit) are prone to optimism and self-delusion. Witness Paddy Ashdown vowing to eat his hat if the Exit Poll prediction of Lib Dem losses was accurate, even though this was one of the respects in which the Exit Poll and the pre-election polls were in agreement. Or remember John Major in 1997: "The difference out on the doorstep with what we are seeing in the opinion polls is very striking indeed – very striking. This election is there to be won, of that I have not a shred of doubt and I believe that we are going to win it... The polls are rubbish." Even the honest politicians are consistently worse at judging public opinion than are the polls.

Or the Press? These days, most newspapers rely on polls to help them understand public opinion. Did the public believe their newspapers before polls were invented (1935)? Before proper opinion polls, the media interviewed party activists and reported to their readers what the activists told them. In those days the *Telegraph* seemed always to find a last minute swing to the Tories while the *News Chronicle* would find a last minute swing to Labour. Also remember that in 1945, before the reputation of the then-solitary Gallup poll was sufficiently established that anybody took any notice of it, it was the press that was unanimously of the opinion that Churchill would be re-elected easily. Attlee won a landslide, the press speculation far further from the truth than the polls have ever been.

It is sometimes argued that there are other indicators of the forthcoming general election result which are more reliable than the voting intention polls – although most of them seem to be based, directly or indirectly, on poll findings (if not of voting intentions then of economic optimism, attitudes to the leaders, best party on certain key issues or some other political opinions). That so many different observers have so many different pet theories is perhaps revealing in itself. Matt Singh of Number Cruncher Politics published alternative projections based on a number of different indicators before the election[199], and the one that turned out to

---

[199] Matt Singh, 'Is There a Shy Tory Factor in 2015?', *Number Cruncher Politics*, http://www.ncpolitics.uk/2015/05/shy-tory-factor-2015.html/.

give a very close prediction of the eventual Conservative lead was based on Ipsos MORI's satisfaction ratings for the two leaders. But although that worked in 2015, it has not been entirely infallible. It was MORI's first political client, in fact, who found himself embarrassed by relying on precisely that principle: "Perhaps you can point to the last occasion on which a party won with its leader trailing behind the other leader in personal ratings – particularly if you find he was trailing nearly two-to-one behind the other leader," he said.[200] That was Harold Wilson, basking in his comfortable ratings lead over Ted Heath in June 1970; a fortnight later, he had lost and was out of office.

But in any case, even if these other predicting methods were infallible they would not make the polls redundant. They can't tell you who votes which way, or why, or what might make them change their minds. At best, they may warn when the voting intention polls have gone wrong; but they are no substitute for the information the polls can provide so long as they are right.

We are unhappy with the performance of the polls in 2015. But we will not stop polling, nor should we. We are not perfect, and sometimes things go awry, but we are all of us trying our best and even our imperfections do not make a case for abandoning the effort. Understanding public opinion is a worthwhile aim and, we believe, an integral and indispensable part of democratic politics; and surveys are the only way to do that.

---

[200] Harold Wilson speaking at a press conference on 2 June 1970, quoted in David Butler and Michael Pinto-Duschinsky, *The British General Election of 1970* (London: Macmillan, 1971), 159.

Margins of error

We should conclude with a word on the 'margin of error'. This is something which is often discussed but almost as often misunderstood. The margin of error is usually taken as being another name for what statisticians call the 'confidence interval', but that is a misunderstanding of the practical aspects of conducting opinion polls. Our colleagues in the USA have begun to talk in terms of an alternative, the 'credibility interval', which may be a more useful way of treating the matter.

But it is with the confidence interval that our explanation should start. The confidence interval is a statistical calculation, and strictly speaking it applies only to surveys using probability sampling – in other words, where it is known exactly how likely every person was to be asked to take part in the survey. Then, provided the only possible source of error is bad luck in picking the wrong people to take part, it is mathematically straightforward to calculate exactly how probable it is that the difference between the estimate taken from the survey and the true figure for the whole population falls within any given range.

Let's take a very simple example. Most people know that the probabilities in games of chance can be precisely calculated – we know exactly how likely it is that you will be dealt a Royal Flush in poker or that red will come up seven times in a row on a roulette wheel. Sampling in a survey is, in effect, exactly like being dealt a hand from a huge shuffled pack of cards. But let's cut the complications to a minimum, and consider what happens when we throw two ordinary dice and add the numbers together. The lowest possible score is 2, if we throw a double one, the highest is 12, if we throw a double six, but the likeliest score is 7, because there are six different combinations that add up to 7. We know there is just 1 chance in 36, a 2.8% chance, that we will throw 12, a double six, but 6 chances in 36, 16.7%, that we will throw 7 in one way or another.

Now suppose we try to predict the outcome before we throw the dice. The likeliest total is 7, but it is still much more likely than not that we will throw a different total; however, if it's not 7 it is more likely to be near to 7 than a long way away. It is almost an even chance (44%) that we will throw 6, 7 or 8; a two-thirds chance (67%) that we will throw between 5 and 9. And it is very likely that we will throw a score between 3 and 11, which will happen 17 times out of 18, a 94.4% probability.

This is very similar to what we mean when we talk about the confidence interval of an opinion poll. The conventional measure is the 95% confidence interval, the prediction that has 19 chances out of 20 to be right, which is obviously not very far away from the 17 out of 18, 94.4%, chance of throwing between 3 and 11 with two dice. We could say that the 94.4% confidence prediction for the dice throw is 7 plus or minus 4, in other words between 3 and 11. But we are still saying that 7 is the single likeliest outcome, and that it is not impossible that we will throw a 2 or a 12, just that it won't happen very often. In the same way, the "headline" prediction from the opinion poll is the likeliest single number, but the real figure might easily be a little bit higher or lower than that; and, one time in twenty, it will be even further away from the prediction than the "margin of error" suggests. (The margin of error for opinion polls is often quoted as being "3 per cent", which is a – badly inaccurate – shorthand way of saying that a poll finding of 50% really means 50 plus-or-minus 3; but 50 is the likeliest single figure, and one time in twenty the true figure will be lower than 47 or higher than 53.)

But we are making an important assumption here – these probabilities only hold if the dice are fair. Suppose one of the dice is loaded: in that case we don't know any more that it is equally likely to throw a 1, 2, 3, 4, 5 or a 6. The chances of throwing a double six may not be 2.8% any more. More difficult still, suppose we don't know whether the dice are loaded or not – perhaps we don't think it's likely, but we don't know for certain. How likely is it now that we will throw between 3 and 11? To work that out we would need to know:

- how likely that throw would be with the fair dice (OK, we already know that);

- how likely it would be with the loaded dice (and perhaps we know enough to make a reasonably accurate guess at that); and

- how likely it is that the dice we are about to throw are loaded rather than fair.

That is the tricky bit. It is not a matter of mathematical probabilities at all, but something we would have to judge from the circumstances, who we were playing with, what chances they had had to switch the dice, and what number we thought that they wanted us to throw.

Making predictions from opinion polls is exactly like this. We never have a guarantee that we are playing with fair dice – and even if they have not been deliberately loaded they may not have been so perfectly made that the chances of throwing each number are exactly equal. The confidence intervals that are frequently quoted for opinion polls assume a perfect probability sample where the exact likelihood of each person taking part in the poll is known, and the measurement of each participant in the poll can be made with perfect accuracy. But even with the purest (and most expensive) surveys, this is never true in practice. Not everybody who is asked to take part in the survey will agree to do so, and we don't know how different those people who do take part are from those who don't. And the measurements are unlikely to be precise, either: easy enough if we are trying to tell how tall the population is, and we can take a tape measure to our respondents, but not so easy if we want to predict how they will vote tomorrow and do not know how exactly their answers to our questions will be reflected in their behaviour 24 hours later.

This all implies that the 'margin of error', if the concept is to have any useful meaning, cannot just be about the 95% confidence intervals. They assume perfect dice – pure random sampling with 100% response rates and perfect interpretation of respondents' answers. No pollsters use pure random samples (they are simply not practical for the purpose) and even if we did we could not approach 100% response rates. As a pure matter of practicality, we know we cannot exclude the possibility of sampling biases, non-response biases, questionnaire biases or mis-projection of behaviour from survey responses; all we can do is attempt to minimise all of these. All of those may contribute to polling error, but our experience is that many times their errors cancel each other out.

We know perfectly well that we can't expect to be able to get away with saying "well, the sampling variation was well within the confidence intervals and none of this other bias is our fault", and nor should we. The effects of the biases will be part of the error as well as the effects of the sampling variation, unless we are lucky enough to find they cancel each other out. (And we should explain here that when we talk about 'bias', we do not mean that any pollster has a preference for one result over another or that the polls are ever crafted to produce specific outcomes: 'bias' is the term for a measurement being systematically likely to be inaccurate in one direction rather than the other. It is not the pollsters that are biased, but the real-world influences that interfere with our attempts to make accurate measurements. The dice are loaded, but it is not we that have loaded them.)

But this means it is wrong to expect that all the poll errors will be randomly distributed, that a three per cent error in one direction is no more likely than a three per cent error in the other direction. That applies to the sampling variation, the good or bad luck in drawing a representative sample for an individual poll, but it doesn't apply to systematic biases: if Labour supporters are more likely than Conservatives to say that they will vote when they don't intend to do so, that will affect all the polls at the same time, and in the same direction. At any one election it is entirely likely that most or all of the poll errors will favour the same party, and it will only be by unlikely chance that the 'poll of polls' is more accurate than the individual polls.

Different polling companies adopt different solutions to minimise the effect of bias on their polls, and this can create a systematic difference in their results, often called a 'house effect'. House effects are usually fairly small, perhaps a matter of one or two percentage points difference in party's share of the vote at most, and you can't reliably detect them in a single poll because these differences are quite small enough to be cancelled out by the random sampling variation – just as you can't tell whether the dice are loaded from a single throw, but you might be able to from several hundred throws when sixes keep coming up more often than is natural. These house effects mean that in the long-term, some companies' polls are likely to be more accurate than others, but because their accuracy can only be tested once every five years we are never likely to know for certain which is which.

So when we say as a rule of thumb that polls should be treated as having a three per cent margin of error, we have to include within that the errors arising from any forms of bias as well as the sampling variation, allowing for the practical imperfections of polling as well as the theoretical probabilities in a perfect world. By still quoting that three per cent figure in those circumstances we are in fact setting ourselves a very demanding standard (which, unhappily, we failed to meet 2015 for the Labour and Conservative Parties). But it is wrong to assume that we can go further than that, and expect that as well as all the polls being within three per cent there should be one that overestimates the Conservative lead for every one that underestimates it. The world doesn't work like that.

Towards 2020

The next General Election is scheduled to take place on 7 May 2020: but what implications will the results of the 2015 General Election and the subsequent elections of new Labour and Lib Dem leaders have for the main political parties over the next five years?

The Conservatives, enjoying a majority of only 10 seats, will need to hold onto the seats they gained in 2010 and 2015. A number of factors will impact on whether or not they can really do this: some within the party's control, such as the choice of the next Conservative leader (and presumably Prime Minister just before 2020); others which any government only has a limited ability to control, in particular the performance of the economy. But the Conservatives' fortunes in 2020 will also depend on how well the Labour Party responds to its second successive defeat.

2015 was another terrible election year for Labour. Arguably, it was far worse than 2010, given that the party failed to make any progress in key Conservative-Labour marginal seats (despite five years of Coalition austerity and the collapse of the Lib Dem vote) and the humiliation of losing all but one of its Scottish Members of Parliament to the SNP. For Labour to gain power at the next election, either through gaining a majority of seats in the new House of Commons or through becoming the largest party to "lock out" the Tories, they will need to make very significant progress in the English and Welsh seats currently held by the Conservatives, and to rebuild in Scotland.

There are a number of factors that we can be fairly sure will have an impact on voters and their decisions in 2020. By the time of the next general election, the leaders of the three major national parties (still counting the Lib Dems of course!) will be different to the ones who fought in 2015. David Cameron committed himself to stepping down, and Ed Miliband and Nick Clegg resigned immediately following the 2015 election. This is a similar situation to that which occurred in 2010 when Brown, Cameron and Clegg were 'fresh' leaders, none of them having campaigned in a general election as party leader. The 2010 election saw more people emphasise the importance of the image of the leader in helping them decide how to vote than ever before in the period that MORI has been polling. We look at the challenges facing the new party leaders in more detail below.

The EU referendum

The referendum on whether the UK should remain in or leave the European Union has the potential to be a major factor in how people decide to vote at the next general election. Almost all polls in recent years have found majority support for staying in the EU (our most recent, in October 2015, found 52% who would vote to stay in and 39% to leave[201]), and the experience of past referendums both here and around the world has been that when there is a swing in opinion, it tends towards the status quo[202]. The economic security arguments for keeping EU membership seem to make sense to the majority of the public, and – as in 1975 – many in the political and business world are likely to argue the same way with perhaps a few exceptions such as Lord Bamford of construction company, JCB. The likeliest outcome, therefore, must be that Britain will vote to stay in.

Nevertheless, such an outcome cannot be taken for granted. More than half the public say they could still be persuaded to change their minds on how they will vote[203]. UKIP has already shown that the issue of immigration has the potential to mobilise anti-EU sentiment, and developments in the EU's response to refugee migration from Syria and elsewhere since the summer of 2015 could transform the way that some of the voting public view the membership issue. And even when majorities have indicated their preference for retaining EU membership, we have also found that the type of European community that most British people would prefer is only a common (economic) market, with no element of

---

[201] Ipsos MORI interviewed 1,021 GB adults by telephone on 17-19 October 2015. More details at https://www.ipsos-mori.com/researchpublications/researcharchive/3641/Stays-lead-narrows-in-EU-Referendum-debate.aspx#gallery[m]/1/, accessed 9 November 2015. Ipsos MORI trend data on attitudes to Britain's membership of the European Union can be found at https://www.ipsos-mori.com/researchpublications/researcharchive/2435/European-Union-membership-trends.aspx.

[202] For a relevant and instructive discussion of the dynamics of public opinion in recent referendums in Ireland, see Jane O'Mahony, 'Ireland's EU Referendum Experience', *Irish Political Studies* 24 (2009): 429–446.

[203] Ipsos MORI Political Monitor, October 2015 – see note 201.

political union. (Table 49.) It is not impossible, therefore, that opponents of the EU might find a productive way to reframe the debate about Britain's place in Europe before the decision has to be made.

Table 49: Britain's relationship with Europe

Q. Which of these options best describes your own preference for Britain's future role in Europe?

	June 2015 %	October 2015 %
Britain and other member states of the European Union moving towards closer political and economic integration	14	12
Britain's relationship with Europe remaining broadly the same as at present	31	26
Britain returning to being part of an economic community, without political links	33	37
Britain leaving the European Union altogether	13	18
Other	1	*
None of these	1	1
Don't know	6	5

Base: c. 1,000 British adults 18+ in each survey
Source: Ipsos MORI Political Monitor

Moreover, it seems to be an essential part of David Cameron's strategy, as it was of Harold Wilson's, to renegotiate the terms of British membership so as to find some 'concessions' he can present to the voters as bait to persuade them to reaffirm the European project once more. In theory, there need not be much substance to these, so long as they can be presented enticingly enough to the floating voters but, at the very least, he needs the co-operation of the leaders of other European countries to allow him to spin the situation to his advantage. If they continue to play hardball, in public as well as in private, playing Nigel Farage's game rather than David Cameron's, calculating that British withdrawal from the EU is an impossibility and they can therefore safely humiliate the British government, they risk a miscalculation (which would be even more disastrous for them than for David Cameron).

A decision by the British public to vote to leave the European Union would have a considerable impact on domestic politics. Not only would it represent a failure of Cameron's leadership (and probably force his early departure from office, especially if he has campaigned to remain in the EU), it could provide the pretext for the SNP demanding and getting a

249

second referendum on Scottish independence, given Scottish support for remaining in the EU. A decision such as this is one of the few factors we see that could lead to an early general election, since it has the potential to split the Conservatives and smash their slender parliamentary majority, if Cameron's leadership skills prove inadequate to avert this disaster or if external events tear matters out of his control.

The same might conceivably happen if a vote to stay in the EU splits the Conservative Party, and if the Eurosceptic wing of the Tories felt betrayed by their leader campaigning to remain in the EU, but in that case the Labour Party might have more freedom of movement to decide whether an early general election was to their benefit or not, since there would be no political imperative for Labour to make common cause with Eurosceptic rebels.

What would happen in those circumstances, given the as-yet-untried provisions of the Fixed-term Parliaments Act, is uncertain. If the rebels joined the opposition in voting for a motion of no confidence in the government, a general election would not automatically follow, as would previously have been the case. With a Eurosceptic leader in Jeremy Corbyn, it is not inconceivable that Labour could demand the opportunity to try to form an alternative government without an election. Presumably it would fail if brought to a vote, but the only way it could be formally brought to a vote would be for the Crown to dismiss Cameron from office and invite Corbyn to attempt to form a ministry[204]; in which case Corbyn rather than Cameron would go into the subsequent election as Prime Minister! We stress, however, that whilst this situation is possible, it is a remote contingency, but it does nevertheless underline the important point

---

[204] The Act provides that Parliament will be dissolved (and an election will follow) if a motion of no confidence in the government is passed and no further motion expressing confidence in the government is then passed with 14 days. Because the provisions hang on confidence in a government, a new government must take office before the 14-day clock can be stopped, unless of course the old government can persuade MPs to reverse their decision. Since the appointment of a Prime Minister remains a royal prerogative, no procedures are laid down to determine what steps must be taken to determine the viability of an alternative potential government before it can be appointed and allowed to meet the Commons, but the constitutional logic would seem to be in favour of the benefit of any doubt being given to the aspiring new PM, and allowing the Commons to determine his fate, rather than proceeding directly to a new general election with no chance for him to test his strength.

that an early election might make nonsense of calculations about which leaders will contest the premiership in 2020.

If there were an early election provoked by a Conservative rebellion over Europe, it might be natural to suppose that the European issue would be the sole one over which it was fought, but single-issue British elections are rare: even the general elections of 1910, centred on the 'People's Budget' and the powers of the House of Lords, which would perhaps offer the nearest parallel, were affected by many other issues as well. Leadership – Cameron against Corbyn, if that were the line-up – could hardly fail to be of importance and to range over much wider ground than just EU policy. Economic policy would likely continue to be central, especially if Britain by having just committed to leaving the EU had entirely redrawn the economic landscape. Moreover, if the Labour leader were Jeremy Corbyn and he retained his current opposition towards the EU, Labour could hardly fight the election on a policy of reversing Cameron's errors and negotiating re-entry; nor could Cameron, or his successor as Conservative leader were he supplanted, easily defy a clear public judgment on their own policies and promise an immediate second referendum to reverse the decision.

So an election that immediately followed a referendum vote to leave the EU might be fought with neither major party being a natural refuge for Europhiles. Might that cause a formal split in the Conservative or Labour parties? A huge swing back to the Liberal Democrats? Or might the voters ignore the issue and vote on other matters entirely? Or might a new centrist, pro-business, pro-EU party be born out of this mess? If Britain goes down this road, we find the consequences very difficult to predict indeed, particularly in the longer term.

Assuming that the outcome of the EU referendum does not result in an early general election, the potential for Europe to be a salient, political issue in 2020 should still not be underestimated. This is not so much that two or three years after the referendum the public will believe Europe is one of their biggest concerns when coming to cast their vote, as that the political impact of the campaign may not by then be resolved. One of the defining (and damaging) public perceptions of the Conservative Party since the early 1990s is that it is a 'divided' party. Part of David Cameron's electoral success to date has been to reduce this perception of the Tories, but a referendum on the very issue that most divides the party has the potential to do long-term harm, especially if a successful 'yes to Europe' vote wins by a narrow majority. Of course, the potential for Europe to cause – or rather expose – a split is not confined to the Conservatives. If Labour's new leadership advocates a vote to leave the Union, Labour may also feel the political pains well after the campaign is over. Nevertheless, in all likelihood, more important to the 2020 election result will be how the parties are rated on the issues that are nearly always most salient for the voters – in 2010 and 2015 these were the economy, immigration, public services and welfare.

And finally, of course, are the events that will surely happen – both foreign and domestic – over the next few years that none of us can today predict. For the most part, the political impact of these events will be most obvious from how well the government is seen to respond to them: the public may not necessarily give extra credit for a government that handles events competently ("isn't that what the government is supposed to do?"), but even a generally popular government can quickly come unstuck where they are seen to lose control of events.

The Conservative leadership

The Fixed-term Parliaments Act provides David Cameron and his successor with a higher level of comfort than has been the case with previous prime ministerial changes between elections. Assuming that Cameron is able to choose his date of departure, say in 2019 or early 2020, any political pressure or demand for the new Conservative prime minister to seek a fresh mandate will be much reduced. Gordon Brown's experience in 2007 illustrates perfectly well how poisoned a chalice that prime ministerial prerogative can be.

Labour's experience in securing its third successive election victory in 2005 illustrates a potential problem for the Conservatives seeking a renewed mandate in 2020. Between 1997 and 2005, Labour's share of the vote dropped from 44% to 36% – a drop of 8 percentage points. Anything like that scale of movement away from the Conservatives in 2020 will almost certainly mean the loss of power. Yet we should not assume the same will happen at the next election. David Cameron proved in 2015 that it is possible to buck long-term historical trends. In addition, the Conservatives will be looking to gain a popularity boost from their new leader. This certainly helped the then governments in 1955 when Anthony Eden replaced Sir Winston Churchill and in 1990 when John Major replaced Margaret Thatcher. Yet, as both Eden's and Brown's prime ministerial careers demonstrated, the switch to a new leader will not necessarily revive a governing party's fortunes: if they don't do the job well, or if the public does not think that they are doing it well, their popularity will plummet. In each case the party got a brief 'bounce' from the novelty of the new leader, but was soon enough (like Tigger) 'unbounced'.

The process for electing a Conservative leader is twofold. Conservative Members of Parliament hold a series of ballots from nominated candidates in order to finalise a shortlist of two – those being the two candidates with the most support from their parliamentary colleagues. In 2005, David Cameron and David Davis qualified, with 90 and 57 votes respectively, to go onto the ballot paper for the membership vote ahead of Liam Fox (eliminated at this stage after receiving the support of 51 MPs). The ultimate decision on the leader is therefore up to Conservative Party members. In 2005, almost 200,000 members voted in that ballot, electing David Cameron with a two to one majority over David Davis (68% to 32%).

At the next leadership election, the Conservatives will be unlikely to want to widen the electorate to include associate members or supporters (Labour's decision to do this and provide votes for those willing to donate £3 has been a painful experiment for some in the party). Nevertheless, the challenge for the Conservatives will be to elect a new leader that can appeal to a wider supporter pool than its own electoral base; their experience of electing leaders whose greatest appeal was in the consonance between their own views and those of the grassroots activists – William Hague and Iain Duncan Smith – was not a happy one (although both men have proved themselves to have much more substance in their performance as ministers since 2010 than was apparent while they were leaders of the opposition). This breadth of appeal has been one of the most important characteristics of Cameron's success (and also Tony Blair's). It is most likely then that when the leadership election comes around, the country will be looking for someone who has the same ability to appeal to voters as Cameron has certainly had, but likely also to be someone who appears much different to him.

The task facing the Labour Party

The election of Jeremy Corbyn as leader of the Labour Party in September 2015 is a clear sign that the vast majority of the party (although not the parliamentary party) interpreted that year's election defeat as the consequence of not offering a clear-enough, anti-austerity, left-wing alternative to the Coalition Government.

True, there were plenty of opinion polls during the past five years showing the public disliked austerity and there was strong opposition to several of the key policies implemented by the Coalition. In addition, as Table 50 illustrates, over the past several years there has been a rise in the number of people who would describe their political views as "Left" (from 23% in 1999 to 29% in 2015) and a smaller decrease in the number of self-identifying on the "Right" (from 22% to 20%).

Table 50: Left, right and centre

Q. Some people describe their political views as being left wing or right wing. How would you describe your own views?

	Oct 1999 %	Oct 2010 %	Oct 2013 %	Jan 2015 %
Left wing	8	9	9	11
Left of centre	15	15	18	18
Centre	38	33	29	30
Right of centre	12	16	20	14
Right wing	10	8	9	6
Don't know	17	19	15	21

Base: c. 1,000 British adults 18+ in each survey
Source: Ipsos MORI Political Monitor

In itself, a change like this might not be surprising; people do, after all change their political opinions, sometimes in quite dramatic numbers over a short period of time. But if the number of right-of-centre sympathisers has decreased, you would probably expect that to be accompanied by falling support for the political parties on the right. The strange thing in this case was that this did not happen. The voting intentions of the participants in the 2013 and 2015 polls, for example, were very similar: in October 2013 we found the Conservatives on 35%, Labour on 35%, the Liberal Democrats on 9% and UKIP on 10%; in January 2015, the Conservatives had 33%, Labour 34%, Liberal Democrats 8% and UKIP

11%. No significant movement, or a sign of any difference between the two polls beyond ordinary small sampling variations – certainly nothing that would remotely reflect a nine-point fall in the proportion of the public who consider themselves right of centre. And the General Election results show that the Conservatives can win, even where fewer people see themselves ideologically on the Right. Perhaps, more than anything, this reiterates much research that shows most voters – particularly swing voters – do not think in 'Left-Right' terms, and certainly do not discuss or frame their political choices in this way. So those who believe there is a growing, left-wing, anti-austerity 'silent majority' in Britain should be careful how they interpret opinion data such as this. It may well be that it is people's perceptions of what constitutes 'left wing' or 'right wing' thinking rather than their own views that are changing. If people feel the political centre of gravity is moving to the right and perhaps leaving them behind, will this eventually cause their votes to gravitate to Labour? Or will they feel pressure to move rightwards too?

Further, much of the evidence from the last parliament suggests that most people accepted the need for austerity (even where they were critical of how it was being implemented, particularly in terms of fairness) and large proportions of the public continued to blame Labour for the need for austerity in the first place.

Looking ahead to 2020, of all the issues Labour needs to address in order to stand a chance of winning back the floating voters the most important is to demonstrate that it is capable of managing the economy – and this includes that it understands public concerns about too much spending on public services (and too much waste, particularly in welfare). Few Corbyn-backers are likely to agree with Tony Blair on many topics, but his comments quoted in *The Times* in July 2015 seem entirely appropriate here:

> "After the 1979 election... the Labour Party persuaded itself that the reason why the country had voted for Margaret Thatcher was because they wanted a really left-wing Labour Party. This is what I call the theory that the electorate is stupid, that somehow they

haven't noticed that Margaret Thatcher was somewhat to the right of Jim Callaghan." [205]

Part of the rebuilding of the party – and of demonstrating that it has learnt the lessons of its two most recent defeats – will be to consider what of the Conservative Cameron 'settlement' it is prepared to accept. New Labour did this effectively before 1997, deliberately campaigning to build on (or at least tame) the Thatcherite economic and public service reforms rather than undo them. The Conservatives attempted the same – and to some extent succeeded – in 2010, accepting, for example, a whole range of Labour policies that it had previously opposed including the National Minimum Wage, increased funding for the NHS and overseas development and a more liberal social policy.

By 2015, Labour had failed to demonstrate to the public that it understood the reasons for its defeat in 2010, and did not do enough to show it had a better approach to tackling people's concerns than the Conservatives. If it cannot win the argument on the Tories' agenda, it must move the agenda on to some issue on which it can win, and the only way to do this may be to concede the Tory victory on the economic question. But if Labour neither moves on, nor finds the key to winning without moving on, it will lose again, and again, and again.

The other core failure of Labour between 2010 and 2015 was leadership. As we have seen in pages 51–61, through the election and subsequent decisions of Ed Miliband, Labour allowed itself to be portrayed as too left-wing to appeal to the moderate Conservative supporters it needed to win back marginal seats; and Miliband offered no personal appeal to stop the sweep of the SNP in Scotland. Compounding this, Miliband as a leader – a Prime Minister in waiting – was a failure. The party appears to have made the same mistake with the election of Jeremy Corbyn as leader.

Ipsos MORI's first measure of public reaction to Corbyn as Labour leader was in a survey conducted on 19-22 September 2015. This showed that slightly more people were dissatisfied (36%) than satisfied (33%) with his performance to date as Leader of the Opposition. This 'net score' of –3 is the lowest recorded for a new Leader of the Opposition since MORI

---

[205] Michael Savage and Lucy Fisher, 'If Your Heart Is With Corbyn Get a Transplant, Says Blair', *The Times*, 23 July 2015, 8–9.

started tracking this question at the start of the 1980s. By way of comparison, at the same stage in Ed Miliband's tenure, his 'net satisfaction' score was +19.

On a wider measure of Corbyn's image, we also found that more people said they "do not like him" (55%) than do (37%); those who say they voted Conservative at the general election dislike him by 77% to 18%, and those who did not vote at all – the group where he must look for new support if he cannot win over Tories – by 48% to 30%. And although he was popular with the majority of those who had voted Labour, the immediate reaction of three in ten was that they did not like their new leader. This seems to be further evidence that despite his widespread victory among Labour members, supporters and affiliates, he has so far not been able to widen that appeal to those voters that determine who wins at a general election. Add to this the clear evidence that he does not start out with the confidence of his own parliamentary party, and the task facing him if he hopes to become Prime Minister in 2010 is as daunting as for any party leader in decades.

It also appears that the Labour brand has been damaged by the election of Jeremy Corbyn. The main changes in Labour's image between April and September 2015 were all negative. By September 2015, three in four (75%) felt that Labour was "divided" (up 32 points), "out of date" (55% – up 19 points) and "extreme" (36% – up 22 points). On the crucial question of whether Labour is "fit to govern", just 35% of the public in September said it was (5 points down from April) and 21 points lower than saying the same about the Conservative party. But it is the perceptions of division which seems to most differentiate the two parties in the minds of the public. By September 2015, twice as any people would use the term "divided" as an accurate description of the Labour party (75%) as of the Conservative party (38%)[206]. As we – and many others – have pointed out many times before, "divided parties rarely win elections". The challenge is twofold for Labour, therefore. First, the early polling indicates that its new leader has a huge task ahead in persuading people he is personally right for

---

[206] Ipsos MORI interviewed 1,255 GB adults aged 18+ by telephone on 19-23 September 2015. See also Ipsos MORI's 'likeability' trend data at https://www.ipsos-mori.com/researchpublications/researcharchive/2543/Like-the-Leader-Like-their-Party.aspx?view=wide, accessed 6 November 2015.

the job as Prime Minister. And second, if Labour's brand has been severely damaged – as the Tories was in the early 1990s through divisions and splits – it may take more than one leader to repair it to such a state where the public see them as a government in waiting.

At the time of writing, it can be argued that it is too early to form a definitive picture of Labour's new leader and the impact of him on the public's wider view of the party. The first 'real' test will be in the May 2016 elections. By that time, however, the public will have had time to view Jeremy Corbyn, and for many people first impressions – particularly negative ones – really do count. Moreover, the deputy leader, Tom Watson, and Corbyn's shadow Chancellor, John McDonnell, are both for different reasons under attack by a hostile press and, without pre-judging any of the outcomes, it seems very likely that one way or another within a few months' time the public's views of the Corbyn Labour Party may have already crystallised into a clear and stable opinion that will determine once and for all whether it has any chance of winning in 2020.

In the slightly longer term, it seems almost inconceivable that there will not be a formal challenge to Corbyn's leadership at some point in the current parliament. Indeed, many commentators are treating it as a foregone conclusion that he will not lead the party into the next election, and at the moment a good many of the public think that should be the case: 42% think Labour should change its leader before the next general election, 32% that it should not. (Even among those who voted Labour, the majority against ousting Corbyn is only 40% to 38%.[207])

But even supposing such a challenge succeeded, there is an obvious danger that the ensuing civil war in the party would be far more damaging to its electoral chances even than retaining Corbyn as leader. In 2003 the Conservatives achieved a bloodless coup in similar circumstances when Iain Duncan Smith was ousted in favour of Michael Howard, rather to the surprise of most observers who expected a bloodbath; but the Conservatives have always had a more pragmatic tradition and, importantly, the party rules left the rank-and-file members who had voted for IDS powerless to intervene when Howard was nominated unopposed. A putsch against Corbyn may not end so peacefully. For one thing, if he

---

[207] Ipsos MORI interviewed 1,021 GB adults by telephone on 17-19 October 2015.

declines to go quietly, Labour MPs do not have the power that the Conservatives had in Duncan Smith's case to stop him running again by a simple majority, to be judged by the same electorate that has already given him a landslide once. (And, besides, Howard lost the general election anyway.)

Conclusion

These preceding pages have outlined three key decisions that must be made before 2020 and which will all have an impact on that year's election: by the whole voting public on whether the UK will remain a member of the EU, by the Conservative Party on who is to succeed David Cameron as leader, and by the Labour Party on whether Jeremy Corbyn will lead them into the election (and, if not, who will do so instead). In each case, the way in which the decision is reached may have much of a political impact as the decision itself.

But these are by no means the only uncertainties on the way to 2020. To these we can add the uncertainty of what will probably be a radical and disruptive review of the parliamentary boundaries, but which is likely to work substantially in the Tories' favour (unless the opposition parties find a way of blocking it again, which would mean the election being fought on boundaries more than twenty years old).

The Liberal Democrats, too, pose a conundrum. Plainly there is room for a substantial centre party in British politics, and for a party that can count on the protest votes of those who object to both the Conservatives and Labour, but neither role need necessarily fall in the future to the party which has filled them in the past. There is at least a possibility that the Liberal Democrats' loss of credibility with many of those who supported them until 2010 is irreparable. The protest votes went mostly to UKIP, the Greens and the SNP in 2015; if they stay there, separated from the centre party vote, the psephological landscape is fundamentally altered, and this works once again to the advantage of the Conservatives. The Conservatives have been plagued since the 1960s by losses to the Liberals and their successors in otherwise secure strongholds where Labour has been unlikely to make progress. Can Tim Farron rebuild that threat in five years? Or at all? Surely not while UKIP and the Greens continue to draw as many votes in England as they did this time around.

Of course, the last time Labour swung so sharply to the left after an election defeat, in 1979, one result was the break-away of the SDP, re-aligning the political battle and ultimately working to the revival of the Liberal Party, but transforming it in the process. These possibilities are at the back of everybody's minds again, but history rarely repeats itself so neatly. Labour can comfort themselves with an alternative precedent, that when the Tories last won re-election with a small majority and fundamental fault-lines over Europe, they had soon fallen out so badly among themselves that the majority evaporated and they went down at the next election to their worst defeat in almost a century.

UKIP's future is equally unpredictable, although presumably closely bound up with the outcome of the EU membership referendum. Either a resounding victory or a convincing defeat for the Eurosceptic cause might undermine the case for UKIP's continued existence, even though it is no longer quite the single-issue party that it once was. A close decision either way, however, will leave the issues of Britain's relationship with the rest of Europe firmly alive and UKIP's *raison d'être* intact – but that is not to say that UKIP's support may not fall, or rise, considerably in the process. The elevation of the European issue to being the chief subject of political debate in the run-up to the referendum may well cause perspectives to change and votes to swing.

Finally, we need to consider the Scottish National Party. They will surely retain their majority in the Scottish Parliament in the 2016 election, but how far they can maintain their momentum until 2020 is less certain. Assuming they can find no pretext to force another independence referendum, which would certainly be a game changer, can they achieve enough at Westminster to persuade the hordes of former Labour supporters who voted for them in 2015 that another SNP vote in 2020 will not be wasted? The state of the Labour party in Scotland suggests that the SNP probably have little to worry about over so short a timescale as five years, but they would be unwise to become complacent – which was, to a great extent, what did for Labour.

Sometimes after one general election the outcome of the next seems already a foregone conclusion – although even then the glorious uncertainty of British politics has often sprung a surprise. This time there seems to be uncertainty around more of the elements than usual, with the party system in a state of flux after the biggest election-on-election shifts in voting support for decades. And that is before we take into account whatever unforeseen events circumstances throw up, and how the government deals with them. We can't forecast who will win the election of 2020. But it is going to be interesting watching and finding out.

Appendix: Editorial cartoons and the 2015 election

Kent Worcester[208]

Editorial cartoons are a familiar yet easily overlooked feature of the political landscape. They are popular with many readers and have enlivened the pages of countless magazines and newspapers. With luck and timing they can also be surprisingly effective. A well-crafted political cartoon can elicit a chuckle, evince a groan, provoke an outcry, publicise a cause, wound its subject, change a mind or two, and sometimes even encapsulate the public mood.

Many aspects of contemporary editorial cartooning are rooted in artistic and commercial practices that date to the eighteenth and nineteenth centuries. Political cartoonists continue to combine caricature, symbolism, text, and humour to make fun, skewer the prominent, and take sides in public controversies. While specific styles and conventions have gone in and out of fashion, the basic visual-linguistic ground rules of the editorial cartoon can be traced back to pre-industrial times. Perhaps the only truly radical innovation since the era of James Gillray and Isaac Cruikshank has been the advent of the web, with its disruptive impact on both the newspaper industry and the craft of cartooning, as pencils and brushes make room for tablets and software.

In keeping with long-established traditions, the political cartoons of 2015 typically deployed irony, whimsy, and scorn rather than facts or nuance. By definition, the medium's restrictive canvas precludes any form of extended dialogue. But the pragmatic activity of visual-verbal encapsulation can produce striking results. The famous claim that every picture "tells a story" and "is worth a thousand words" speaks to the ways in which humorous and polemically charged editorial cartoons can unpack and dismantle

---

[208] Kent Worcester is a professor of political science at Marymount Manhattan College, New York. He is the author, editor, or co-editor of eight books, including *C.L.R. James: A Political Biography* (1996), *The Social Science Research Council, 1923-1998* (2001), *Arguing Comics: Literary Masters on a Popular Medium* (2004), and *The Superhero Reader* (2013). He would like to acknowledge the helpful research assistance of Kerry Colville at Ipsos MORI.

candidates, policies, and parties, and shed light on the underlying mechanics and dynamics of political life. As the nineteenth century essayist Ralph Waldo Emerson observed in his journal, "caricatures are often the truest history of the times".[209]

By their very nature, elections generate unforeseen incidents that dawdle in the public sphere – gaffes, pratfalls, and other unforced errors that give cartoonists and journalists something to draw, write, and laugh about. The 2015 British general election had its share of such moments, from Natalie Bennett's 'brain fade', and Labour's eight-foot limestone slab, to six-year-old Lucy Howarth's dramatic interaction with the Prime Minister. While these kinds of tempests inspired plenty of responses from the pens, and tablets, of cartoonists, policy issues and constitutional questions were also summoned during the election campaign. The economy, immigration, Scotland, the National Health Service, and the European Union all figured in the election's graphic output. Another recurrent theme was that of leadership – who was qualified, or perhaps more importantly unqualified, to hold or retain power. At the same time, the rise of UKIP, the surge of the Scottish Nationalists, Labour Party infighting, and the unravelling of the Tory-Lib Dem coalition all lent the election a compelling sense of drama, as did the uncertainty of the outcome.

There was not exactly a shortage of source material for editorial cartoonists to draw on, in other words. The election involved an unusually large number of parties, and party leaders, which gave cartoonists abundant opportunities to transform mannerisms, body language, and facial expressions into comedy and political symbolism. If we include Plaid Cymru, the Greens, and the SNP, all of which were represented in the ITV and the BBC leaders' debates, three of these party leaders were women – Leanne Wood, Natalie Bennett, and Nicola Sturgeon. This alone gave the election a distinctive aspect as far as the optics were concerned. The proliferation of competitive parties, the deepening of the England-Scotland schism, and the increased prominence of women in leadership roles each left a mark on the election's graphic commentary.

---

[209] Quoted in Stephen Hess and Milton Kaplan, *The Ungentlemanly Art: A History of American Political Cartoons* (New York: Macmillan, 1968), 141.

Political cartoons turned up in broadsheets and tabloids alike, usually in black-and-white but sometimes in colour. They were typically single-panel graphics, often with an emphasis on one or two talking heads or a single figure. Some were organised around a pair of panels, so that the second panel could offer a humorous and unexpected contrast with the first. A few were wordless, a fair number were diminutive 'pocket cartoons', and some were massive graphics that dominated the page. Throughout the election, for example, the *Guardian* and the *Independent* showcased the work of Brian Adcock, Steve Bell, Dave Brown, and Martin Rowson by ceding them substantial acreage on the opinion pages. The scale of the imagery let readers know that these cartoonists were part of the paper's brand. Editorial cartoons came in all sorts of shapes and sizes, serving in some cases as incidental features and in others as central design elements. In this sense there was a significant degree of continuity between print cartooning during the 2015 general election and that of previous election cycles.

Whether they popped up on the front page, the editorial page, or in news columns, political cartoons and illustrations could be found in national, regional, and local newspapers, as well as free commuter papers and weekly leftist papers. Cartoons also appeared in major political and business magazines, and their web counterparts. Upwards of several hundred editorial cartoons featured in print outlets during the campaign, most of which were created by one of a couple of dozen or so commercial artists, some of them holding full-time staff positions but the majority employed on a freelance basis.

At least a few online current affairs sites commissioned original work by editorial cartoonists, such as politicalbetting.com, which utilised the graphic art of Martha Richler ("Marf") in 2010 and 2015 (Cartoon 4). Numerous web designers and bloggers uploaded and linked to political cartoons on their websites, of course, and also used clip art, Photoshop, and other software programs to fashion home-grown graphic content with a political edge. Even trying to estimate the total number of cartoons and graphics that were posted online during the election and that never made it into print would be difficult: the phrase "political cartoons 2015 British general election", entered into Google, yields "about 1,960,000 results", while the phrase "2015 UK general election cartoons" produces "about 3,600,000 results".

Cartoon 4: Marf, *politicalbetting.com*, 13 April 2015

Labour's worst nightmare ...

"FISCAL RESPONSIBILITY"

VOTE LABOUR

sigh

hi there.

... the naughty undecided voter.

The focus of this chapter is on newspaper editorial cartooning as opposed to magazine or online cartooning (or, for that matter, mini-comics, comic books, or graphic novels). It places a special emphasis on cartoons that were published in nationally distributed UK dailies during the five-week period between 1 April and 7 May 2015. Cartoonists were developing their styles, honing their jokes, and refining their caricatures before the first of April, of course. The ideas and imagery of the election's cartoons built on tropes, fixations, and gestures that had been worked out long before the formal campaign began. In this sense, the line that separates pre- or post-election cartooning from cartoons that appeared during the campaign itself is somewhat arbitrary. But campaigns bring a heightened level of public awareness to the work of journalists, and cartoonists, and cartoons published during the election were more likely to engender discussion and scrutiny than those produced outside of the campaign's glare. Cartoonists themselves are often provoked and inspired by the intense rush of the political joust.

An approach that emphasises newspapers with national distribution is inherently selective and partial. It neglects the efforts of cartoonists whose work shows up in papers that are produced outside London, including Iain Green (*The Scotsman*), Steve Camley (*Herald Scotland*), Jack Knight (*Lancaster Guardian*), and Stevie Lee (*Belfast Telegraph*), as well as the work of Paul Dallimore (London *Evening Standard*). And it overlooks cartoonists whose work mainly appears in weekly, bi-weekly, or monthly magazines, such as Tom Humberstone (*New Statesman*), William McPhail (*New Statesman* and *The Week*), Jacky Fleming (*Red Pepper*), Nicholas Garland (*Spectator*), Stephen Collins (*Prospect*), Robert Thompson (*The Oldie* and *Radio Times*), Kevin ('KAL') Kallaugher (*Economist*), Tim Sanders (*Socialist Worker*), and Grizelda, the veteran female cartoonist whose work appears in the *New Statesman* and the *Spectator*, and sometimes the *Independent*. Furthermore, focusing on newspaper cartooning discounts the inimitable contributions of *Private Eye*, from its snarky photo-comic covers to its deep bench of graphic contributors.

There may be good reasons for tackling a piece of the puzzle rather than the whole, however. Mounting a comprehensive study of UK political cartooning in the digital age would require an enormous expenditure of time and effort, and daily newspapers have long played and continue to play a central role in vetting and distributing political graphics. With this in mind, I have collected and collated some 312 cartoons that were originally printed in one of nineteen nationally distributed dailies and their Sunday counterparts in April and early May 2015. In alphabetical order, they are the *Daily Express*, the *Daily Mail*, the *Daily Star*, the *Financial Times*, the *Guardian*, the *Independent*, the *Independent on Sunday*, the *Mail on Sunday*, the *Mirror*, the *Observer*, the *Sun*, the *Sun on Sunday*, the *Sunday Express*, the *Sunday Mirror*, the *Sunday People*, the *Sunday Telegraph*, the *Sunday Times*, the *Telegraph*, and *The Times*. I have reluctantly left out the *Morning Star* on the grounds that its distribution is patchy. But Britain's only credible socialist daily publishes several notable cartoonists, including Martin Rowson, who also works for the *Guardian*, Ben Jennings, Rob Amos, and Lou McKeever ('Bluelou'), who is currently the sole female cartoonist on the staff of a daily UK newspaper.[210]

Although it is by no means complete, the figure of 312 accounts for the vast bulk of cartoons published by British papers during the 2015 general election and offers a sense of the scale of print-based cartooning in the period under review. Mined as cultural data, these 312 cartoons provide a basis for generalising about the messages, values, and norms expressed by editorial cartoonists during the past election. We should be able to say with some confidence, for example, whether depictions of a given party leader were friendly, neutral, mildly satirical, or hostile, for example, or whether the issue of Scottish independence came up rarely, occasionally, or frequently. As far as London-based papers are concerned, at least, the general trend-lines should be clear.

The range of styles on display in these 312 cartoons is enormous, from the exuberant linework of the *Daily Star/Sunday Express*'s Scott Clissold, and the bold inkiness of the *Daily Mail*'s Stanley McMurtry ('Mac'), to the painterly renderings of the *Independent*'s Dave Brown. In many cases, compositions focused almost entirely on faces, and upper bodies, while in others the imagery included lavish backgrounds. Some of the work featured delicate lines while other pieces were blunt and sometimes strident. A few cartoonists favoured a minimal approach, both in terms of the sparing use of text and the relative absence of visual details. Others could be garrulous with language and/or lines. As a general rule, cartoons printed in the tabloid papers tended to march straight to the point while those that turned up in the broadsheets were more likely to employ literary, historical and art-historical allusions. It hardly seems accidental that some of the most sedate and tasteful imagery was published in the *Financial Times*, whose readers were presented with Ingram Pinn's studiously detached, 'cool' graphics, to invoke Marshall McLuhan's distinction between hot and cold media.

---

[210] According to Wikipedia, the truly marginal Workers Revolutionary Party still publishes a daily paper, *The News Line*, but judging from the WRP's website the paper does not use cartoons.

The subject matter of these 312 cartoons most often involved politicians, but not always. Nearly three-quarters (222 out of 312, or 71%) depicted party leaders, individually and in groups. Forty-eight (15%) showed ordinary voters shopping, drinking, watching the telly, lying in bed, or talking to pollsters. Nearly a dozen combined these two elements by showing politicians dealing with people on the street. Traditional visual icons such as the cricket pitch, the publican, the Union Jack, the Houses of Parliament, and Number Ten were common but were by no means ubiquitous. These signifiers of Englishness, and sometimes Britishness, appeared in roughly one out of ten cartoons (31, or 10%). A smaller number referenced Scottish national symbols, such as the thistle, tartan, bagpipes, and the St Andrew's Cross (21, or 7%). In over a dozen cases (16, or 5%), cartoonists aimed at the media rather than voters or elected officials, mocking on-air personalities and experts rather than politicians. Nine of the cartoons (3%) left out people altogether and used maps, flags, talking animals, and even, on one occasion, talking submarines, to tell their story.

Stark distinctions in terms of tone and sensibility could be discerned. Some of the political imagery conveyed a cynical stance vis-à-vis the electoral process. Other images concentrated their fire on specific leaders and their parties. While a number of cartoonists were consistently partisan, others made a point of switching targets from time to time. The connection between the perspective adopted by an individual cartoonist, and the editorial stance of the paper in which his or her work appeared, was straightforward in some instances but not others.

Much of the time, newspaper cartoonists highlighted facial expressions above anything else – David Cameron's bland insouciance, Nicola Sturgeon's fierce determination, Nick Clegg's haggard game face, and Nigel Farage's maniacal grin. Cartoons that spotlighted one or two candidates – most often David Cameron and/or Ed Miliband – represented over 50% of the total number of pieces collected for this study. Ninety-six of these cartoons (31%) focused on Cameron, while 79 (25%) concentrated on Miliband. Only 9 cartoons (3%) were primarily devoted to the Liberal Democrat leader, whereas 14 cartoons (4%) centred on UKIP's Farage. Sturgeon could be spotted in the foregrounds or backgrounds of 34 cartoons, 11% of the total; women in general were represented in 122 of the 312 cartoons (39%). Forty-seven (15%) made light of three or more party leaders, often in debate settings, while 16 (5%) mocked figures from the recent past like Tony Blair and John Major, both of whom received mixed reviews for their campaign interventions. Twenty-four cartoons made fun of the media (8%), while 12 (4%) depicted members of the royal household. The latter came in one of two varieties: cartoons in which the Queen wryly commented on the election to her husband, Prince Philip, and cartoons about the Duchess's pregnancy.

Unfortunately for Her Majesty's Opposition, Ed Miliband came in for a special measure of ridicule – his hair, eyes, lips, teeth, and gait were all relentlessly mocked in the period between April Fool's and polling day. Even his table manners, and lightly furnished home kitchen, invited graphic ridicule. While Cameron appeared in a greater number of cartoons, as many as half were neutral or mildly favourable in their treatment of the PM. Cameron often came across as smug, but only rarely unhinged. The same cannot be said of the cartoons that featured Miliband, who was generally depicted as a klutz, buffoon, hysteric, or bug-eyed loon. In the *Sun*, for example, Steve ('Brighty') Bright reimagined the Labour leader as a naked would-be emperor, with knobbly knees and a hairy posterior, while in the *Sunday Express* Scott Clissold portrayed him as a terrified man-child with buck teeth and sweat dripping down his face. Bob Moran of the *Daily Telegraph* made him look petulant, Morten Morland of *The Times* drew him as a stubborn child, and in a couple of cartoons Dave Brown (*Independent*) depicted Miliband as literally adrift at sea. Christian Adams (*Telegraph*) spoke for many when he drew the party leaders as the seven dwarfs (Cartoon 2, p. xv). Cameron was Stuffy, Farage was Tipsy, Clegg was Needy, Sturgeon was Dozey, Wood was Tiddly, and Bennett was Proxy. The only one to retain a name from the Disney version – Dopey – was also the candidate whose caricature was least flattering: Ed Miliband.

Even cartoonists employed by the *Mirror*, the country's largest-circulation pro-Labour paper, made Ed Miliband look a bit odd. A freelance illustration by Martin Rowson, for example, published by the *Mirror* during the middle of the campaign, showed Miliband walking away unscathed as Cameron fell in the mud. For once the portrait of the Conservative leader seemed overtly hostile – he's grossly overweight, covered in filth, and seems to be wearing women's shoes, for some reason. But while the image could be plausibly coded as pro-Labour, the depiction of a triumphant Miliband was not exactly flattering, since in this version he still retains a crazed look in his eyes and oversized choppers. Another regular *Mirror* contributor, Charles Griffin, broke with these conventions and devoted very little attention to Miliband's teeth, hair, and eyes, but managed to make him look dour and shady all the same. Peter Brookes of *The Times* came up with the most visually striking of these caricatures, turning Miliband into an exaggerated version of Wallace from Wallace and Gromit. With the exception of the *FT*'s Pinn, whose mild-mannered drawings cast all of the party leaders in a respectful light, it would have been difficult to find editorial cartoonists who didn't at least occasionally treat Miliband as a punching bag.

Cartoon 5: Kerber and Black, *Daily Mirror*, 2 April 2015

The Conservative HQ had less to worry about when it came to cartoons. While David Cameron was sometimes represented as vacuous, pudgy, or self-satisfied, he rarely came across as villainous. The worst that Brown, Griffin, Moran and most other cartoonists could do was to portray the Prime Minister as out-of-touch. In Brian Adcock's cartoons for the *Independent*, Cameron seemed a little overwhelmed, and in Christian Adams' work he came across as a bit foolish. Neil Kerber and David Black (*Mirror*), the most consistently pro-Labour of all the cartoonists working for big-circulation papers, gave Cameron a comically exaggerated jawline. (Cartoon 5.) Chris Riddell (*Observer*) often portrayed the Conservatives as an alliance of fat cats and ogres, but his caricatures of Cameron were mild. Peter Brookes' imagery suggested that there was a certain level of anxiety, or at the very least irritability, lurking beneath Cameron's smooth exterior. Steve Bell (*Guardian*) was perhaps the Tories' least-favourite political cartoonist, since he made of habit of drawing Cameron as if he were sheathed in a condom, which made him look like he was made out of plastic and implied that he was a dickhead. Boris Johnson and George Osborne also turned up in some of these cartoons. With his salad-bowl haircut, Johnson resembled Ringo Starr circa 1965, especially in Michael Heath's delightfully eccentric sketches (*Mail on Sunday*). Osborne usually carried a sombre expression. In contrast to the imagistic fury aimed toward Ed Miliband, none of these blows, with the possible exception of Bell's, landed with any real force.

The Scottish Nationalists similarly benefitted from comparatively agreeable visuals. While bagpipes, the St Andrew's Cross, and the thistle occasionally served as visual shorthand for the Scottish question, for the most part the emphasis was on SNP leader Nicola Sturgeon, who most often resembled the cat who had just swallowed the canary. In a couple of dozen cartoons, Sturgeon smiled, grinned, smirked, or gloated as her political adversaries stood about looking helpless. Measured in terms of facial expressions, the SNP leader seemed to be enjoying the election more than anyone else so far as cartoonists were concerned. She could come across as formidable, and perhaps even scary, but these are hardly liabilities in the political arena.

Some of the most dramatic cartoons to appear during the election revolved around the vexed relationship between Nicola Sturgeon and Ed Miliband. In a dozen or so cartoons Sturgeon was shown inflicting damage on Miliband, sometimes physical, most of the time political. In one wordless graphic, by Gary Barker of the *Daily Mail*, Sturgeon's taut long arm held the rope that was strangling the Labour leader. This was exceptionally brutal in terms of its conception if not execution, since the artwork itself was rather graceful. More representative of these images was the cartoon by Peter Schrank (*Independent on Sunday*) that featured a television set showing a debate in which Sturgeon tells Miliband, "Together we can lock David Cameron out of Downing Street", while Cameron reclines with a drink in his back garden, musing to himself, "Keep this up Nicola, and I'll be staying put". (See Cartoon 3 on p. xvii.) The SNP and its leader were now forces to be reckoned with, in the cartoon world and beyond. By contrast, neither the Greens nor Plaid Cymru attracted anything approaching this level of cartooning coverage. Their leaders were almost always seen in the context of the television debates – two out of seven people standing behind podiums. They provided material for good-natured caricature but not much more.

Nick Clegg had a dire election so far as cartooning was concerned. Most of the time he was either not in evidence or lurking in the background. When he occupied the centre-stage the portrayal was uniformly negative. In one cartoon by Peter Brookes, for example, he was a miserable-looking doormat for the entrance to Number Ten. In Scott Clissold's work, Clegg was almost always drenched in sweat. Steve Bell turned Clegg into a defenceless hedgehog that had been abandoned on the side of the road by the Liberal Democrats' campaign bus, while Bob Moran placed Clegg in a wig and a dress, with a despondent Cameron standing alongside him/her. Freelancer Andy Bandery, in the *Independent on Sunday*, depicted him as a surly youngster. Most of the time Clegg looked fearful, or hapless, rather than angry.

Another party leader who might have wondered whether newspaper cartoonists were out to get him was Nigel Farage. As the consummate 'outsider' Farage probably have relished their scorn, however. In almost every case, Farage was drawn with a cigarette in his mouth, sometimes with a pint of bitter in hand. The lit cigarette seems to have been baked into Farage's avatar. In many cases, the most prominent feature was his enormous grin, which suggested that he was bold, confident, and possibly deranged. Dave Brown went further than most by giving him warts, leering eyes, and a camel's mouth. In one of Brown's cartoons, Farage pitches a cigarette carton labelled "Manifesto Lite", while in another the

UKIP leader is dressed as the Grim Reaper, bending over the inert body of an NHS patient. Scott Clissold drew him as a deluded knight on a white horse, carrying the flag of St George, while Christian Adams imagined him as a clapped-out runner whose hair was on fire. In a couple of cartoons he resembled a British version of Homer Simpson. While UKIP supporters no doubt bristled at these kinds of depictions, Farage himself did not seem to mind and was probably a lot of fun to draw.

Cartoon 6: Tim Sanders, *Independent*, 5 May 2015

Although cartoonists mainly directed their ire against party leaders, in over a dozen cases their target was the system rather any single individual or party. The *Guardian*'s Andrzej Krauze, for example, created a wordless illustration in which a generic male candidate rests in the hands of the real power behind the throne, a greasy banker in an even more expensive suit. Neither the candidate nor the crowd he's waving at notices he's a puppet.

Another respectable man in a suit, this time in a pocket cartoon by Tim Sanders (*Independent*), told his female friend, "I can't be bothered to vote in this election". "You should", she replied, "you're the candidate". (Cartoon 6.) A similar sense of humour was evident in the work of Jeremy Banx (*Financial Times*) who drew middle-aged voters saying things like, "I can't make up my mind if I'm apathetic or undecided" and "This election is so unpredictable even I don't know how I'll vote" (see Cartoon 1 on p. xii). Matt Pritchett (*Telegraph*) canvassed similar territory: in one of his slender cartoons, a voter tells a pollster, "I'm a Don't Know. But I'm a very passionate, pumped-up Don't Know". This form of agreeable wit seems tame, however, in comparison to a more deeply cynical piece like "The Cannibals", by Dave Brown, which portrayed the seven main party leaders as naked, Goyaesque flesh eaters. Now this was an image that was designed to linger in the reader's mind.

Dave Brown was by no means the only cartoonist who was firing on all cylinders during the election. Peter Brookes also comes to mind as someone who turned out a succession of timely graphics that were elegant, cutting, and smart. While Brookes' rendition of Ed Miliband as Wallace was amusing, his pen cut deeper than most when it came to David Cameron. In one particularly insightful strip, he used ten panels to dissect the inner life of the Prime Minister. For seven panels the PM is at rest, his eyes closed. In the eighth panel a raged-filled Cameron bounces into the air, his arms flaying about. In the ninth panel he goes back to sleep, and in the final panel he lifts one eye open and says, "See? I can do passion!"

Like Brookes and Brown, Martin Rowson and Steve Bell were also prolific, skeptical, and visually unpredictable. Looking to the past for inspiration, Brown, Rowson, and Bell sometimes favoured classical paintings as reference material. The most arresting of these cartoons was arguably Steve Bell's. Titled "After Caravaggio", it showed three grim figures bathed in shadow – Nicola Sturgeon, David Cameron, and Ed Balls. (See Cartoon 7.) In this version of Caravaggio's 1607 masterpiece, "Salome with the Head of John the Baptist", Sturgeon carries the sword while Cameron brandishes the silver platter that holds Ed Miliband's severed head. This image could be interpreted as sympathetic to the Labour leader, but it seems unlikely that anyone at Labour Party headquarters was going to plaster it on a poster or t-shirt. Gerald Scarfe (*Sunday Times*) was yet another broadsheet cartoonist with a distinctive aesthetic and a raft of historical and literary allusions whose work was simultaneously decorative and disturbing. One of his pieces transformed the seven party leaders into Fabergé eggs. Sturgeon, of course, was "Scotch Egg". "Egg Farage" was "cracked and rancid". The "Welsh Egg" was "fresh from the valleys" while "Green Egg" came with ham. Once again the Liberal Democrat leader Nick Clegg looked despondent; he was "Clegg of Toast". Cameron got off relatively lightly: he was "Egg Cameron (pickled)" while "Egg Miliband (scrambled)" had bleary eyes, a runny nose, and a creepy set of teeth.

Cartoon 7: Steve Bell, *The Guardian*, 30 April 2015

Copyright Steve Bell, used by permission

A prominent newspaper cartoonist who enjoyed an exceptionally fruitful election was Stanley McMurtry, better known as "Mac". Born in 1936, McMurtry was granted an MBE in 2003 for his services to the newspaper industry. He has worked for the *Daily Mail* since 1970. He has described himself 'apolitical', and sees his function as making the "dreary news copy of the daily paper brighter, by putting in a laugh".[211] Mac is a clever, funny cartoonist, but Labour supporters would have been puzzled about the apolitical part. He certainly did not hold his punches. An elderly couple in a doctor's surgery: "If Miliband's lot get elected we'd like to sign the 'Do Not Resuscitate' forms". Tony Blair emerging, vampire-like, out of a coffin that is surrounded by piles of money: "Be warned! Voting Tory will bring economic chaos...er, for the rest of you". Perhaps his most memorable cartoon was set at "The Sadist & Masochist Club: Pain, Humiliation & Self-Inflicted Suffering R Us". This wonderfully farcical graphic shows a roomful of misshapen misfits hitting their heads with hammers, punching themselves with boxing gloves, and placing their hands inside mousetraps. One smiling club member says, "Yeah. Roll on tomorrow. I'm voting Labour too". Left-leaning cartoonists came up with any number of literate, provocative, and visually appealing cartoons during the 2015 general election. Few if any could match Mac when it came to cranking out entertaining, punchy, and politically devastating single-panel cartoons.

Further Reading

Timothy S. Benson, *The Cartoon Century: Modern Britain Through the Eyes of its Cartoonists* (New York: Random House, 2009).

Timothy S. Benson, *The Best of Britain's Political Cartoons 2014* (London: Scribe Publications, 2015).

Mark Bryant, *Dictionary of Twentieth-Century British Cartoonists and Caricaturists* (Farnham: Ashgate Publishing, 2000).

Cartoon Aid Trust, *The 1000 British Cartoonists of the Century* (London: Cartoon Aid Trust in Association with Beer Davies, 2000).

James Chapman, *British Comics: A Cultural History* (London: Reaktion Books, 2011).

Vic Gatrell, *City of Laughter: Sex and Satire in Eighteenth-Century London* (London: Walker & Company, 2007).

Paul Gravett and Peter Stanbury, *Great British Comics* (Worthing: Aurum, 2006).

Jeet Heer and Kent Worcester (eds.), *Arguing Comics: Literary Masters on a Popular Medium* (Jackson, MS: University Press of Mississippi, 2004).

Jeet Heer and Kent Worcester (eds.), *A Comics Studies Reader* (Jackson, MS: University Press of Mississippi, 2009).

Michael Wynn Jones, *The Cartoon History of Britain* (London: Tom Stacey, 1971).

Edward J. Lordan, *Politics, Ink: How America's Cartoonists Skewer Politicians, from King George III to George Dubya* (New York: Rowman and Littlefield, 2006).

---

[211] These quotations are taken from McMurtry's Wikipedia page.

Victor Navasky, *The Art of Controversy: Political Cartoons and Their Enduring Power* (New York: Knopf, 2013).

Nick Newman, *Private Eye: A Cartoon History: Five Decades of Classic Cartoon Art* (London: Private Eye Productions, 2013).

Monika Nowicka and Janusz Kazmierczak, 'Leading British Politicians in The Times' and the Guardian's Cartoons, 2010-2013' *International Journal of Comic Art* 17.1 (Spring/Summer 2015): 299-335.

Helen Walasek (ed.), *The Best of Punch Cartoons: 2,000 Humour Classics* (New York: The Overlook Press, 2008).

Kent Worcester, 'Editorial Cartoons and the 2010 Election' in Robert Worcester, Roger Mortimore, Paul Baines and Mark Gill, *Explaining Cameron's Coalition: How It Came About: An Analysis of the 2010 British General Election* (London: Biteback, 2011).

Kent Worcester (ed.), 'The State of the Editorial Cartoon: A Symposium', *PS: Political Science and Politics* 40.2 (April 2007).

Index

Also available from IndieBooks

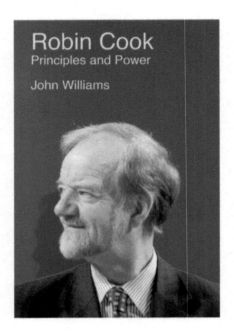

Robin Cook's early death robbed British politics of one of its most distinctive and principled stars. Ten years on, his struggle to reconcile those principles with the realities of power remains as relevant as ever. In this intimate, behind-the-scenes portrait, John Williams, who as press secretary was at Robin's side during three dramatic and turbulent years as Foreign Secretary, shows the reality of a man of strong beliefs facing the compromises and accomodations of New Labour. He reveals the inner workings of modern power-politics, from the European Union to Palestine. And he reflects on what today's politicians and voters can learn from Robin Cook: a man who believed that, despite everything, politics can still be a force for good.

"...a must read for scholars, practitioners and "laypeople" alike. It provides a ring-side seat into the sense and sensibility dilemas of British Foreign Secretary the late Robin Cook during the early and challenging Blair years ... It is a significant contribution to the litera-ture about how Cook utilized information in support of government outcomes ... and a handbook of lessons to be learned."

Professor Robert Sharp